TAMERLANE AND THE JEWS

This book provides a general introduction to the history of Jewish life in fourteenth-century Asia at the time of the ruler Tamerlane (Timur). After defining the origin of the Central Asian Jews, the author describes the attitudes towards them and the historical consequences of their relationship with Tamerlane.

In founding an empire, Tamerlane had delivered Central Asia from the last Mongols and brought the nations of Transoxania within the orbit of Persian civilization. Left alone to live within a large stable empire, the Central Asian Jews prospered under the leadership of Tamerlane, absorbing the empire's spirit into their language and culture.

Michael Shterenshis was a lecturer at the Finnish College in Jerusalem, and teaches now at the AMHS School, Hod HaSharon, Israel. Previously, he worked as a cultural assistant for the Embassy of the Republic of Uzbekistan in Israel, and as a research fellow at the Hebrew University of Jerusalem. His interests cover the history of Central Asia and the history of the Jews, as well as Jewish and Asiatic medicine and the history of religion. He is a widely published author of scientific works on Jewish and Asiatic history, as well as the history of medicine.

TAMERLANE AND THE JEWS

Michael Shterenshis

RoutledgeCurzon
Taylor & Francis Group
LONDON AND NEW YORK

First published 2002
by RoutledgeCurzon
11 New Fetter Lane, London EC4P 4EE

Simultaneously published in the USA and Canada
by RoutledgeCurzon
29 West 35th Street, New York, NY 10001

RoutledgeCurzon is an imprint of the Taylor & Francis Group

Typeset in Times by
Keystroke, Jacaranda Lodge, Wolverhampton
Printed and bound in Great Britain by
TJ International Ltd, Padstow, Cornwall

British Library Cataloguing in Publication Data
A catalogue record for this book is available from the British Library

Library of Congress Cataloging in Publication Data
A catalog record for this book has been requested

ISBN 0–7007–1696–3

THIS BOOK IS DEDICATED TO
MY PARENTS,WHO HAVE SPENT
ALL THEIR LIFE IN UZBEKISTAN,
WITH LOVE AND GRATITUDE.

CONTENTS

MAPS AND ILLUSTRATIONS

Maps

Plates

PREFACE

The purpose of this book, is to provide a general introduction to the history of Jewish life in Asia during the fourteenth century, mainly at the time of the last great World conqueror Timur (Tamerlane). I have endeavoured to present the main facts about Timur's attitude to the Jews and the Jews' attitude to Timur. This topic, as an aspect of the history of the Jews, the history of Timur and the Timurids, or as the general history of Asia, has never before been investigated and is the first published work on this subject.

I have tried to present the material in moderate compass and without too many technicalities, to avoid the form of a literary essay or a philosophical treatise, or even an exposition of the scientific historiographer's viewpoint. It has been my aim to draw attention to this unknown period in Jewish history and the history of Central Asia.

However, all the regular scientific organisation of the material, notes, bibliography, indexes, is maintained in a way usual for standard scientific research. At the same time, transliteration of Turk, Arabic and other Oriental names has been simplified and dots, bars, definite articles, and other diacritical marks have been omitted. Most of the dates are given in years of the Christian era (AD). Oriental and Jewish words that occur in the book have brief definitions in the text in order to make this book intelligible to those who have no specialist knowledge of Oriental history.

ACKNOWLEDGEMENTS

Financial support

This book is the product of a long process, during which I have received help and support from many individuals and institutions. Above all, I am indebted to Boris Kandov, Agrotec Company, whose enthusiasm and love for the history of the Jews in Uzbekistan encouraged me to write this book.

My research in Israel was conducted with the support of the Joshua and Hannah Leibowitz Fellowship Fund. My research in Uzbekistan and the final stage of writing the book were funded by Joseph 'Kobi' Ben-Gur, the head of Flex International Manufacturing and Trading Ltd, and by Avi Manor.

I have also received continuous and generous financial support from Dov Rappaport, the head of RPA Port International Ltd, from Yoram Shaked, a businessman, and from the Caspi Aviation Company of Israel.

Scientific, technical and spiritual help

This book would probably never have been written, far less published, had it not been for the interest shown by Mr Rustam Issaev, the Ambassador of the Republic of Uzbekistan to Israel when we met in Tel-Aviv.

A very special thank you also to Gilgi Hauser, Tel Aviv, for her professional, creative and highly valued editing, even when she was in Europe.

Prof Gary Ferngen, University of Oregon, read the manuscript with a critical eye and suggested many valuable improvements, as did David Mehler, from Tel Aviv, in the initial editing. The Amir Temur Foundation in Tashkent, Uzbekistan, provided me with valuable sources.

Dr Dilorom T. Usupova from the Uzbek Institute of Oriental Studies assisted me in my research in Tashkent, Uzbekistan, and Dr Vladimir Mesamed from the Truman Research Institute in Jerusalem helped me with translations from the Persian and Judeo-Persian. I should like to thank Sheikh Abdul Aziz Musa Bukhari of Jerusalem for his help in the translation of Arabic texts.

My younger daughter Julia was born in July 1999, and I thank her for her tactful behaviour from the very first day of her life that permitted me to finish the manuscript.

A NOTE ON SPELLING AND TRANSLITERATION

Despite the clear definitions of the *Encyclopaedia of Islam*, different spellings of Oriental geographical and historical names can be found in scientific and popular literature. The generally accepted regulations on transliteration of Arabic script is good for the Arabic language, less successful for Persian and Turkish, and least successful for Chagatai Turkic, Old Uzbek, and the modern Uzbek and Tadjik languages. The object of the English transliteration of names in this book in the above-mentioned languages, therefore, is to cause the English reader as little trouble as possible. In order to avoid misunderstandings, several names that are frequently used in this book should be clarified.

Tamerlane – Timur: the original name of the main hero of this book, Timur (Tu. *Temur*, 'iron'), has been corrupted, via the Persian Timur-i Lang ('Timur the lame'), into the European forms *Tamerlane* (Engl.) or *Tamerlan* (Fr.).

In addition to these forms some others have been used throughout the centuries:

- *Tamorlan* – by Ruy Gonzalez de Clavijo, Spain, 1403–6.
- *Thomor* – by B. de Mignanelli in 'Vita Tamerlani', 1416.
- *Tamburlaine* – by Christopher Marlowe, England, 1587; it was also used by the modern English writer Hilda Hookham in 1962.
- *Tamerlano* – by Giosafat Barbaro, Italy, 1436–78. This Venetian merchant used other spellings too: *Tamberlan*, *Tamburlan*, *Tamberlano*, and even *Zamberlan*.
- *Tamerlanes* – J. Du Bec, France, 1595.
- *Tamerlanis* – J.-H. Boeckler, France, 1657.

Different European historians and novelists used these variations. In Oriental sources Timur was *Timur* or *Timur-i Lenk* (sometimes spelled as *Timur-i-Lank*). Latin transliterations can be *Timur*, *Timour*, *Temoor*, even *Demir* (Turkey). The current Uzbek spelling is Temur.

Chingiz Khan: this spelling suits the actual pronunciation the best. Other variations are: *Chinggis Khan*, *Jengiz Khan*, *Genjis Khan*.

There are several variations in the spelling of names that are used in this book. Examples are:

- Samarkand – Samarcand, Samarquand.
- Bukhara – Bokhara, Boukhara.
- Khorezm – Khwarizim, Khwarizm, Carizme (Gibbon).
- Tashkent – Tashkend, Shash. The current Uzbek spelling is Toshkand.
- Uzbeks – a nation in Central Asia of Turk origin. The given spelling is based on the Uzbek pronunciation. Variations: Uzbegs, Ozbegs.
- Khazars – Chazars.
- Bayazet – Bayazid (the Turkish Sultan, d. 1403)

Other names for Central Asia are Meverannahr (Arab), Transoxania, Transoxiana (from 'Oxus' – another name for the Amu-Darya river). Sometimes it can be called Turkestan. However, 'Turkestan' has a broader geographic meaning.

The majority of Oriental names are spelled as is generally accepted in academic literature, with as little use of diacritical marks as possible. I tried to avoid different spellings of the same words in different languages. For example, the word 'history' is *Ta'rīkh* in Arabic, *Tārīkh* in Persian, and *Tarikh* in Old Uzbek. Therefore I have used the simplest form of transliteration.

INTRODUCTION

Many great rulers can be evaluated according to their attitude towards the Jews. This statement is true both for Europe and for Asia. In the case of the great Asian warrior and statesman Timur (Tamerlane, 1336–1405) there are two questions that have not been researched, Timur's attitude to the Jews, and the Jewish attitude to the personality of Timur.

While Timur has enjoyed much attention in historical studies of Asiatic history of the fourteenth and fifteenth centuries, the history of Jews in Central Asia of this period has been almost completely neglected. Approaching the time of Timur's rule, we should state that there is a shortage of Jewish historical works covering this period. We do not have even travellers' diaries or sketches. In fact, after Benjamin of Tudela and Rabbi Petachia of Ratisbon, who both travelled through Asia in the twelfth century, there are no further writings of Jewish travellers that could shed light on the Jewish Diaspora in Central Asia over the next three centuries. What few sources there are derive from the Jewish communities themselves.

The reign of Timur falls in the period between 1370 and 1405. At the end of his life Timur owned all the land from Damascus in the west up to the Chinese border in the east, and from the Volga river in the north up to the city of Delhi in the south. Timur created an empire with the centre in Samarkand that he transformed into the pearl of Asia. Timur originated the dynasty of Timurids. His descendants ruled in Central Asia, Persia and the neighbouring areas for the next 200 years.

Several historical works have been written about Timur. He has been the hero of several novels and plays.[1] The English poet Christopher Marlowe wrote two poems about Tamerlane in the sixteenth century.[2] Edgar Allan Poe wrote a poem entitled 'Tamerlane' in the nineteenth century.[3] Händel composed the opera 'Tamerlano' in 1724.[4] Nevertheless, although nearly every British, Israeli or American schoolboy knows something about Chingiz Khan, he does not know anything about Timur.

Indeed, the recent *World History* textbook published by McDougal Littell (1999) presents a ten-page description of Chingiz Khan (Genghis Khan) and the Mongols, and gives Tamerlane less than half of a page.[5]

Timur's attitude to the Jews has never been investigated. It is necessary to start from the very beginning and to research the subject thoroughly. Jewish history and the history of the nations of Central Asia are linked together. A vivid example can be taken from Barthold's *An Historical Geography of Iran*:

> There are also in Hamadan a fair number of Jews . . ., both local and from Baghdad; . . . The attitude of the local population towards the Jews, according to Curzon, is exceedingly hostile, although the Muslims venerate the Jewish sanctuaries in the city, the presumed tombs of Esther and Mordecai. The cupola crowning the building has, according to Curzon, the character of an undoubtedly new structure; the bodies are kept in wooden coffins covered with Hebrew letters. Ker Porter heard that the present mausoleum had been built after Timur's time and was restored in the seventeenth century. Near it was the tomb of the famous eleventh-century philosopher Avicenna (that is, Abu Ali Ibn Sina).[6]

So the tomb of Ibn Sina, the national pride of the people of Uzbekistan, is located very close to the tombs of the Jewish legendary heroes, Esther and Mordecai.

Timur himself was sometimes compared with biblical personages. Ghiyas ad-din Ali, Timur's court biographer, wrote in his fawning *Diary of Timur's campaign in India*:

> There was a message from beyond with a meaning that this building will be the World indicator because the whole world is in one dress and the whole army is in one body [of Emir Timur] . . . [This is not a hyperbole], because the Most High Creator testified in the glorious Koran that Ibrahim [Abraham], the friend of Allah – let it be the Merciful's benediction on him! – had a tribe of true faith, and this was said about one man on a basis of glory and nobility of all [his] people![7]

Another example can be found in Ibn Arabshah's *Tamerlane or Timur the Great Amir*. Ahmed Ibn Arabshah, an Arab historian of the fifteenth century, who himself counted Timur as a wicked person, published a letter written by Timur's son Miranshah to his glorious father. Miranshah wrote:

> But where are you, if you are compared with Noah and his mourning over his family and his good service and piety [.] and with David, who had a great kingdom and yet was constant in full observance of the Divine commands and worship and praise of God Almighty and with Solomon, his successor, and his dominion over men and jinns and birds and beasts and winds.[8]

All such comparisons arose from the Koranic verses and the Jewish origin of David and Solomon was not taken into account by Miranshah.

Where Central Asia is located

As a geographical expression the term 'Central Asia' tends to elude precise definition. The currently accepted definition of Central Asia encompasses the five newly independent Muslim states of the former Soviet Union namely, Uzbekistan, Turkmenistan, Kazakhstan, Tajikistan, and Kyrgyzstan. Geographically some of these states, notably Kazakhstan, belong more to Inner Asia, whereas Afghanistan and northern parts of Iran, such as the province of Khorassan, are part of Central Asia. In the pages that follow, the term 'Central Asia' is used primarily to describe the area comprising Uzbekistan, Tajikistan, Turkmenistan, and the southern parts of Kazakhstan. The core of this area is the land between two major regional rivers, Syr-Dariya and Amu-Dariya (ancient Oxus). These rivers run almost parallel and end in the Aral Lake. For most of our period Central Asia was a bridge between the Muslim and non-Muslim parts of Asia. This land was populated by a diverse range of races and creeds. Here Muslims met Chinese, Buddhists, Shamanists and other pagans, Nestorian Christians and Russian Orthodox Christians, Jews, and many other people of different religions.

Neighbouring Persia, modern Iran, also deserves our attention. Today it is merely the shadow of its former greatness, but it must have been an extraordinarily interesting land when the name of Persia stood for all that was most excellent in the arts and, above all, in the difficult art of living. The ancient Persian Empire was destroyed by Alexander, but five hundred years later, under the dynasty of Sassanids, the Persians restored the ancient realm of Xerxes and Cambyses. They restored the Zoroastrian faith to all its former purity and made the desert flower with the roses of Isfahan. Unfortunately, for several centuries afterwards, Persia was a poor and badly administered country. Its geographical location hardly offered any blessing; in fact it was very much of a curse. It is a desert, but when a desert is situated on the main road, which in turn is part of a land bridge connecting two of the most important parts of the world, then that desert will forever be a battlefield and a bone of contention between opposing interests. This reasoning was especially true at the time of Timur and the Timurids.

Most of the Jewish communities in these territories were far older than Timur's empire. Those that lasted after the Timurid dynasty were no more than a dim memory. Timur's rule was a brief episode in the long history of the Jews of Central Asia.

The history of the Jews has one geographical regularity, the farther east we move from Europe and the Mediterranean the less knowledge there is on Jewish history. It is therefore necessary to clarify the origin of the Jews in question.

Who are Asiatic Jews?

There are four groups of Jews one can speak of regarding the Orient:

- The Ten Lost Tribes
- Rabbinic Jews
- Karaites
- Jews by blood who converted or accepted Christianity or Islam.

I will not speak about the Ten Lost Tribes here. The lost is lost. This topic, no matter how fascinating, is based on speculation. Several books have been written, and many people have wanted to speculate on the destiny of the Ten Lost Tribes of Israel, who were carried away by the Assyrians in 722 BC. Even the numerous attempts to find remnants of the Ten Lost Tribes have never been able to prove where they are now located; all we know is that they disappeared somewhere in Asia.

Seventy years ago Hendrik Willem Van Loon commented sarcastically on the subject of the Ten Lost Tribes in his *Life and Times of Rembrandt*:

> Meanwhile in another corner of the room the good Rabbi was endeavoring to prove his point by a weird mixture of geographic and philologic and messianic information and was trying to make his hearers believe that the existence of such places as Dankhar and Dango and Dano showed the probable route taken by the tribe of Dan on its way from Palestine to the East. The argument sounded rather far-fetched to me. If Dankhar and Dango were to be accepted as evidence of the Israelites having been in Asia, how about Danzig and Danemark and the Danube as living testimony to their presence in Europe on their way from the old promised land to the new one?[9]

As recent as 1992, David Law tried to prove the same points in his book *From Samaria to Samarkand: The Ten Lost Tribes of Israel*[10] by trying to show that Samarkand, for example, was named after Samaria, the capital city of the northern kingdom of Israel. Speaking of Mongols and Turks, such speculations could be numerous. Indeed, one of the main Mongol tribes that became a part of the Mongol nation had the name of Karaites[11] and the name of one of descendants of Chingiz Khan was Dayan Khan.[12]

The other three groups of Jews should also be taken into account on an equal basis. One cannot concentrate only on Rabbinic Jews. Such an approach could significantly impoverish Jewish history.

The Karaitic movement was born in Asia. Karaites (Karaims) were a sect within Judaism that rejected the Talmudic authority and based itself on the individual interpretation of the Holy Scriptures. Karaism originated among the Babylonian Jews in 767. It flourished in Persia, Central Asia and Eastern Europe from the ninth to the twelfth centuries, spreading from Persia to Palestine, Egypt, and into Europe.

Walter Fischel mentioned 'The Rabbanite Jews and Karaite Jews' in his article on the Jews of Central Asia (Khorasan) of 1945. 'The Jews of Khorasan,' he wrote, 'similar to the rest of the Oriental Jewish Diaspora, were divided into two distinct groups, the Rabbanite Jews and the Karaite Jews.'[13] He did not, however, mention the third group, the Jews that converted to other religions, mainly to Christianity and Islam. Just as in Europe, there were Jews in Asia who were so anxious to climb the social and political ladder that they felt constrained to convert to the dominant faith. Islam kept its doors wide open for the whole of the Jewish community, although in practice it was only individuals who crossed the threshold.

We cannot ignore these people. Some of them played a visible role in the history of medieval Asia. Let us examine, for example, Persia of the thirteenth century when it was conquered by the Mongols. There were three prominent personalities – all Jews by origin: Rashid ad-Din (Fadl Allah Rashid ad-Din Tabib, of Hamadan, 1247–1318) was a minister in Mongol Persia and a great Persian historian. He was of the Islamic faith, and was killed by his court enemies. Sa'd (Saad) ad-Daula ibn as-Safi (b. Abhar, d. 1291), a physician, became Vizier of the entire Mongol Persian Empire in 1289. He practised Judaism and he too was killed by his court enemies. Bar Hebraeus, Gregory (Abu al-Faraj ibn Harun, 1226–86) was a son of a Jewish physician named Aaron and lived in Asiatic Turkey and Persia. Being a prominent theologian, historian and philosopher, he was of the Christian faith. In 1264 he became Primate of the Eastern Jacobites. His best known work is his historical writing *Chronicle*. He was not killed.

Jews of different religious orientations contributed to the history of the Asiatic Jews and I shall include all of them, although the Khazars will be mentioned only briefly. This tribe of Turk or Finnish origin, which settled in the south-east of European Russia during the Barbarian invasion of Europe, adopted Judaism about AD 750. In fact, Judaism was adopted mostly by the nobility. Judaism of the Khazars influenced the religious situation in Asia but the history of the Khazars in general does not go into the mainstream of Jewish history. By the time of Timur, the Khazars had already disappeared as a nation.

The Jews, who are the subject of this book, like any other Jews of the Diaspora, lived a life in great part determined by the behaviour of the non-Jewish society around them, as expressed in its laws, its customs, its economical possibilities, and its administrative and political institutions. The behaviour of the Jews towards their neighbours was conditioned by the behaviour of the neighbours towards the Jews and by examining this relationship one gains an understanding of their attitude to each other.

The topic of Timur and the Jews is a sensitive one. A critical approach to the subject is essential. Russian sources of the Soviet period, with very few exceptions, can not be counted as reliable works.[14] Western historiography of Timur's time almost completely ignores the history of the Jews in Central Asia. Jewish sources traditionally point out the ill fate and oppressions of *dhimmi* (or the *zimmi*, the Jews and Christians in Islamic lands) by the Muslim majority. Modern Uzbek historiography is not yet developed. This book presents the current knowledge on the subject; however, serious research on the topic of Timur's attitude to the Jews is necessary to fill the gap in the history of the Asiatic Jews and in the history of Timur.

PROLOGUE

Legends

Legend 1: Timur was bad for the Jews

'At the end of the month of November when the Hebrew inhabitants wished to celebrate a certain feast, as was the custom among them, and fearing that they would be despoiled by the hordes of Thomor [Timur], they crowded into the temple with devotion and fear. For greater protection they carried there all their portable goods and valuables, for example their moneys, jewels, gems and things similar to these. At this time there were in Thomor's army certain warriors who knew quite well the Hebrew idiom. Knowing all this, and it is believed, with the consent of Thomor, they went well armed and in semi-Jewish dress for the purpose of visiting the temple as they said. They came with their faces bent toward the ground, entered the temple with Hebrews prayers on their lips, and said, "We are of your people, Hebrews even as you are". Those foolish men listened readily to their facile talk about the Sacred Books, the Psalter, the Talmud, and all the Judaic scripture, and they joyfully believed all, especially when they heard that they understood the Talmud, because it was an obscure book and known to but a few, a book which corrupted, falsified, and perverted almost the whole Bible. These men said that they served their Most Serene Lord and had come to the temple to worship out of fraternal love, a love, rather, that a dog has for a dog, and to protect those Hebrews and their possessions. They said that they had come to them with new and eternal brotherhood for the future and they demonstrated a silent reverence for the temple. They added that Thomor wished to despoil the city [Aleppo] and persuaded them to bring all their possessions to the temple because that was safer. They promised with the brotherhood of wolves and with feigned love that they would protect all. These foolish Jews, depriving of their reason, believed everything that was told them and gave boundless praise to God seeing that Hebrews had been so greatly honored beyond what was customary. They rejoiced so with mingle pride that they fell to blaspheming in grand style the Christian princes who did not honor the great worth and the activity of their false Machabes as he was doing. In their temple they poured forth beyond measure the most devoted prayers for the exaltation of so glorious a Prince, for these foolish men did not know what a future day would bring forth.

When their homes had been emptied and the temple filled, the fictitious Jews entered the temple. Each of them was armed with a cruel sword, and beginning with the oldest even to the youngest, they slaughtered all the Jews, even the women. Some few young and beautiful girls were spared and these they violated in the temple. But the other were killed, and when the temple had been polluted with foulness and gore, they emptied it of its treasures and divided up the spoils, laughing over the folly of the Hebrews. Thomor had men who were distinguished and skilled in Arabic, Greek, Hebrew, and in every language, as well as in Astronomy, Geometry, Incantations, Magic, and well informed in every kind of knowledge of that sort.'

(B. de Mignanelli (1416) *Vita Tamerlani*, Constance. English translation W.J. Fischel (1956) 'A New Latin Source on Tamerlane's Conquest of Damascus (1400/1401)', *ORIENS* IX, 2: 213–14)

Legend 2: Timur was good for the Jews

'They [Jews of Bukhara] then gave to Wolff the following account of themselves:

"When the God of Israel stripped up the spirit of Pul, king of Assyria, and the spirit of Tiglath-Pilneser, king of Assyria, they were carried away, even the Reubenites, and the Gadites, and the half tribe of Manasseh, and were brought into Halah (which is now called Balkh), and Habor (which is Samarcand), and Hara (which is Bokhara), and to the river Gozan (which is the Ammoo, also called Jehoon, and by Europeans called Oxus [modern Amu-Daria]). They lived in this empire for centuries, untill they were expelled by the Tshagatay, the people of Genghis Khan; and then they settled in Sabz-Awar, and

Nishapoor in Khorassan; and, centuries afterwards, the greater part returned from Sabz-Awar to Boukhara, Samarcand, and Balkh. And Timoor Koorikan (called falsely by the Europeans, Tamerlane) gave them a great many privileges; and, at Balkh, the mother of cities, he gave them a whole beautiful quarter of their own, with a gate to enclose it; and so they lived in peace and prosperity. One of the prime ministers, who was called "the second after the king" (in Hebrew, *Shenee-lamelek*) and was the chief secretary to royalty, was a Jew from Germany.'

(J. Wolff (1861) *Travels and Adventures of the Rev. Joseph Wolff, D.D., LL.D.*, London: Sauders, Otley, and Co., vol. II, pp. 12–13)

What, indeed, happened in reality between Timur and the Jews? This book will try to deal with this question.

Part I

HISTORICAL BACKGROUND

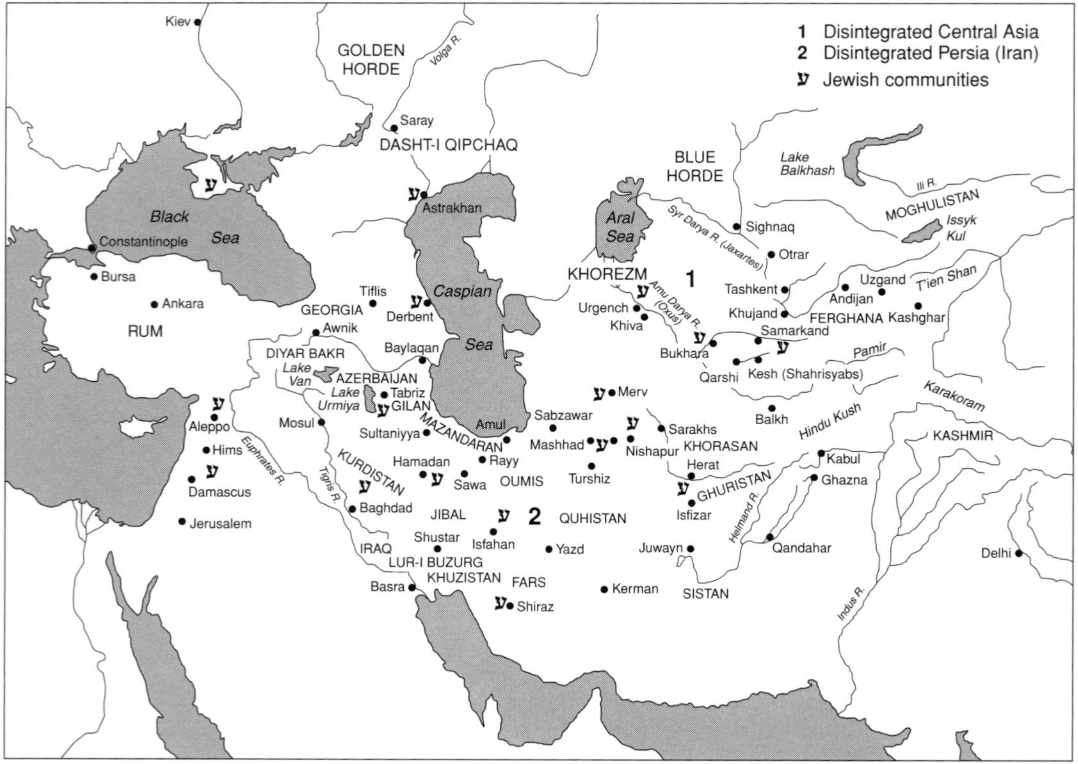

Map 1 Asia in the fourteenth century before Timur

1

THE FOURTEENTH CENTURY IN ASIA

What this portrays

Think, in this batter'd Caravanserai
Whose Doorways are alternate Night and Day,
How Sultan after Sultan with his Pomp
Abode his Hour or two, and went his way.
(*Rubáiyát of Omar Khayyám*, rendered into
English verse by Edward Fitzgerald)

The fourteenth century is a dim, indistinct and obscure word combination for each of us who has no special historical knowledge of that period. When we read phrases like 'it had happened in the fourteenth century' or 'he lived in the fourteenth century' each of us creates a distinct and somewhat different picture about that era.

We could not do without dates but unless we are very careful, dates play tricks on us. They are apt to make history too precise. During the fourteenth century Europeans did not relate to dates in terms of BC and AD so there was no conscious notion of that century either in Europe or in Asia; in Europe the book of Joseph Justus Scaliger, *Opus de emendatione temporum*, a foundation of modern chronology, was only published in 1583. At the same time, the Muslim world did not live according to the Christian calendar, and dated itself by the years and centuries of the *Hijra*, or Mohammed's 'emigration' from Mecca to Medina; the Muslim era begins in AD 622. Eastern Christians in Arab lands used the so-called 'Greek chronology'. Following these chronologies the year of AD 1400 was the year of 803 of Hijra and the year of 1711 of the Greek Era. If we recall that Dante composed his *Divina Commedia* in 1307, that Petrarch was crowned a poet on the Roman Capitol in 1341, that Boccaccio wrote the *Decameron* in 1348, we may assume that the fourteenth century was indeed a pleasant century to have been born into. But there is a need to be aware of the differences in human psychology of the peoples who lived then.

First of all, the people of the Middle Ages, both Europeans and Orientals, never thought of themselves as free-born citizens, who could come and go at will and shape their fate according to their ability, energy or luck. On the contrary, they considered themselves part of the general scheme of things, which included emperors and serfs, popes and heretics, sultans and dervishes, heroes and swashbucklers, rich men, poor men, beggar men and thieves. They accepted this divine ordinance and asked no questions. The exceptions were some solitary philosophers such as Jean Buridan (1300–58). In this, of course, medieval people differed radically from modern people, who accept nothing and who are forever trying to improve their own personal financial and political situation.

To the average man and woman of the fourteenth century, whether Christian, Muslim, or Jew, the world hereafter – a Heaven of wonderful delights and a Hell of brimstone and suffering – meant something more than just empty words or vague theological phrases. They accepted this as reality and the medieval dervishes and knights spent the greater part of their lives in preparation for it.

Contemporary people regard a noble death after a well-spent life with the quiet calm of the ancient Greeks and Romans. After three score years of work and effort, we go to sleep with the feeling that all will be well. But during the Middle Ages, the King of Terrors with his grinning skull and rattling bones was man's steady companion. He woke his victims up to terrible tunes on his scratchy fiddle, he sat down with them at dinner, he smiled at them from behind trees and shrubs when they took a girl out for a walk. If you had heard nothing but hair-raising yarns about cemeteries, coffins and fearful diseases when you were very young, instead of having listened to the fairy stories of Andersen and Grimm, you, too, would have lived all your days in dread of the final hour and the gruesome Day of Judgement.

Alas, the fourteenth century contributed heavily to peoples' fears. In 1299 pestilence struck Persia and thousands died. In 1316 England and Ireland were devastated by pestilence. In 1332 the bubonic plague erupted in India. Due to the limited contact between Asia and Europe there was little trade and tourism to the Orient and for the next fifteen years the plague was confined within Asia. We have no precise figures of the human loss in Asia but in China alone millions were said to have died. The Black Death finally devastated Europe in 1347 and by 1349 a third of the population had been killed in England. This Black Death became history's greatest disaster with an estimated seventy-five million dead. After that, repeated outbreaks of plague decimated Egypt, the British Isles, Persia and France from 1358 to 1370. Finally, from 1382 to 1385 the pestilence called the 'Fourth' gripped Ireland and once again thousands died.

Sometimes, fear of the future filled peoples' souls with humility and piety, but more often it influenced them in opposite ways and made them cruel, unsentimental and overtly religious. First, they would murder all the Jews in a ghetto, or all the women and children of a captured city, then they would devoutly march to a holy spot – it did not matter if it were a Christian church or Muslim *mazar* – and with their hand gory with the blood of innocent victims, they would pray that the merciful heaven or Allah forgive them their sins.

In general, fourteenth-century Europe was in a bad state both politically and economically. The crusaders' zest had dispersed a hundred years previously and the great wanderlust was still a hundred years ahead. Russia was in a bad state too. Divided into several small principalities, which were under either Mongol or Lithuanian domination, Russia was still at the very beginning of her future centralisation. From the time when the long-lasting Christian–Muslim West–East controversy began, the overland route to the profitable Orient was gradually being closed. For several centuries following the great Arab conquest, a permanent state of war existed between the two cultures. However, the thirteenth and fourteenth centuries helped to partially overcome these sad circumstances.

Asia, during the same period, was better off. It was richer than Europe, had bigger states, and more goods to offer. Also, all three major powers of the Orient of that time, the Mamluks of Egypt, the Ottoman Turks and the Mongols, were much stronger militarily than the European states.

Marco Polo is usually mentioned as the first European to have visited Asia, but there had been others before him. As so often happens in the realm of geography, it was another war rather than peace that widened Europe's knowledge of the Asiatic map. Although historians have generally regarded the Mongol invasion of the thirteenth century into Central Asia and countries further west as an unmitigated disaster, it may also be seen as having been partially beneficial. The Mongol armies may have been motivated solely by lust for conquest and destruction, but out of this evil sprang a positive development when they rent asunder the veil which had for so long shut off Central Asia, Persia and other Islamic countries from the West. A result of the Mongol invasion was the establishment of new contacts between the East and the West, which were slow at first and encumbered with all the handicaps of ignorance on both sides.

The Eastern traveller was said to have left home and gone on the road for religious, political and (or) commercial reasons, or just to quench his thirst for adventure. The same held true for the Western traveller. The horror that was created in Europe by the Mongol conquest and attacks on Eastern Europe in the middle of the thirteenth century led the Pope and the kings of France and England, to send missionaries and emissaries to the court of the Great Khan. They hoped to put an end to the Mongols' aggression in Europe, of converting them to Christianity, and establishing trade routes between the East and the West. Thus, in 1245 Pope Innocent IV sent a delegation headed by a Franciscan friar, John Pian de Carpini, to the Great Khan. A few years later another friar-traveller, William of Rubruck, was sent out as the representative of Louis IX, King of France.[1] Yet these friars were not the first Europeans to visit Central and Middle Asia in the Middle Ages. The Jewish merchant, Rabbi Benjamin of Tudela, whose period of travels extended from AD 1160 to 73 also visited about 300 different cities in Europe, Asia and Northern Africa. His diary, written in Hebrew, was edited after his death and given an introduction by Eliezer Gershon. However, it was first printed only in 1543 in Istanbul, entitled *Massaot shel Rabbi Binjamin*.[2]

Within a very short period of time, Benjamin of Tudela was followed by Rabbi Petachia of Ratisbon who, like his predecessor, was a highly motivated merchant and who visited his Jewish brothers living in other parts of the world in order to acquaint himself with their condition. His objective was to write down what he saw and heard in order to inform his people, the house of Israel.[3]

After Carpini and Rubruck, the Latin mission, which had started in the late thirteenth century, continued to head toward the East until the mid-fourteenth century.[4] But 'although the best travel books belonging to this period were written by missionaries, the real impetus to travel was the lure of trade, and the most frequent journeys to Persia, India and Cathay were made by merchants'.[5] The greatest of them all was Marco Polo, whose two journeys through Persia and Central Asia, occurred between the years 1271 and 1294.

At the beginning of the fourteenth century all these expeditions finally made Europe 'Asia-conscious'. The East was no longer a closed book to the West, but as yet was still an unknown quantity. It must be borne in mind when studying the medieval history of Asia that the 'traffic' was not merely from West to East; there were also travellers in the opposite direction, including Jewish merchants. On the whole, a good deal less has been heard of these visitors from the Orient partly because they were fewer in number, and partly because their accounts did not, in the majority of cases, become widely known, if at all, in Europe.

Often the background or interest of a traveller differed from the purpose of travel, or the travel itself was of a multipurpose nature. Rabbi Benjamin of Tudela provides the best example; his primary object was to visit the synagogues of the principal cities through which he passed, and to describe the number and condition of the Jews whom he found in them.[6] As a merchant he was interested in acquiring commercial information. On the other hand, the friars who were sent to Inner Asia in the Middle Ages, besides having missionary purposes, were also bearers of political messages or acted as emissaries sent to establish trade relationships. This combination and diversity of purposes and interests widened the scope of information gathered by the travellers.

Visitors who came to Central Asia on religious missions or those with religious backgrounds, focused more on the spiritual beliefs of the people, searching for similarities and differences between Christianity, Judaism and Islam. Sometimes Buddhism, Shamanism and Zoroastrianism were also taken into account. These travellers were more interested in assessing facts about the religious minorities of the country, how they lived, population statistics, areas of concentration, their religious activity, and how all of the above affected the authorities. Alas, there are significant time gaps concerning these journeys and several periods are not covered at all.

The Middle Ages were 'internationally minded'. Europeans of the thirteenth or fourteenth centuries rarely talked of themselves as Germans or Frenchmen or Italians. Indeed, there were several German states, French principalities and Italian independent cities. They said, 'I am a citizen of Munich or Bordeaux or Genoa', and belonging to one and the same church, they felt a certain bond of brotherhood.

The history of Central Asia also centred on empires and tribes, and the concept of nation and nation-state to denote triangular relationship between territory, ethno-cultural identity and political authority is very recent in this region. Indeed, Timur (Tamerlane) created an international empire but at the same time he counted himself as a descendant of the Barlas tribe.

Going back to the time of Timur, the major events of human history were moving from Europe to Asia. Europe was divided and weak. The best days of chivalry and crusading had gone. Attacked by the Mamluk Sultans of Egypt, by Ottoman Turks and by Mongols, Europe had become an armed camp by the time Timur appeared on the scene.

In his well-known book *Tamerlane* Harold Lamb wrote about this:

> There is today near a junction of the Trans-Siberian railway a stone obelisk bearing on one side the word Europa and on the other Asia. In Tamerlane's day this stone would have been placed some fifty degrees of longitude farther west, about in the suburbs of Venice. Europe proper would have been no more than a province of Asia. A province of barons and serfs where the cities as a rule were no more than hamlets and life – so says the chronicler – an affair of murmuring and misery.

> We know the setting of the European scene of that century, but not the man who rose to dominate the world. To those Europeans Tamerlane's magnificence seemed unearthly and his power demoniac. When he appeared at their threshold, their kings sent letters and envoys to 'Tamburlan the Great, Lord of Tatary'.[7]

Europe tried to learn about Asia as much as possible. Some of the earliest contacts between Timur's empire and the West were made by Franciscans and in particular, Dominicans. In March 1377 Johannes de Galonifontibus, a Dominican, was appointed Bishop of Nakhichivan, a town in modern Azerbaijan. In August 1398 Pope Boniface IX made him Archbishop of Sultaniyya.[8] This city was located in Persia, modern Iran, and was for some time Timur's headquarters. Timur, after his great victory over the Ottoman Turks near Ankara in July 1402, sent Archbishop Johannes on a mission to Venice, Genoa, London and Paris with tidings of his triumph.[9] Timur sent letters to Henry IV of England and Charles VI of France, in which he proposed to conclude treaties for the granting of reciprocal privileges for the merchants of his realm and for those of England and France. Both kings replied with suitable terms and congratulated Timur on his brilliant victory.[10] On his return to Persia, Johannes de Galonifontibus remained at Sultaniyya until his transfer to the Crimea in about the year 1423.[11]

What did Europeans know about Asia and its people at the beginning of the fourteenth century? Not too much. Travellers' descriptions, and let us remember that printing appeared only in the fifteenth century, were rare and obscure. Carpini tried to frighten his readers. He wrote of the Mongols:

> When they are in battle, if one or two or three or even more out of a group of ten run away, all are put to death; and if a whole group of ten flees, the rest of the group of a hundred are all put to death, if they do not flee too. In a word, unless they retreat in a body, all who are in flight are put to death. Likewise if one or two or more go forward boldly to the fight, then the rest of the ten are put to death if they do not follow and, if one or more of the ten are captured, their companions are put to death if they do not rescue them.[12]

There was little consideration for human life at that time; also story-telling and legends from distant places were not taken seriously. We can see this in an example relating to Marco Polo. When in 1275 young Marco finished his trans-Asiatic trip and arrived in China, he became a favourite of the Mongol court at Peking. He was made governor of a province, received titles and honours, but after two decades he became homesick and so returned to Venice.[13] His neighbours, not in the least interested in his stories, nicknamed him Marco Millions, as he was forever telling them how rich the Khan was, and how many golden statues there were in this temple or that, or how many silken gowns the concubines of such and such a prime minister owned. Why should such yarns be believed, when it was well known that even the wife of the Emperor of Constantinople had only a single pair of silk stockings?

That was the psychology of Europeans. It was very hard to believe that some dirty Mongols in remote Asia lived much better than the Christians. And Marco Millions might have died and his story might have died with him if Venice and Genoa had not engaged in one of their little quarrels just then, and if Marco, as commander of a Venetian galley, had not been taken prisoner by the victorious Genoese. He remained in prison for a year, sharing his cell with a citizen from Pisa by the name of Rusticiano. This Rusticiano had had some experience as a writer and quickly recognising the publicity value of the great Polo story, he pumped Marco dry for information. Taking down everything Marco told him, he gave the world a book that is read as much today as when it was first published in the fourteenth century.

Polo was honest and correct in his recollections. But unfortunately there were other traveller's diaries, some of which were just fiction. The best example is *Mandeville's Travels*. This book was written in French in about 1357, possibly in France and probably not by 'Sir John Mandeville'. Nothing else is known, and little more can be inferred about the immediate origins of the book. The book was absolutely fictional and immediately successful. This 'Mandeville' wrote that the Mongols, whom he called *Tartariens*, all dressed in 'clothes of gold', that the men's and women's appearance was the same and that 'the folk of that contree begynnen alle hire thinges in the newe mone'.[14]

Being unable to discern and separate true information from false, Europeans, including kings and popes, were still ignorant to some degree about the real Asia in the fourteenth century. That is why Timur became a superman and an epic hero in their minds when they first heard of him. The real history of Asia in the fourteenth century was unknown to them.

In reality this history was a difficult one. The Mongol Empire had reached its zenith in the previous century. In the fourteenth century it was already divided into several states, which were called *hordes* or *uluses*. The Golden Horde, for example, covered the modern south-eastern part of Russia, western Siberia and northern Kazakhstan. Central Asia was a part of Chagatai ulus, and Chagatai (Jagatai) was a son of Chingiz Khan. During the second half of the thirteenth and the first half of the fourteenth centuries the Mongol ruling class and its Turkish troops gradually assimilated with the original inhabitants of these Inner Asian territories to become the Tatars of later times. Islam became the dominant religion there only in the fourteenth century and the Tatar language, a mixture of Mongol and old Turk languages, began to evolve as Latin in Europe. During the reign of Khan Uzbek (1313–40) and his son Janibek (1342–57), the Golden Horde became a fully-fledged Islamic state, but with numerous non-Muslim subjects.

In the division of Chingiz Khan's empire, Central Asia (*Mawarannahr* in Arabic sources) and eastern Turkestan (Kashgaria and Semirechie, that are closer to China than Central Asia) formed the ulus of Chagatai, named after his second son. The history of Chagatai ulus is extremely obscure and much of the chronology must be considered provisional, the source material is inadequate and even the numismatic evidence fragmentary. But it is clear that in this ulus its population was able to retain nomadic traditions far longer than in conquered China and Persia (Iran) or even the Golden Horde. In the fourteenth century the river Amu-Daria was a frontier between Chagatai ulus and the Mongol Il-Khanate of Persia. By the time of Timur both these states had already disintegrated and several smaller principalities were involved in permanent wars for local superiority.

In fact, by the time of Timur's first steps on the political scene, there were three strong powers in Asia at the borders of Europe, the Mongol Golden Horde, the Mamluk Sultanate of Egypt, and the state of Ottoman Turks.

The Mamluks, literally 'possessions', were mercenary slaves from the Black Sea region and became rulers of Egypt in 1250. The Mamluks were enslaved by purchase or captured outside the Abode of Islam – Islamic law forbade the enslaving of one Muslim by another – and then raised to be Muslims and soldiers; they were fiercely loyal on both scores. They had been the backbone of the Egyptian Abbasid dynasty caliphs' armies since the ninth century and many of them were Turks. Mamluks' accomplishments were considerable. They held most of Syria, Palestine and Egypt against the apparently invincible Mongols, winning a crucial victory at Ayn Jalut in Galilee (this site is now in Israel) in 1260. They also drove off the last of the Crusaders from the Holy Land with the capture of Acre (Acco) in 1291. However, one hundred years later, in Timur's time, they were not as strong as before.

The founder of the dynasty of the Othmanlis, or Ottoman Turks, which existed till 1918, was Osman (Othman), born in 1258. His father was Ertoghrul (called Orthgrul by E. Gibbon), the prince of a wandering tribe of warriors from Turkestan that had converted to Islam. Ertoghrul established himself with his tribe on the borders of the Byzantine Empire, and thought to form his tribe into a nation. He died in 1288 and Osman began his reign by carrying out the policy of his father most successfully. He even dreamt of turning the nation into an empire. Edward Gibbon wrote about him, 'Othman possessed, and perhaps surpassed, the ordinary virtues of a soldier; and the circumstances of time and place were propitious to his independence and success'.[15] These circumstances of time and place helped Osman and his successors ruin the Byzantine Empire, several other minor states and successfully fight with European nations during the entire fourteenth century. By the end of the century, at the time of Timur, the Ottoman Turks were at their zenith.

The states of India and China, however, concentrated on their internal affairs and were not at all aggressive during Timur's period.

Even though the period of Timur and the Timurids is not our immediate past, splinters of this glorious epoch can be seen even in Great Britain. Several metallic candlesticks, cups, jugs, a vase for flowers, a gold-plated pattern and inkpots are displayed in the British Museum. The master's name and the year of production are engraved on the inkpots and a craftsman, 'son of Ali Riza', made some of these items in 1386. A rare nephrite cup engraved with the name and title of Timur's grandson Ulugbek is also kept in London. The British Museum also exhibits a metallic jug of another Timurid, Hussein Baikara, made in 1497 (AH 903) that is covered with a carving and a subtle Arabic inscription. In Edinburgh Royal Museum in Scotland, an unusual shaped clay sputum cup made by Isfahan craftsman Mirak Hussein Yazdi in 1444 is on display, and according to the tradition of that time the cup is polished with white paint. There are numerous Timurid items also in Paris, Rome, New York, Istambul, Moscow and even in Lisbon.[16]

For the Jews, the fourteenth century was not at all a good period. In 1306 King Philip IV expelled the Jews from France. In 1349 Jews in Germany were persecuted because of the epidemic Black Death of 1347–54, which affected the Jewish communities as badly as all the others in Europe. Three hundred and fifty Jewish communities were destroyed in Germany at that time. This disaster gave further incentive to the Jewish migration to the East that had begun during the Crusades. Finally, in 1391 the Catholic Church in Spain initiated its struggle against the Jews, which led to their expulsion under the Grand Inquisitor Torquemada in 1492. Another persecution of the Jews in France took place in 1394; England was not involved in these pogroms because the

Jews from England had been expelled much earlier, in 1209. The Jews in Asia had no such complications, as we shall see in Chapter 2.

The fourteenth century was, perhaps, the last great century for Asiatic history and the Asiatic domination of the world, and of course the last great Asiatic figure was Tamerlane.

2

THE JEWS IN ASIA PRIOR TO TIMUR

> The history of Jewish settlements in the different parts of Central Asia since the Islamic conquest is still shrouded in great obscurity.
>
> (W.J. Fischel 1945)

How the Jews dispersed throughout Asia

Jews are Asians. They have their roots in Asia, they flourished in Asia, and they dispersed mostly in Asia.

It is possible that already in the first century BC the number of Jews outside of Palestine was greater than the number within it. No reliable figures exist, and the estimates vary greatly. It is probable, however, that there were between two and three million Jews in Palestine and a somewhat larger number in the different lands of their dispersion.

These Jewish communities came into existence in a variety of ways, and they differed greatly in size and importance. Some of them, like the immense community in Babylonia, began with the groups of captives who were torn away from their native land during the wars between Assyria and Babylon. Other Jewish settlements in the cities on the Mediterranean coasts and on the islands originated with Jewish traders who chose to remain in places where their travels had brought them. Jewish captives were added to these settlements and after being ransomed by their brethren or having purchased their own freedom, they became members of the communities. Some of the communities like those of Egypt and Babylonia counted their numbers in millions, while others, in the outlying parts of the Roman Empire, may have contained a few families only.

Wherever they settled, the Jews became prominent not only in the industrial, agricultural and commercial spheres, but in civic and political affairs as well. They usually acquired and made full use of the rights of citizenship. They held political office and served in the military and naval forces. In Egypt and Babylonia, in particular, they were known for their military prowess. Colonies of Jewish soldiers defended the frontiers of Egypt against the Ethiopians (the Elephantine Island colony), and the Babylonian Jews were also selected to serve as frontier guardsmen.

There are direct links between Babylonian Jewry, Persian Jewry and the Jews of Central Asia. With regard to the Jews of Babylonia, two facts are of particular importance. First, they constituted the largest Jewish community of the Diaspora;[1] second, while the others were exposed to Hellenistic influences, Babylonian Jews were not or almost not exposed to these influences. The Babylonian Jews lived in a country that was not part of the Roman Empire, and when later a Roman emperor attempted to conquer it, he met with the most desperate resistance from the Jews. The Jews participated in the rebellions against Trajan in Mesopotamia in AD 116.[2] This community had grown enormously since the days of Cyrus when part of it had left to support and help create the second Jewish State. At first the Jews lived in dense communities in fertile regions between the river Tigris and the Euphrates. Later, when Mesopotamia became a province of the immense Persian Empire, Jews were able to travel and to settle down practically everywhere within its borders. There is, for example, an ancient Jewish cemetery said to date from the second century AD not far from Shiraz in modern Iran.[3] For our story it is important to know that the Persian Jews took an active part in organising the silk trade. They owed this benefit to the evident support of the local kings.[4]

The question of the first Jewish appearance in Central Asia is itself divided into two separate questions. First, when did the first Jews visit this part of the world? Second, when did a substantial Jewish community settle down in the region?

Alas, there are no definite historical sources that can help us in answering these questions. We can speculate that the first Jews visited Central Asia before the time of Alexander the Great. Most probably this happened during the existence of the ancient Achaemenid Persian Empire in the fifth and fourth centuries BC. In its zenith, the Achaemenid dynasty ruled all the lands from Egypt to the northern Central Asian land of Khoresm, which means that 99 per cent of the Jews, made up its subjects at that time. Tolerant in religious matters with an inclination towards monotheism, the Achaemenians were particularly well disposed towards monotheistic peoples, above all the Jews. The Persians developed the old Semitic idea of some kind of survival after death into a belief of immortality. This belief penetrated into Jewish doctrines, and through this filter Zoroastrianism influenced Christian theology. Being within the borders of a huge state and having no restrictions in wandering, some Jews could penetrate Central Asia as far as Khoresm. There are, in fact, definite records about people moving in opposite directions. For example, Khoresmian troops took part in the great Greek–Persian war of 480 BC. If the Khoresmian soldier, Dargman, carried out his military duties in the Jewish garrison of Elephantine Island in upper Egypt,[5] it is therefore certainly possible that some brave Jewish merchant also travelled far in the opposite direction, to Central Asian *terra incognita*.

If some historian definitely proves that there were Jewish troops in the army of Alexander the Great, we will be able to state that some Jews marched through Sogdiana, Central Asia, in the fourth century BC. By the same token, if some historian proves that some Jewish veterans of Alexander were given land in Sogdiana, we would be able to say that we know the exact date of the first Jewish settlement in Central Asia. Without this knowledge we can only move on to the most recent period of pre-Islamic Iran.

Fourth century BC was the era of the Persian kingdom of the Sassanid dynasty. In addition to the semi-legendary Esther, the Jewish wife of Xerxes I (486–465 BC), Sassanian Persia, a state practising several religions, presented Jewish history with another, absolutely real, Jewish queen, Shushan-Dukht, wife of the Sassanian king, Yazdigird I (AD 399–420).[6]

This fact does not mean, of course, that Persian Jews lived without any troubles. From time to time, but not too frequently, there were anti-Jewish riots and persecutions. Already Yazdigird II (AD 438–59) persecuted both Jews and Christians at the end of his reign. One of these riots took place in Isphahan under king Peroz (AD 459–84). The riot was sparked off by uncontrolled rumours of the murder of two Zoroastrian priests by Jews.[7] Pre-Islamic Persia at that time was a state with numerous cults that fought each other, creating paramount problems for the Jews, and in addition to Christians and Jews there were Zoroastrians, Manichaeans and Mazdakites.

Zoroastrianism is a religion with a dualistic theology of two gods, the Good God, Ahura-Mazda or Ormuzd, and the Evil God, Angra-Mainyu or Ahriman. These gods are forever fighting each other and the Zoroastrian ritual places great importance on the divinity of *Atar* (fire). The Manichean faith is another dualistic religion based on a mixture of theological and metaphysical ideas with a system of two Roots or basic principles of Light and Dark, and the three Moments of Past, Present and Future. Light is divine, and each man possesses a divine spark of light. The Manicheans practised baptism and communion and received absolution and a remission of sins before death. They rejected Judaism and considered Moses and the Prophets to be devils and their god the lord of darkness. Mazdaism (from Mazda, the Great Creator) was another Persian religion, based on Zoroastrian principles but centred on Ahura Mazda. All these religions found their route to Central Asia also by way of the Silk Route.

In general the Jews were very loyal to the Persian rulers. At the beginning of the seventh century AD, the Jews watched the Persians attack the Orthodox Christian Byzantine Empire with great expectancy and joyfully welcomed the conquest of Jerusalem in AD 614.[8] The Jews learned the Persian *dari* language and there is evidence that at a very early date the Jews were writing *dari* in Hebrew characters.[9] In 632, the Byzantine Emperor Heraclius ordered all the Jews in his dominions to convert to Christianity. As a result, many Byzantine Jews fled to Persia and to Central Asia. Although the Jews were less bothersome than the Manichaeans to the Zoroastrians, they did antagonise the Christians, and being dependent on the fluctuating religious preferences of the Persian kings, the Jews did not resist the Arabs too much when the Islamic armies arrived.

The Arab conquest of Persia and Central Asia gave historians more reliable information on Jewish history in the region that can be found in historical accounts by Arab scholars of the time. In general, the Arab conquest was a convenient event for the Asian Jews. The Jews gained in strength under Islam not only in Babylonia, their national and religious centre during the last pre-Islamic centuries, but also in Palestine, Egypt, Persia and Central Asia; in Muslim Spain and in many adjacent countries, the Jews increased in number and influence.[10]

The Jews were not foreigners to the Arabs; they had lived among them in Arabia for ages. The anti-Jewish suras of the Koran contained dangerous tinder for fanaticism, but for a long time that tinder seldom kindled. Having achieved the status of a world power, Islam proved to be tolerant. The Muslim civilisation developed a high culture, and it is very well known that the children of Israel made notable contributions to it.

However, the Arab Empire had erected a mighty barrier around all Christian lands and Central Europe had been cut off from Egypt, the Near East and other Asian territories. The Jews alone were still in a position to mediate between the Christian West and the Muslim East. This position gave them some advantages that will be discussed later.[11]

When the Arabs conquered Persia in the middle of the seventh century, people who were in accordance with the precepts of the Koran were recognised as ‘People of the Book’, allowing the Jews and Christians to continue in their former faith as *dhimmis*. This term only applied to followers of recognised religions. All the other religions were counted as pagan and a Muslim was obliged to fight against their followers in the holy war of *jihad*. *Dhimmis*, however, were obliged to pay the special additional poll-tax for non-Islamic citizens of Islamic countries – *jizya*.[12] In case a non-Muslim was a landowner, he was also obliged to pay the tax of *kharaj* for his land.

That is why Islamic rule in Persia, especially in the early days of the conquest, sat more lightly upon Christians and Jews than the previous Zoroastrian rule in Persia. At first only Christians and Jews were counted as *dhimmi*, because they were specifically mentioned in the Koran. Later, however, Zoroastrians were also counted in the ranks of 'People of the Book'[13] as these Zoroastrians were dispersed throughout Central Asia too. In Bukhara, Zoroastrians sacrificed a cock each day of *Navruz* (the New Year) at the tomb of the legendary king and hero Siyavush. These Bukharian Zoroastrians lived with their Jewish neighbours and Nestorian Christians in the same city.[14] Later, the Muslim treatment of the Jews, Christians and Zoroastrians in Persia and Central Asia varied in accordance with the policies of the caliphs and the attitudes of different local governors.

Zoroastrians did not stop to fight other religions, including Judaism and Islam, after the Arab conquest. The treatise *Skand-Gumanik Vicar* became their last ideological book to set up a true faith. This book tried to prove the superiority of Zoroastrianism over Judaism, Christianity, Manichaeism and Islam.[15] Under these circumstances it was natural for the Muslims to co-operate with the Jews. When the Arabs defeated the Sassanian dynasty, they found an intact system of Jewish self-government in Persia, led by the exiliarch, a truly political official and rich landowner. This self-government became even more important under the caliphs.

Having conquered Persia, the Arabs moved to Central Asia in the eighth century. Much less is known about the Jews in Central Asia in comparison to the Persian Jews. Modern books on the history of Diaspora[16] or on Jews in Muslim countries[17] usually disregard the subject. A book on the subject of Central Asian Jews was published in Russia in 1995.[18] This book also disregarded the subject of early Jewish presence in the region, as it concentrated mainly on the preceding 200 years of Jewish history in Asia.

However, there are some indicators of Jewish presence in Transoxania. From 1937 to 1947 the Russian archaeologist and historian S. Tolstov, spent years of field work in the northern part of Central Asia called Khoresm, which was an independent state before the Arab conquest. Using his archaeological evidence and analysing historical sources, mainly Arab history of Tabari,[19] Tolstov became aware of a Jewish presence in Khorezm during the pre-Islamic period. He discovered that Khorezm religious leaders of the early eighth century were called *habr* (pl. *ahbar*) in Arabic, which means a Jewish scholar or learned rabbi. Tolstov excavated coins from that period that had inscriptions in the Khorezmian language written in the Hebrew alphabet. There was also a trefoil on the coins similar to the trefoil on the current Israeli Shekel. All this permitted Tolstov to name the Khoresmian religion of the early eighth century as 'syncretic Judaism'.[20]

The conquest of Central Asia by the Arab general Qutaybah from AD 708–18, was the last Arab action towards the east. This bloody war was important for the Arabs. The crossing of the Syr Darya river was an epoch-making event, as this river, rather than the Amy Darya river, formed a natural political and racial frontier between settled Iranians and nomadic Turks. Its crossing constituted the first direct challenge by Arabs to Mongoloids and by Islam to Buddhism. Bukhara, Balkh and Samarkand had Buddhist monasteries and in Samarkand and Bukhara the fire temples and idols were demolished.[21] The Jews, being a 'People of the Book', were in a favourable situation during these religious struggles. However, Tolstov realised that the Khoresmian Jewish religious leaders fled north from the Arab armies and met the Khazars.[22]

We will not dwell upon the history of Khazaria here. This huge state flourished on the banks of the river Volga on the Caspian Sea. There are other works on the subject of Khazaria in which Judaism was a state religion.[23] I want only to mention that the existence of a Jewish state right in the middle of this huge Asian continent was very impressive, and the influence of this state on the neighbouring nations was significant. In fact, the Khazars, who themselves accepted Judaism around AD 750, were not the only Asian nation of this religion. We know from the Franciscan traveller of the thirteenth century, Plano Carpini, that there was at least one more Asian tribe, named Brutachi, that also acknowledged the Judaic faith.[24] These Brutachi, or Burtashi, took part in a great Mongol–Russian battle at Kulikovo Pole in 1380, serving in the Mongol army.

It is usually said that Judaism came to the Khazar steppes of the modern Volga river area by way of the Byzantine Empire and the Crimean peninsula of the Black Sea. While Tolstov's idea of Judaisation of Khazaria through Central Asia sounds plausible, some additional study needs to be conducted on the subject. Tolstov published some of his materials in English[25] and therefore found a Western advocate for his ideas, V. Altman, who also considered that there were reasons to believe that Judaism 'was brought to Khazaria in the eighth century [the century of Arab conquest!] through Khorezm'.[26]

Believable or not, two facts are certain; first, Jews lived in Central Asia before the Arab conquest; second, Khorezm was the immediate southern neighbour of Khazaria. The last statement is supported by the famous letter of Joseph the king of Khazaria to a Spanish Jew, 'the head of the Assembly, Hasdai, the son of Isaac, son of Ezra', in which the king described the southern borders of his kingdom.[27] An Arab genealogist of the beginning of the ninth century, Ibn al-Kalbi (d. AD 819), made both the Khazars and the Khoresmians descendants of the biblical Isaac.[28]

For our story, it is important to understand about a possible indirect Jewish influence on the Turks through the Khazars. This idea was expressed by D. Dunlop in his *History of the Jewish Khazars*. He draws our attention to the fact that the Turkish tribe of Oghuz (Ghuzz) was closely related to the Khazars. These Turks had a chief called Seljuk (history places the Seljuk Turks later). The sons of Seljuk were called Mika'il, Yunus, Musa and Isra'il. Dunlop assumes that these names, especially Isra'il, indicate a Jewish Khazar influence on the Turks.[29] However, there is also another theory that postulates a Muslim origin of these names.[30] In any case, there were close connections between the Khazars and the Turks. Bar Hebraeus (AD 1225–86), a Syriac historian and religious leader of Jewish origin, wrote in his *Chronography*, a subchapter on 'the beginning of the Kingdom of the Saljuks in Persia'. He was very specific in his description of Turk–Khazar relations. Seljuk himself was in great favour at the court of the Khazars' king until troubles transpired with the queen.[31]

In general, Jews and Judaism were not something strange and unknown for nomadic and semi-nomadic tribes of Inner and Central Asia. Judaism, so much oppressed in Medieval Europe and the Byzantine Empire, was one of the recognised religions, equal in rights to any other faith in Asia. That goes for the Jewish presence in India too.[32] In Muslim Central Asia the great scholar al-Biruni (AD 973–1048), himself a native of Khorezm, wrote on comparative religion in two of his main books, *India* and *Chronology*. He wrote on all known religions, including Judaism and even the faith of the Samaritans. It is obvious from reading his works that he had some Jewish informants, as Biruni himself mentioned his contact with Jewish teachers in *Chronology*. He quoted the Old Testament frequently. He knew Jewish festivals such as Yom Kippur, Hanukka, Purim, Pessach and others. He even mentioned the Jewish sects of the time other than the Rabbinic Jews and Karaites, such as the Miladites, Maghribis and the Alfaniyya.[33] Another great Central Asian scholar of that period, Abu Ali Ibn Sina (Avicenna), a physician and 'the Aristotle of the East', was said to have been of Jewish origin himself,[34] but this is pure speculation.

Before Benjamin of Tudela's famous travels to the East, an Arab historian and traveller of the tenth century, Abu-Abdallah al-Mukaddasi (al-Makdisi), mentioned Persian Jews in his book, *The Best Division to Know Countries*, written in AD 985. This scholar was born in Jerusalem and knew Palestine well. That is why he mentioned that the town of Marv (Merv, now in Turkmenistan) resembles Palestinian Ramla more than other cities.[35] In a subchapter entitled *General Description of Khorasan*, he wrote that in Khorasan 'there are many Jews and only a few Christians'.[36]

There are no such clear indications from historians about the presence of the Jews in Central Asia, nor is there archaeological evidence of a Jewish presence there, in contrast to archaeological evidence such as a cemetery tombstone dating from AD 898 from the Jewish settlement, Chufuth-Kale, in the Crimea.[37] However, according to local tradition it is mentioned that the first synagogue was built in Bukhara in the eighth century.[38] Up to the time of Benjamin of Tudela, the Jews in Muslim Persia and Central Asia were members of the 'protected' communities, *dhimmi*, living in their own quarters. They enjoyed freedom of religion and appointed their own religious officials, subject probably to the confirmation of the sultan and his officials. Their usual limitation, such as the wearing of distinguishing markings on their clothing (usually yellow) and restrictions to bear arms and ride horses, are well known. At the same time, Jews were largely occupied in trade and commerce,[39] as well as in medicine. The prominent philosopher and physician of this age, Abu'l-Barakat Hibat Allah al-Baghdadi (d. 1152), was known, for example, to the poet Umar Khayyam, whose *Rubayat* is famous all over the world.[40] There was also the Jewish tax-farmer in Basra, Ibn Allan, who prior to 1079–80 had farmed some of the private domains of the caliph.[41] Unfortunately he was killed in a local riot. In Central Asia, Muslim rulers of the eleventh century had a slogan, 'to keep agreements with *dhimmi*', and let the Jews live peacefully.[42] I need to mention here that at the early stage of the Arab conquest of Central Asia, the Sogds, a nation that inhabited Central Asia at that time, was obliged to pay poll-tax (*djizya*) and land-tax (*kharaj*) too, until the Sogds became Muslim.[43]

When Benjamin of Tudela started his journey, the Jews, moving by way of the Great Silk Route, had already explored Asia from the Near East to China.[44] Benjamin of Tudela travelled through the Middle East in about AD 1170. There are two English translations of his diary, that of A. Asher of 1840 and of M.N. Adler of 1907.[45] Therefore the following paragraph has two versions. Asher's version is as follows:

> Seven days from thence Giva [Asher thought that this is Khiva in Khorezm, Adler thought that this is Ghazna in Persia], a large

> city on the banks of the Oxus, containing about eight thousand Jews. Very extensive commerce is carried on in this place, to which resort traders of all countries and languages; the country about it is very flat.[46]
>
> Five days from thence, on the frontiers of the kingdom [Persia] stands Samarkhand, a city of considerable magnitude, which contains about fifty thousand Jews. The Prince Rabbi Obadiah is the governor of the community, which includes many wise and learned men.

Adler's version states:

> Thence it is seven days to Ghaznah the great city on the river Gozan, where there are about 80,000 Israelites [against Asher's 8,000]. It is a city of commercial importance; people of all countries and tongues come thither with their wares. The land is extensive.
>
> Thence it is five days to Samarkand, which is the great city on the confines of Persia. In it live some 50,000 Israelites, and R. Obadiah the Nasi is their appointed head. Among them are wise and very rich men.[47]

It is hard to translate the Hebrew language, 8,000 can become 80,000 and 'learned men' can be changed into 'rich men'. Bukhara is not mentioned. It is obvious from the text that Benjamin did not visit Samarkand himself as no real description of the city is present. Therefore the number of 50,000 Jews seems to be an exaggeration. Indeed, the city of Isphahan, a well-known large city with numerous Jewish inhabitants, had, according to Benjamin, 15,000 Jews (both Asher and Adler agree on that). The huge community of Baghdad had 40,000 Jewish inhabitants.[48] Samarkand could have had 50,000 Jews, or 15,000, or 5,000, but one fact is certain: there was a sizeable Jewish community in the largest city of Central Asia fifty years before the Mongol conquest.

Benjamin's statements are confirmed according to a local oral tradition, where the Jews took part in constructing the aqueduct to supply Samarkand with water in the twelfth century.[49]

Then the thirteenth century came and the Mongols appeared.

Jews and Mongols

The spiritual, social and economic climate of the Muslim world, generally favourable for the Jews, underwent a profound transformation during the course of the thirteenth century. In addition to the Spanish Reconquista, the Mongol hordes swept across Asia into the Muslim East, leaving a path of devastation in its wake. In 1219–21 Chingiz Khan defeated the Khorezm state and conquered Central Asia. On 10 February 1258, Hulagu Khan, a grandson of Chingiz Khan, took Baghdad after a brief siege, executed the local caliph along with many members of his family, and put an end to the Muslim power. Damascus fell in 1259.[50]

There are psychological and historical links between Chingiz Khan and Timur. That is why the Mongol attitude toward the Jews is so important for the subject of this book.

First of all, the Jews were not complete strangers to the Mongols. Moving eastwards by the Great Silk Route, Jews had settled in China between the seventh and the thirteenth centuries.[51] The first synagogue was erected in 1163 in Kaifeng[52] (before Chingiz Khan's conquest of northern China) and was rebuilt in 1279 during the reign of the Mongol ruler of China, Kublai Khan.[53] The Mongols knew of the Jews before Chingiz Khan's great expedition towards the west. These Chinese Jews were silk traders with Persian roots.[54]

In addition to the synagogue that was rebuilt in China during Kublai's reign, Marco Polo tells a story about Kublai's religious tolerance:

> This [kissing the Holy Scriptures] was his usual practice upon each of the principal Christian festivals, such as Easter and Christmas; and he observed the same at the festivals of the Saracens, Jews, and idolaters.
>
> Upon being asked his motive for this conduct, he said: 'There are four great Prophets who are reverenced and worshipped by the different classes of mankind. The Christians regard Jesus Christ as their divinity; the Saracens, Mahomet; the Jews, Moses; and the idolaters, Sogomombar-kan, the most eminent amongst their idols. I do honour and show respect to all the four, and invoke to my aid whichever amongst them is in truth Supreme in Heaven.'[55]

There is no evidence that the Mongols persecuted Jews in any part of their domains, and the domains were vast indeed, from the Far East up to the German borders. A significant number of Jews became citizens of the Mongol Empire. William of Rubruck saw Jews in many cities of the Caucasian region and in Persia in 1254.[56] Brother Andrew of Perugia, of the Order of Friars Minor, mentioned the Jews of China in his letter written in 1321:

> In this vast empire there are verily men of every nation under heaven and of every sect; and each and all are allowed to live according to their own sect. For this is their opinion, or I should say their error, that every man is saved in his own sect. And we can preach freely and securely, but of the Jews and the Saracens none is converted.[57]

Marco Polo also mentioned a small Jewish community in Tiflis (modern Tbilisi in Georgia).[58] There were also Jews, mainly merchants, in Russia and Crimea at the time of the Mongol conquest.[59]

And the Jews of Central Asia? Alas, after Benjamin of Tudela's brief reference, the Jewish historical sources mention neither Bukhara and Samarkand nor the other cities of Central Asia for several centuries. However, there was a Jewish scholar, Solomon ben Samuel, in Urgench (Gurganj, the city in Khorezm). He wrote a Hebrew–Persian dictionary in Urgench in 1338. The dictionary survived[60] and we know that Jews, even learned Jews, had been living in the region under Mongol rule at the time of Timur's childhood.

The most curious medieval travel book, *Mandeville's Travels* of 1357, (Timur was already twenty-one by then), was a mixture of new geographical knowledge with fables, and it mentioned the Jews only once and then in connection with Bukhara. The unknown author of the *Travels* wrote about the Jews in the twenty-ninth chapter of his book, dedicated to the countries 'that ben beyonde the land of Cathay'. In this chapter he placed the Jews between Bukhara (Bacharye in the book) and some mountains near the Caspian Sea at the Tartar province of Caldilhe. They were identified as the Ten Lost Tribes who, however, still spoke only Hebrew.[61] 'People were then on the whole more drawn to fabulous tales than to factual narrations,' was a general comment on the book by one of its editors.[62] However, Khorasan, Khoresm, Samarkand, Turkmeniya and Turkestan are mentioned in the book in addition to Bukhara. Also the question arises why did the author place Jews in Central Asia and not in India, China or Siberia?

Medieval Muslim historians did not speak about the Jews of Central Asia under Mongol rule. Abu Omar al-Jauzjani (1193?) told a story about a religious struggle in Samarkand under the Mongols in his historical work *Tabakat-i Nasiri* (1260). According to this story, Christians and Muslims of Samarkand, being involved in religious strife, tried to gain Mongol support against each other. The Mongol Berke Khan accepted Islam himself and then helped the Muslims against the Christians in 1259.[63] As a result, the Christians were oppressed and Berke was hailed by Jauzjani for his Muslim zeal. However, we have no similar stories about Jews and perhaps Samarkand Jews were not involved in any significant religious struggle.

During the Mongol wars people of all nations died indiscriminately. After the war Jews probably encountered few problems with the Mongols. Some of the Jews, such as Sa'd al-Daula and Rashid ad-Din, sustained careers at the Mongol court in Persia. Indeed, for the Jews of Persia the second half of the thirteenth century was a period of unusual freedom and opportunity. The early Mongols (*Il-Khans*), who had ruled Persia sincc the 1250s were pagans, Shamanists. They did not recognise the distinction between Jews, Christians and Muslims. They were hostile to Sunni Islam for political reasons and openly showed favour to Jews, especially during the reign of Arghun Khan (1284–91). Judaeo-Persian literature also flourished under the Mongols. The Torah was translated into the Persian language, and Jewish writers all used the Hebrew script exclusively.

This does not mean, however, that there were no riots at that time. Syriac Christian historian and religious leader Bar Hebraeus (1225–86), the son of the Jewish physician Aaron, wrote in his *Chronography* about an attack of some bandits in 1286:

> And they put to the torture not only the Christians but the Arabs also, and they made a mock of their women, and sons, and daughters in the mosques before their eyes.
>
> And when they had made an end there they went to the quarter of the Jews, and they looted their houses and plundered all their community.[64]

We see from this description that this was a usual bandits' attack and not an anti-Jewish pogrom. Also the bandits were 'robbers and brigands, Kurds, Turkmans, and Arabs' and not at all Mongols. Bar Hebraeus even mentioned that Mongols and Kurds were in strife.[65]

The first real anti-Jewish pogroms took place in Tabriz and Baghdad in 1291.[66] Once again the resident population of the cities was involved but not the Mongols. Then, in 1295, the Ilkhanid dynasty became Muslim under the rule of Ghazan Khan. Another pogrom followed in 1296 under the command of Ghazan and Emir Nauruz. Ghazan gave orders to destroy all Christian churches, Jewish synagogues, fire temples and Buddhist pagodas.[67] Bar Hebraeus mentioned:

> Now this persecution had not dominion over our people alone [Christians], but also over the Jews, and it was twice as fierce, many times over, on the priests who were worshippers of idols.[68]

Once again the persecution was not entirely anti-Jewish. In fact, this second appearance of Islam in Iran again made the Jews *dhimmi* with *djiziya*, *kharadj*, humiliating them. 'Christians were not to appear in public without having a zonar, or peculiar girdle, about their waist, nor Jews unless they wore a special head-dress'.[69]

As it was written in the Persian *Divan of Sana'i* in the twelfth century:

> For the Jew in this arena fearless casts himself amain,
> And the Brahmin in this temple burns his idol at the shrine.[70]

For the Jews, the main benefit of the Mongol invasion was that Mongols did not make any distinction between them and all the other conquered nations. In medieval Europe, Jews usually were discriminated from the local nations. They either received privileges from a king, becoming 'king's serfs', or were persecuted up to expulsion from a country. The Mongols did not give the Asian Jews any privileges and did not persecute them either. Such was the Jewish situation at the time of Timur's arrival. As we will see later, Timur was wise enough to maintain this order.

Map 2 Timur's empire

3

TIMUR (TAMERLANE)

The brightest personality of the fourteenth century

> The career of Timour as a conqueror, is unparalleled in history; for neither Cyrus, nor Alexander, nor Caesar, nor Attila, nor Zenghis Khan, nor Charlemagne, nor Napoleon, ever won by the sword so large a portion of the globe, or ruled over so many myriads of subjugated fellow-creatures.
>
> (Sir Edward S. Creasy, *History of the Ottoman Turks*, London, 1878, p. 45)

Francis Galton mentioned Timur in his famous book *Hereditary Genius*.[1] He had no doubt that Timur was a genius, he only doubted that his genius was hereditary. Galton's contemporary John Pool echoed, 'Though born only a petty chieftain, Timur, by his remarkable genius for war, quickly forced his way to the front rank of Eastern conquerors.'[2] Timur, though, became famous not only because of his genius for war. We might call such a person 'a brilliant general', or consider a talented politician as 'an outstanding statesman', and we could also call an outstanding organiser 'a talented manager'. But we would not title that person as a genius. In the case of Timur, as I see it, his genius was the result of an accumulative combination of his talents in statehood, military affairs, politics and general management. Timur was not a thinker; he was a doer with a special talent for precise planning and enormous energy to execute his plans.

The pre-Timurid history of Central Asia can be divided into several periods. The first is from the Stone Age until the Persian invasion of the sixth century BC. During this period some Asian nomads settled at the banks of two large rivers, the Amu-Dariya (Oxus) and Syr-Dariya (Jeihun), and formed the first primitive states. The second period lasts from the Persian invasion to the invasion of Alexander the Great in the fourth century BC; during this period Central Asia was under the political and cultural influence of Persia. After Alexander the Great's campaigns (330 BC) the Baktrian kingdom was established in Central Asia and Greek culture was introduced to the region, but Baktria was then replaced by the nomadic Kushan kingdom that ceased to exist in the first half of the third century AD. In this period Buddhist religion and elements of Hinduism were spreading throughout Central Asia, then in the middle of the sixth century AD the Turks came to the region. In the very beginning of the eighth century the Arabs occupied the land of Central Asia and the period of Islamisation began. This lasted until the Mongol invasion of Central Asia at the beginning of the thirteenth century (from 1218 onwards). Timur, in fact, liberated Central Asia from the last Mongol rulers.

Timur was born on 8 April 1336 (25 Shahban 736 of the Muslim *Hijra* calendar) in the settlement Khodja Ilgar near Kesh (present-day Shahrisabs in Uzbekistan).[3] His name, which was very common in those days, has caused historians a great deal of trouble and, to make matters worse, his name has frequently been misspelled and confused with others of the same name. An example of mistaken identity can be found in Christopher Dawson's *Mission to Asia* where the name of Tamerlane is attributed to another Timur, Timur Khan of China (1294–1307).[4] It is easy, however, to avoid such complications when reading the historical literature on the subject. Timur usually was mentioned with specific titles of Amir (Emir), kurakan (*kurkan*), or *sahibkiran*. Only occasionally was he called Timur beg and never Timur Khan. The term *kurakan* in fact is a Mongol word, which means son-in-law. Ibn Arabshah gave an explanation of it in his biography of Timur:

> But after conquering Transoxiana [another name for Central Asia] and rising above his companions, he married princesses and therefore they gave him the surname Kurkan, which in the Mogul language means Son-in-law, since he had gained affinity with kings, and enjoyed the highest authority in their courts.[5]

Indeed, this term was not understood outside the Turko-Mongol world. That is why the term *kurkan*, as a surname (not a title!) attributed to Timur, appeared very often, for example, in the Mamluk sources.[6] In fact, Timur accepted the title when he married a widow of his ally, brother-in-law and later enemy Amir Husain (Khuseyn or Hussein). This woman, Saray Mulk Khanum (Bibi-Khanum), was the daughter of Kazan Khan who himself was a descendant of Chingiz Khan. Therefore this title was very important for Timur because it was indicative of his relations with the family line of the Chingizids. I should mention here that the title *Khan* was attributed only to Chingizids by their blood line at that time.[7]

As for *Sahibkiran* (or *Sahib-Qiran* from Persian sources), it was just a panegyric title meaning born under the lucky star. This title was an astrological metaphor and used by the Mongols before Timur.

However, these titles help a reader of literature on Asiatic history of the thirteenth and fourteenth centuries to distinguish without a doubt Timur–Tamerlane from Timur-malik, Timur Qutlugh, Timur-shah, Toghul Timur, Timurtash and other prominent Timurs of the time. The name Tamerlane is the sixteenth-century European corruption of the Persian Temur-i-lenk, Timur the lame, a name given him because of a slight limp, usually explained by injury in an early battle or occasionally as a tubercular infection.

According to Khwandamir, the genealogy of Timur descends to our Biblical Noah. This Timurid historian wrote in 1524:

> The Axis of the Sultanate and Caliphate Amir Temur Kuragan was the son of Amir Taraghai, son of Amir Burkul, son of Elangir Noyan, son of Amir Ejil, son of Qarachar Noyan, son of Amir Sughuchachan, son of Erdamchi, son of Baysunghur Khan, son of Dutummanan Khan, son of Buka Khan, son of Bodhonchar Qa'an, son of Alanqoa. As was recorded truly in the first section of this volume, Alanqoa was of the lineage of Qayan, whose descent stems from Japheth the son of Noah.[8]

This Noah's distant relative by the line of Japhet lived at the same time as Richard II of England, Charles VI of France, Dmitriy Donskoy and Vassiliy I of Russia, and Bayazet I of Turkey. His motto was *Rasti, Rusti*, that is, 'Truth is safety', according to Ibn Arabshah's translation,[9] and 'Justice and Power', according to our current understanding.[10] Timur belonged to the Mongol tribe of Barlas which settled in the valley of the small river Kashka Darya only in the beginning of the fourteenth century, intermingling with the Turkish population, adopting Islạm, and gradually giving up its own nomadic ways.

Marcel Brion started his book *Tamerlan* with a table entitled 'Le mémorial des siécles'.[11] He named Timur 'the man of the century' for the fourteenth century. According to him, Muhammad was the man of the seventh century, Louis XIV the man of the seventeenth century, Napoleon of the nineteenth and Lenin of the twentieth century. Unfortunately the official histories of Timur – written at his command by his court historians and at the court of his son Shah Rukh – say nothing about Timur's early years. The real history starts from 1360.

In 1360 and 1361 the khan of the neighbouring state of Moghulistan, another Timur, called Tughluq Timur, campaigned in unstable Central

Asia. One of his followers was the future 'man of the century'. After the attack on former Chagatay Ulus, Tughluq Timur presented his brave captain Timur with the Kashka Darya *tumen* (a province that could send ten thousand warriors to an army). But Timur soon broke off relations with the foreign khan and his son Ilyas Khodja, who had been left to govern Central Asia.

Being now an amir (a ruler) of a rich *tumen*, Timur, in 1361, contacted one of the pretenders to power in the region, the chieftain of Balkh, Amir Hussein, sealing the relationship by marrying his sister. We know already that Timur also married Hussein's widows afterwards. During the whole decade of the 1360s Timur fought with Hussein against the Moghulistan armies and then against Hussein himself. Finally this series of long-lasting local wars made Timur the sole ruler of Central Asia. Between 1360 and 1370 Timur created both a political machine and a new kind of army that were rooted in the political background of Central Asia. In 1370 a meeting of the military chiefs and nobles of the tribes proclaimed him the only ruler of a reunited and centralised state that was within the approximate borders of Chagatay Ulus. As the ulus was, in fact, a Chingizid's domain, Timur proclaimed Soyurghatmish, a real descendant of Chagatay, a puppet khan for sitting around doing nothing.[12]

Thenceforward he extended his dominions by ruthless warfare, slowly at first, then with increasing momentum, the 'marvelous Mohammedan power of mushroom growth', as John Pool described it.[13] Inside Central Asia, Timur created a new kind of composite army, a new pool of military technology including the first cannons.

In 1370 Timur made Samarkand, an ancient city with almost 2000 years of history, his capital and finally restored its walls that had been ruined by Mongols almost 150 years before. The main support of Timur's administration came from the warlike nomadic and semi-nomadic Mongol nobility of Central Asia. Conscious of the need to broaden his social base, Timur tried to befriend the local land-owning nobility, the urban notables, and the Muslim clergy. He chose the descendant of the Prophet Muhammad, Said Baraka, to be his spiritual adviser.

Timur made a great effort to reorganise his army. He combined the traditional military system of the Mongols with tactical and technical innovations. In Timur's time, gunpowder was still an innovation as it was only invented in 1313 by the German Grey Friar Berthold Schwarz, yet Timur was the first among the Eastern military leaders to use guns at war. Timur's regular inspections of the army helped to whip his soldiers into a very efficient fighting machine.

A lot has been written about the cruelty of Timur's wars. However,

Plate 1 Samarkand, the capital of Timur's empire, was built by craftsmen of different nationalities. This Djami Mosque of the fifteenth century is one of the most vivid samples of Timurid architecture

Voltaire saw it in another light, 'There is one circumstance which may give us an advantageous idea of Tamerlane's character, which is, that we find him, through the whole course of this war, strictly observant of the laws of nations'.[14] In fact, these 'laws' were very simple – 'everybody co-operates, nobody gets hurt'. The usual claims were to accept Timur's superiority and to pay a huge tribute. Bold resistance or treasonable politics made Timur very aggressive.

In 1372 Timur launched a campaign against Khorezm. This set of oases in the Kizil-Kum desert had a long and noble history and was the last independent state in Central Asia. The rulers of Khorezm tried to use the controversies between Timur's state and their northern neighbour, the Golden Horde, to their advantage, but it was only a prolongation of an agony and finally exhausted Timur's patience. Several acts of treason with apologies between them were a good provocation and finally Timur seized Urgench, the capital of Khorezm, in 1388, and overthrew the local Sufi dynasty. He moved its inhabitants to Samarkand and had the plundered and devastated city razed to the ground and its site sown with barley. In 1391, however, Timur ordered the restoration of Urgench and this city still exists today in Uzbekistan.

In 1381 Timur attacked Afghanistan. In early spring Timur's forces surrounded the walls of its capital Herat. The ruler of Herat, Ghiyas ad-din Pir Ali, first withdrew into the citadel, but soon, realising his helplessness, he came to Timur's tent and begged his mercy. The mercy was granted and the same fate befell Herat as with other captured cities. A heavy tribute was imposed on it and many craftsmen were deported to Samarkand.

The twenty-year-long period of local wars in Central Asia had come to an end. Now Timur was ready to fight beyond his motherland. Michael Prawdin wrote about this in his comprehensive book *The Mongol Empire: Its Rise and Legacy*:

> Tamerlane's dream was to be a new, a Muslim Jenghiz Khan. This was his obsession, which he pursued throughout life with fanaticism and sanctimoniousness, with audacity and cunning, with cruelty intertwined with a chivalrous spirit. The passion never left him under the burning sun of Syria, or in the ice-bound plains of Russia; never left him amid the febrile fantasies of a sick-bed or when, as a half-blind old man, he set out upon the last and greatest campaign of his life.[15]

One may or may not accept this poetic explanation but another twenty years of wars were just ahead. Tamerlane was a politician turned soldier. Having defeated Afghanistan, Timur now became preoccupied with Iranian affairs.

By the middle of the fourteenth century, the strong Mongol State of Il-Khans of Persia had crumbled into pieces. In Timur's time there was widespread evidence of the collapse of national power. In itself, this might well have aroused the expansionist appetites of neighbouring states much earlier, but with the exception of the Golden Horde they simply lacked the military strength to take advantage of the situation. This statement applies to both the Ottoman Empire, which was in its early stages, and to the Mamluk Sultanate of Egypt, which was military stronger but showed no interest in relatively remote Persia. As to the Golden Horde, this state was involved in the fifteen-year-period of civil strife after the death of several prominent khans.

Seeing Persia in a state of anarchy, Timur made his move. Even modern Uzbek historians agree that the expedition to Iran was prompted by its disintegration and lack of defence rather than by any other considerations.[16] But it was not, speaking in modern terms, an act of pure aggression. By the 1380s Timur's state was a strong, stable, centralised domain. The period of civil wars had come to an end. At the same time the Persians were still in a chaotic state with their almost permanent civil war. That is why some important figures in Iran actually wanted Timur to intervene.[17] Evidence of this can be seen in a letter sent by Mu'in al-Din Jami, the aged vizier of Mu'izz al-Din Husain. In this letter Timur was openly invited to make his way to the northern Persian province of Khorasan. Timur presented himself to the Persian people not as a conqueror but as a liberator and the legitimate successor to the crown.

By the year 1385 Timur had firmly established himself in northern Iran. We can only speculate on what his next step might have been, had Timur been the master of the situation, yet his next move was in reaction to the policy of the Golden Horde. In 1386 Tokhtamish, a real descendant of Chingiz Khan, was the khan of this state. There was a time when Toktamish was counted as Timur's favourite and Timur even helped him to gain the throne. Alas, the Chingizid misused Timur's trust and established himself in the Golden Horde. Now he wanted to establish himself in Iran and in Khoresm too.

Timur was primarily a conqueror, but the period of wars with the Golden Horde was, in general, a period of compulsory fighting for him. He never had it in mind to occupy the territory of the Golden Horde and to rule the Russian princes. For several years Tokhtamish was an aggressor. Already in 1386 he tried to conquer western Iran by way of Caucasus, Tabriz and Derbend, and the towns in Azerbaijan were devastated and robbed; Timur was forced to respond.

In general, Timur's wars with Tokhtamish were successful and the ruler of the Golden Horde was beaten several times. But the Golden Horde was huge and rich and after each defeat Tokhtamish was able to reinstate his army. Finally in 1395, during his last campaign against Tokhtamish, Timur defeated his enemy and destroyed Sarai, the capital of the Golden Horde located on the Volga river.

The full story of the Timur–Tokhtamish confrontation was reflected in an unexpected way in the contemporary Russian historiography. From the thirteenth century and for the next three hundred years Mongols (often Tataro-Mongols in Russian sources) ruled the larger half of the Russian principalities. Each Russian prince (*knyaz'*) was obliged to obtain a special written authorization, *yarlik*, from the Mongol Khan to govern his principality and to pay taxes to the Mongols.[18]

It was very embarrassing for the Russians to tolerate such a state of affairs. In 1380 the Russian prince Dmitriy Donskoy defeated Mamai, the ruler of the Golden Horde, in a bloody battle at Kulikovo Pole. Tokhtamish seized the opportunity, dethroned Mamai, and became a ruler himself. His first revengeful act on the Russians was to set Moscow on fire.

The humiliated Russians were still under Mongol control and taxation when Tokhtamish originated his struggle against Timur. When Timur defeated Tokhtamish, one could assume that the Russians would be happy. But they were not. There is a story of Timur in Russian chronicles.[19] This 'Story on a great miracle of the Vladimir Icon of the Virgin Mary' or 'Story on Temir Aksak' is fantastic.

Just imagine, Timur fights Mongols in Russian lands. The text presents him as the most wicked person possible. Oppressed Russians take a miraculous Orthodox icon out of a cathedral placing it in Timur's way to save the Mongols. The chronicler wrote (in my translation):

> the miraculous icon was taken from the town of Vladimir to the town of Moscow . . . That same time Temir Aksak was in Ryazan' land at the Don river, and he was asleep, and he saw a terrible nightmare as Saints were going down from a high mountain with golden rods in their hands promising him troubles; and suddenly [he] saw a woman, decorated in purple dress, being above the Saints in the air with a huge army, preparing him an evil. He suddenly trembled and got up crying aloud and shivering, asking 'what is that ?'[20]

After this alarming event, the story continues with Timur leaving for home and Russia remaining untouched, the Christian spirit defeating the foreigner.

An explanation of this unexpected move of the Russian soul can be found in the political realities of the time. Mongols were not the sole Russian oppressors: some Russian principalities were under the Luthuanian protectorate. The Lithuanian King Vitovt was an ally of Toktamish and Russian religious leaders of Lithuanian orientation were the source of this story.[21]

Some other chronicles, for example, *Troitskaya letopis'*, present another neutral attitude to Timur's personality. Timur is mentioned in this chronicle three times where it is written that prince Semen Dmitrievich of Suzdal indeed served Timur for some time.[22]

This example shows how we are unable to accurately evaluate the reliability of the primary sources on our subject. We come up against this problem when working with all the other primary sources too. Court histories are flattering, while chronicles of defeated nations are malicious.

Meanwhile, between 1386 and 1404 Timur repeatedly raided the Transcaucasian countries from northern Persia. The kingdom of Georgia, which had gained its political independence after the Il-Khan'a state had broken up in 1335, was witnessing a period of economic and cultural expansion. Georgia resisted Timur with all its might, but he crossed its borders with his troops seven times before Tiflis (modern Tbilisy, the capital of Georgia) fell, and in 1404 King George VII was compelled to acknowledge Timur's suzerainty. Armenia had lost its own statehood before Timur and had gone into decline under the rule of Turk nomadic tribal rulers. Timur's invasion proved to be another calamity for the country.

The conquest of Persia was completed by 1393 and the country was divided into two parts. Timur's son, Shah Rukh, was made a governor of eastern Iran, which included Afghanistan during that period, and his brother Miranshah became the governor of western Iran, including Azerbaijan and Armenia.

Joseph Wolff, a religiously oriented English traveller to Central Asia of the nineteenth century, wrote the following on Timur:

> The Persian historians say on him, that he was not only a world-conqueror, but also a world-holder. Though Alexander the Great was more humane, he is evidently inferior to Timoor as a conqueror; for Timoor's conquests did not only comprise more countries than Alexander's, but he preserved a greater extent of country under subjection. Timoor, moreover, fought not, like Alexander, with effeminate nations, but with brave and warlike people; and besides, he was not given to vice; and also, not having been the son of a king, was the creator of his own power.[23]

Thinking of Timur as a 'world-holder' we need to remember that the purpose of Timur's conquests was not merely to acquire booty but to gain control of the major international trade routes. This aspect is very important when we consider the Jewish merchants who were active in the Europe–Asia–Europe trade.

When historians write about Timur's next move they usually use the term 'the Indian campaign'. But India as a whole was outside Timur's military interest. In fact, the expedition had as its objective only northern India, the Delhi Sultanate. Once again Timur captured a state in the period of its decline. In September 1398 the war with Delhi began. Before the decisive battle in December 1398, Timur ordered the execution of all captives held by his armies – the sources speak of a hundred thousand prisoners – fearing that they would side with the Sultan of Delhi during the battle. The number of 100,000 is so fantastic that once again the question of the validity of the primary sources arises.

The war with Delhi ended with another triumph for Timur and he returned to Samarkand in 1399 holding an immense booty. But let us recall again that he was not as yet the only master of Asia. While campaigning in India, Timur lost many of the cities he had previously seized, including Baghdad and Mosul, due to the activities of the Mamluks and Ottoman Turks. In September 1399 he rode out of Samarkand leading his armies on a new western campaign, that proved to be disastrous for the Mamluks and especially for the Turks.

The situation was serious. Timur had two strong enemies in front of him at the same time. He made his first move towards the Ottoman state and ravaged Azerbaijan, Armenia and Georgia. Then he sharply set out for Syria, that together with Egypt was ruled by the Mamluk sultans. He was opposed by the amirs of Syria but they were defeated in the battle near Aleppo (modern Haleb in Syria), which was captured and laid waste.

Before this happened, the Mamluk state had gained a new sultan, the young boy Faraj, who reigned from 1399 until 1412. There was a time when his father Sultan Barkuk had executed Timur's ambassadors. Timur now sent an envoy to Aleppo with a letter for the new sultan intending to clarify the sensitive situation between the two powerful states. Alas, the Syrian amirs 'ordered the neck of the envoy to be cut off in public', as Ibn Arabshah dutifully recorded.[24] The advice of the amirs to themselves was 'Be bold', but they omitted to add the second half of that famous Persian proverb that admonishes a hero to 'be bold but not too bold'. Ibn Arabshah melancholically added, 'And they prepared for conflict and equipped themselves for war'.[25] After taking several more Syrian cities, Timur laid siege to Damascus in January 1401. Failing to receive assistance from the sultan Faraj, Damascus threw itself at the conqueror's mercy but was sacked and set on fire. Timur did not stay long at the gates of the Holy Land and in 1401 turned eastward to deal with Baghdad. He besieged the city for six weeks and then sacked Baghdad too.

The severe mistakes of the Mamluks did not teach the Ottoman Turks a lesson. Since 1389 Bayazid [Bayazet] I Yildirim (the Thunderbolt) had been ruling the Ottoman state. He was nicknamed Yildirim because of his lightning military successes that had made the Ottoman state the most powerful in Asia Minor and the Balkans by the beginning of the fifteenth century. His political qualities were not, however, so impressive and he exercised the same motto to 'be bold'.

Heading northwards, Timur entered the territory of modern Turkey. He demanded the sultan's submission, but in response, Bayazid marched against him. In the decisive battle of Ankara on 20 July 1402 the Ottoman army retreated and Bayazid was taken prisoner together with his two sons. This victory was the last and the greatest jewel in the crown of Timur's military achievements.[26]

In 1402 Timur sealed the fate of the history of the Crusades by taking the crusaders' last outpost in Asia, the seaport of Smyrna (modern Ismir).[27] By his actions in Asia Minor the fall of Constantinople to the Ottomans was postponed for half a century. Timur's last great military undertaking was to have been his projected campaign against China, but on 18 February 1405, while marching to China, Amir Timur Kurakan ibn Taragay, aged 70, died.

> From the Irtish and Volga to the Persian Gulf, and from the Ganges to Damascus and the Archipelago, Asia was in the hand of Timour; his armies were invincible, his ambition was boundless, and his zeal might aspire to conquer and convert the Christian kingdoms of the West, which already trembled at his name. He touched the utmost verge of the land; but an insuperable, though narrow sea, rolled between the two continents of Europe and Asia; and the lord of so many *tomans*, or myriads of horse, was not master of a single galley.[28]

Yes, Timur was the last great Asian historical personality of the period, just prior to the time of the Great Sea Voyages of Discovery of the fifteenth century. He lived without knowledge of America, Australia, or the Antarctic continent.

Thinking about Timur's sea-ignorance the question may arise how much was Timur still a nomad? Indeed, nomads are people of the land and only of the land. The question is within the scope of this book because nomads usually are more religiously tolerant than nations that are rooted and settled. Timur was a man with a wandering spirit. Samarkand was his capital for thirty-five years but he only spent perhaps a year or two there. It is well known that his court and harem were wandering with him all over Asia and, in fact, the capital of his empire was constantly moving to where his tent was pitched. Timur also possessed qualities of specific nomadic chivalry. Besieging a city, Timur only resorted to military force when negotiations of surrender failed. When this happened he took extremely aggressive action, showing the city's inhabitants little or no mercy.[29] But in speaking about 'blood-bath' episodes in the history of Timur's wars, we should understand that there was nothing outstanding or unusual in such actions in the fourteenth century. This was standard practice for the time.

For example, in 1365, when Timur was still fighting for his future capital Samarkand, the last European crusaders decided to target Alexandria in Egypt. When they broke into the city, the inhabitants immediately began streaming out of the city gates and Alexandria was taken. Once again, as at Antioch in 1097, Jerusalem in 1099, and Constantinople in 1204, these crusading soldiers showed that they had learned nothing from the blood-thirsty errors of their forefathers, and that they were still possessed by the maniac savagery of the *furor Normannorum*. Making no distinction between Coptic Christians, Jews, or Muslims, they put the whole city to the sword, looting and murdering. In vain, King Peter of Cyprus tried to restore order and discipline.[30]

Timur, by the way, never encountered King Peter's complications with the discipline of his soldiers. As a rule, the soldiers of his army were only given permission to plunder a city that had surrendered, and then only after a specific signal, when the officials of the divan had completed their requisitions.[31]

As for Timur's religious tolerance, we have many indications that for a Sunni Muslim he was relatively indifferent in his personal attitude to religion, but he treated the champions of the Islamic faith with obvious benevolence. V. Barthold, writing with a critical approach on the primary sources, pointed out that 'the historians who wrote under Shah Rukh, when the Shari'at [Muslim law] had superseded Chingiz-khan's law, were naturally inclined to exaggerate Timur's piety and religious zeal'.[32] As an example, Barthold revealed that in Syria, Timur took up the cause of the Shi'a Muslims, that made the Syrians regard him as a fervent Shi'a, yet in the Khorasan province of Persia, he re-established Sunni Islam, and in another Persian province of Mazandaran he punished Shi'a dervishes for desecrating the memory of the Prophet Mohammad's companions.[33]

In general, the evidence for Timur's religious beliefs is conflicting some factors suggest a commitment to Islam, others cast doubt upon it. There was even a statement that Timur wore earrings, therefore, he 'practiced both Muslim and Shamanist customs'.[34] However, we know very well that Timur's relations with representatives of Islam – theologians, clergy, dervishes – were always very warm.[35] One could also point to the sums he spent on religious causes, on sacred buildings and visits to Muslim holy places.

Living in a harsh and grim century, the worst for civilisation since the Dark Ages, Timur was himself perforce harsh and grim. Yet, there was a gleam of enlightenment about him. Although illiterate, he created the so-called Timurid culture, which dominated the Islamic world for three centuries and influenced the European Renaissance. Although a nomad, who preferred to live in a tent and be on the move, he spoke two if not three languages (Persian and Turkic, for sure), played chess, liked to be read history to at mealtimes, loved buildings, appreciated porcelain, and carried round a portable bath.

Tamerlane was the greatest political man in Central Asia. The talents of this man covered many different areas of statehood. 'Amir Temur's image as a great statesman, reformer of the Middle Ages, a courageous adherent of justice, and a patron of science and culture, has outlasted many centuries', said the President of Uzbekistan, Islam Karimov, in 1996.[36] Timur's reign from 1370 until 1405 initiated the most active period of Central Asian history. This period, thanks to the impetus imparted by him, was to last to the beginning of the sixteenth century. Timur's influence was so significant that all the history of Central Asia can be divided into before Timur and after Timur periods. The happy combination of the right man in the right country at the right moment is very rare in history. Tamerlane was a realisation of this ideal, as far as Samarkand, Bukhara and Persia were concerned, but the rest of Asia would have been quieter without him. This was the person the Jews of Asia had to deal with in the second half of the fourteenth century.

4

TIMUR IN JEWISH SOURCES

The Worldly Hope men set their Hearts upons
Turns Ashes – or it prospers; and anon,
Like snow upon the Desert's dusty Face
Lighting a little Hour or two – is gone.
(*Rubáiyát of Omar Khayyám*)

If you read ten or fifteen general history books on Jewish history, starting from H. Graetz onwards, it is clearly seen that despite the established idea of the Jewish Diaspora – the dispersion of the Jews all over the world – most recorded historical events and most historians concentrate mainly on the European Jews (Ashkenazim), Mediterranean Jews with Spanish roots (Sefardim), and to a lesser degree on the Babylonian, the Persian Jews. The two last centuries has added American Jews, Russian Jews, and Israelis to this list; Chinese and Indian Jews could be mentioned as an exception – a sort of a curiosity so to speak – and Central Asian Jews are hardly mentioned at all and usually do not even receive a footnote.

The history of the Diaspora is not just a history of the Jews, it is also the history of coexistence and co-operation between the Jews and all the other nations involved with this coexistence. By ignoring the history of the Jews in Central and Inner Asia, modern Jewish historiography, in its mainstream of development, also ignores the history of the Asian nations. As a result, historians specialising in Jewish history will be able to point out the interrelations between the Jews and the Germans, the Jews and the French, the Jews and the Arabs, and lastly the Jews and Spaniards. They will not, on the other hand, be able to say anything definite about Jewish life among the Mongols, Turks, Turkmen and Uzbeks. It will just be mentioned that there are no reliable sources on the subject.

As a result, the nations that coexisted with the Jews in that same vast Asian territory, became themselves obscure in the eyes of Jewish historians. Max Dimont supports this vividly in his book *Jews, God and History* (1962) with the following description on the Mongols:

> In the thirteenth century, the Mongols under Genghis Khan invaded the [Islamic] empire from the northeast. It was not a mystic destiny, which led them west; they followed their cattle. Genghis Khan's Mongols wore ox-hides, ate anything that lived – cats, dogs, rats, lice – and drank human blood for want of anything better. In their first encounter with the Mongols, an army of 400,000 Muslims was defeated. Genghis gutted the city of Bokhara, slew 30,000, and continued his march into the cradle of civilisation, burning libraries, sacking cities, and beheading people, stacking their heads into grizzly pyramids as neatly as the Nazis staked concentration camp corpses. Barbarians, yes! But not untidy. When Baghdad capitulated, 800,000 civilians were put to death, the city laid waste, its wealth plundered, and its women violated and sold into slavery.[1]

Max Dimont seems to forget that prior to their first encounter with the Muslims, the Mongols had conquered and occupied sophisticated China and the Uigur lands. Chingiz Khan incorporated the refined military specialisation of the Chinese into his own armies, studied their scientific knowledge and also accepted the Uigur script. The Mongols were therefore able to develop military strategies and tactics to the highest standards of their time, standards the Muslims were not able to achieve. The Mongols intensified West–East trade routes. They established an administrative system that allowed them to rule over occupied territories for the next few centuries.

In reference to the Mongols in Baghdad, for example, we learn:

> The Mongols were patrons of science and learning generally, and Hulagu, the brother of Mangu Khan, immediately after he had taken and destroyed Baghdad in February 1258, ordered his astronomer Nasir ad-Din of Tus to build an observatory at Maraghah. This observatory stood just outside the town, and in it the famous Il-khani astronomical plates with their tables of calculations were preserved. The library that Bar Hebraeus mentions may have been connected with the observatory . . .[2]

Perhaps the Mongols had not burnt all the libraries, but only every second library.

On the Jews of Baghdad in particular, we do not know whether or not Jews suffered at the siege of Baghdad when the last Abbasid, el-Musta'sim-billah, was captured and executed. One thing we know for sure is that the Mongol Khans employed members of a Jewish family as their physicians and viziers.[3]

When dealing with Timur, the lack of primary Jewish sources does not allow historians the full scope of research. The modern Jewish writer P. Iskhakov dedicated five pages to the history of the Bukhara Jews and how they endured Timur's cruelties. This was done without the use of any primary sources dealing with the history of the sufferings of the Jews at that time.[4]

Timur, though, becomes a frequently mentioned character in some old Jewish legends researched by Jewish historians. Chinese Jews, for example, relate a legend 'that after King Tamerlane had captured Persia, he also captured China, and that many Mohammedans, Christians, and Jews followed him to China'.[5] But we know that the Jews came to China much earlier.

In addition to the legend in the prologue, Joseph Wolff, in the book of his *Travels and Adventures of the 1840s*, recorded another Jewish legend on Timur and also gives a short description of Timur's life, personality and campaigns:

> The dervish Barakat, the Samuel of the Tatars, who had predicted to him [Timur] the throne, invested him with the insignia of the empire, and delivered to him the standard and drum, and added to his name Timoor the titles of *Kurikan* (i.e. great ruler) [in reality, 'son-in-law'], *Szhael Keran* (lord of the age) [*Sahibkiran*, 'born under the lucky star'], and *Jehaan-Geer* (conqueror of the world).
>
> Does this not seem to be an imitation of Isaiah IX? He amply justified the truth of those titles in the thirty-six years of his government.[6]

This inference to the Holy Scriptures is very strong. Indeed, Isaiah 9:6 states, 'he will bear the symbol of dominion on his shoulder, and his title will be: Wonderful Counsellor, Mighty Hero, Eternal Father, Prince of Peace.' Timur should be highly esteemed in this use of Biblical parallels. Wolff then proceeds with the Jewish legend:[7]

> The observations of the Jews . . . about Timoor and Ghengis Khan, are highly probable. During the four times nine years of his government, he returned nine times to Samarcand, in order to refresh his troops and to prepare them for new adventures. He united upon his head the crowns of three times nine countries, which belonged to nine dynasties, whose fate was in the hands

> of the conqueror. [Enumeration of the dynasties is given.] Several of these empires he subdued in one battle, but most of them after persevering and repeated conflicts for several years; he led his army seven times against the Gheets, and five times against Khiva; he subdued Hindostan in one campaign; and in his last expedition to Asia Minor, Bayazeed's fate was decided, which war lasted seven years.[8]

These Jewish legends collected by Wolff in Bukhara 150 years ago appear to be quite favourable to Timur. The Bukharan Jews also told Wolff that Tatars (meaning Turks) were somehow related to the Jews. The word 'Tatar derives from the Hebrew *Totar*, which means "remnant", a remnant of those Israelites who turned to paganism'.[9] Jews without Judaism, so to speak.

What sources do we have in addition to these various legends? The sources are, unfortunately rather meagre. The medieval Jewish chronicles and chronologies[10] skipped Timur's personality and the impacts of his campaigns, with the exception of the chronicles of Rabbi Joseph Ben Joshua ben Meir Ha-Kohen (1496–1577).

Rabbi Joseph was a physician and historian. He was born in Spain and died in Genoa. He wrote *Chronicles*, a historical account of the world from the period of the downfall of the Roman Empire. Joseph Ha-Kohen dedicated two pages of his book to the struggle of Bayazid and Timur in 1400–2.[11] He mentioned the siege of Constantinople, and estimated Timur's troops as an army of 1,000,000 (400,000 of cavalry and 600,000 of infantry), describing the battle of Ankara and the capture of Bayazid. He refers to the famous legend when Bayazid was humiliated by Timur and ate leftovers from Timur's table together with the dogs. It is hard to understand from the text of the *Chronicles* on which side the author's sympathies lay. There is no mention of the Jews in any of those descriptions.

It is interesting to mention that Joseph Ha-Kohen also wrote another book, entitled *Sefer 'Emeq ha-Bakha* (*The Vale of Tears*) *with the chronicle of the anonymous Corrector*, an account of the persecution of the Jews throughout the ages. In this book, he described, step by step, all the Jewish sufferings in France, Spain, Portugal, Germany and Italy in the fourteenth and fifteenth centuries and did not even mention Timur, Bayazid, the Persian or the Syrian Jews. The Jews of Baghdad and Persia are mentioned only in the year 1163 of his chronicle, and Turkey first appears in 1492 in connection with the Jewish refugees from Spain.[12] It seems from this book that there was no Jewish persecution during the empire of Timur.

Another Jew who mentioned Timur was Abraham Ben Samuel Zacuto. This Spanish astronomer, mathematician and historian was born in Salamanca about 1450 and died in Turkey after 1510. The astrological *Almanach perpetuum* was his most famous work. In addition he wrote a historical book, *Sefer Yujasin*, or *The Book of Genealogies*, in which he described the Mongols and Tartars and mentioned Timur in connection with the Spanish embassy of Clavijo.[13] Once again no Jewish persecution is described.

Another short story concerning Timur comes from an anonymous Jewish Rabbi who left his writings as a continuation of an Arabic manuscript by Bahya b. Joseph ibn Pakuda, the most popular Jewish religious philosopher of the Middle Ages. This Rabbi wrote:

> And this is the story of Tamerlane. It was on Saturday the 11th Marcheshwan 1400 when Tamerlane entered Aleppo and burnt the city and took the holy man prisoner and killed old men and children and left for Damascus where he acted in the same way. He returned on the morning of Passover of the year which was 803 of the Hegira and, during that time the holy man came to Aleppo and some Jews remained to read to him and he took refuge in the Kuliga and took no meat except from Sabbath night and day and he continued in this state for seven months when one Friday night the disciples came to read before him and found him dead.[14]

Was this holy man of Kuliga the same man who was taken prisoner? Where did his disciples come from? Were these old men and children who were killed in Aleppo, Jews, Christians or Muslims?

One fact is certain from this description: during Timur's stay in Aleppo some Jewish 'holy man' came to the city and found several disciples 'to read before him'. This holy man then remained a hermit for seven months before dying from natural causes.

There are no documented medieval chronicles written by the Persian or Central Asian Jews, but there is a primary source on the subject from central Asia in the form of a letter written by a Jewish merchant, Yosef b. Musa from Sokhar. The letter, written in Persian,[15] around 1450 could have been written by a Muslim as well as a Jewish man, and this is probably why this letter was not analysed by specialists in Jewish history. It describes some trade events and has several Hebraisms like *sefer* (book), *tora* (the Tora) and *saba* (grandfather). These features enable me to refer to Yusef b. Musa as a Jewish person, although Sokhar was a small settlement near Bukhara with a Muslim majority. Yosef was involved in the local silk trade in and around the area and he mentions Timur in the letter only once:

> His grandfather had a large trade when Taimur the Strong [mighty?] was in full power. The road to China was not safe [at that time] and he did not use the Chinese silk for trade. He used a middle-man in Shash [modern Tashkent] for the trade purposes.[16]

Perhaps this is the only known Jewish source relating to Timur from the area of Central Asia. The European Jewish chronicles did not supply a clear picture of Jewish life at the time of Timur's empire. This is not surprising as the Europeans of the fourteenth to sixteenth centuries knew almost next to nothing about Timur.

Analysing the sources, it appears apparent that no Jewish chroniclers included Timur in the list of the Jewish persecutors, and the local Jewish legends draw Timur in a favourable manner. The Jews who were able to handle 'large trade' during his reign called Tamerlane, 'Timur the Strong' and 'the great ruler'. Indeed, being free from any political ambitions, the Jews of Central Asia sought only the protection of Timur, and they had every reason to favour public order, since any disturbance of it was likely to prove disadvantageous to them.

5

THE JEWS IN HISTORICAL WORKS ON TIMUR

> This Piller placed in memorie of her,
> Where in Arabian, Hebrew, Greek, is writ
> *This towne being burnt by Tamburlaine the great,*
> *Forbids the world to build it up againe.*
> (Christopher Marlowe, *Tamburlaine the Great*,
> the second part, 1606)[1]

Marlowe, due to his empathy and perception of the circumstances of that period, mentioned Hebrew, Arabic and Greek in this famous poem. Secondary sources do not frequently mention the Jews. Harold Lamb, whose *Tamerlane* (1928) became perhaps the most popular biography of Timur in the twentieth century, mentioned the Jews in his narrative when discussing Samarkand, 'a bedlam of tongues, and a babel of varied prayer'.[2] When Hilda Hookham wrote Timur's biography in a more scientific manner in 1962, the Jews are mentioned twice with references to Mignanelli's *Vita Tamerlani* (1414).[3] In both cases these references appear to be inaccurate, as Hookham was not aware that Mignanelli's story about the ill-fated events concerning the Jewish people in Aleppo in 1400 was a retelling of a legend similar to Wolff's story of 1840 about the Jewish prime minister who served under Timur (see Prologue and Chapter 10).

Primary sources have little or no rich material on the Jews either.

Ruy Gonzalez de Clavijo, the Spanish ambassador to Timur, mentioned the Jews of India in his *Narrative of the Embassy* but did not make mention of Timur's empire.[4] In his description of Samarkand, Clavijo carefully described the varied nations seen in the city:

> Of the nations brought here together there were to be seen Turks, Arabs and Moors of diverse sects, with Christians who were

> Greeks and Armenians, Catholics, Jacobites and Nestorians, besides those [Indian] folk who baptize with fire in the forehead, who are indeed Christians but of a faith that is peculiar to the nation.[5]

Here a picture of integral religious tolerance is drawn but without any mention of the Jews.

The famous Arabian historian, Ibn Khaldun, described the conversations he had with Timur in Damascus in 1401 when they were discussing their different viewpoints on King Nebuchadnezzar, the destroyer of the Temple of Solomon, but the Jews are not mentioned here either.[6]

However, another Arab historian, Ibn Arabshah, refers to the Jews four times in his biography of Timur. All these references, though, come from different biblical quotations, and do not shed light on the real situation of the Jews during the time of Timur's empire.[7] For example he wrote:

> And Timur asked, 'What is this madman doing?'
>
> Then he said 'O illustrious lord! Your armies are scattered, like the tribes of Israel, and there are men in them who fashion new religions and are drawn into diverse sects, and are sundered and divided by religion'.[8]

There is, however, evidence of another kind of biblical reference in Arabshah's writings. In the chapter dedicated to 'The wonderful gifts of Timur and his nature and character', Arabshah wrote, 'Timur was tall and of lofty stature as though he belonged to the remnants of the Amalekites'.[9] Is this indeed a flattering biblical parallel?[10]

It is not surprising that the court historians did not mention the Jews in their biographies of Timur. Timurid historiography, Oriental in general character, Persian in particular, practised the medieval tradition of composing the image of an ideal monarch from a canonised set of standards. In the late medieval period the Muslim attitude to the Jews was scornful. Living in isolated quarters, wearing special attire, paying additional taxes, suffering constant humiliation and sporadic pogroms, the Jews were also seen by the Muslims as an unclean people. The time of the Mongols, Timur and the Timurids was a period of 'The Triumph of Etiquette' in historiography.[11] This etiquette did not permit the court historians to even mention the Jews in their writings; the Jews could not be referred to in a biography of the ideal monarch! In general, these court histories, with very few exceptions, are written with absurd exaggerations, recondite words, vain epithets, far-fetched comparisons, tasteless bombast, and represent to perfection the worst style of those florid writers who flourished under the patronage of the Timurids in Persia and Central Asia during the fifteenth century.

In private letters, however, this etiquette was not adhered to so strictly. There is a unique collection of letters, written during the time of Timur and the Timurids, called *Makktubat Taimuriya*, which is housed in the Collection of Oriental Manuscripts of the Uzbek Academy of Sciences in Tashkent. The Jews are mentioned several times in the different letters of this collection, for example, there is a letter by a military commander of low rank, Sharifjan Jafar, written in 1390 (AH 792), in which he describes life in his unit. He writes that they spent one night in a small village near Bukhara that was inhabited by Jews. He does not mention the Jews having any specific responsibility to supply food and clothing to the army.[12]

The most important letter in this collection is a petition composed by several Jewish doctors from Herat, addressed to Shah Rukh, the son of Timur. The letter is not dated and is written in the *dari* language in the first half of the fifteenth century. The doctors request Shah Rukh's permission to apply 'their knowledge in the treatment of various diseases', as they wished to treat the soldiers of the Timurid military garrison in Herat, if and when the soldiers sought their assistance.[13] There is no reply to this petition, and we do not know if permission was granted or not. What is important here is not whether the physicians were indeed granted the permission or not, but that a group of local Jewish physicians were trying to establish themselves by providing their services to the state army.

In 1712 (AH 1124), three hundred years later, when the Timurid dynasty had already ceased to exist, Mirza Rumuz of Bukhara wrote a historical treatise entitled *Taimur-nama*, or *The Book about Timur*. He retold the history of Timur's life and reign with numerous legendary and apocryphal elements. In one place he mentioned that Timur was merciless to idol worshippers, but charitable to all 'recognised' nations including 'even Jews'.[14]

The Europeans were not constrained by Timurid historical 'etiquette' but even they did not write too much on the Jews in the domains of Timur. J. Schiltberger, a German mercenary soldier of the Turkish army, captured by Timur's troops in 1402, wrote about the Jews only once in his memoirs. He mentioned them, presumably as Karaites, in his description of Crimea and the cities of Kaffa and Tana of 'the Tartar domains'.[15] B. de Mignanelly alludes to a story about Jewish sufferings after the fall of Aleppo in 1400 in his *Vita Tamerlani* (1416, see above in the Prologue). W.J. Fischel proved that this story was purely a legend and it will be discussed later in the book.

The famous French medieval chronicle *Chronographia Regum Francorum* also has a very similar story about the Jewish massacre in the major 'Judeorum sinagoge' in the town of 'Bursa' (Brusa in Turkey).[16] Once again the Jews of the city took their wives and children, trying to seek safety in the main town synagogue. But in vain. It is most probable that this story is a shorter version of the same legend that Mignanelli had come across. The chronicle, however, informs us that not all the Jews were killed, for those who survived were told to pay a high tribute and Timur allowed them to live.[17] No other stories of actual Jewish life in Timur's domains can be found in the medieval chronicles.

Even Asian folklore cannot help us too much. Hojja Nasreddin (sometimes called Molla Nasrudin or Nasretdin) is the main folk hero in Central Asia, Iran, Azerbaijan and Turkey. More than 1,300 anecdotes of Nasreddin have been published.[18] There are more than 150 jokes about Timur among them. For example (my translation):

> When Timur grew old he married a young and very pretty girl from the Agalyk village which was not far from Samarkand. Soon the young woman asked him to let her to spend some time with her parents. Timur felt lonely and ordered Nasreddin, 'Go to Agalyk and bring my wife back.' 'Yes, my lord!' answered Nasreddin.
>
> He returned with Timur's wife the next day. Timur was angry, 'I should not send you, an old man on a slow-moving donkey.'
>
> After a while, the wife went to Agalyk again. Being impatient, Timur this time sent a young warrior on a strong horse to bring her back. His wife returned to Samarkand only after a week. Timur was puzzled, 'Your slow donkey, Nasreddin, was quicker than my best stallion.'
>
> 'One should know whom to send after a young woman,' Nasreddin muttered quietly.[19]

Among all these funny stories, which have been collected over the centuries, there are only three anecdotes where the Jews are mentioned, including the famous joke about Nasreddin and the greedy Jew, but none of these jokes are connected to Timur.[20]

The notes on the poll-tax (*djiziya*) could once again be helpful as indirect evidence of a Jewish presence in the state. *Djiziya* was mentioned in Timur's court histories, but not always in connection with the empire of Timur. Describing the situation in Turkey while Timur was fighting Bajazet, Timurid historians criticised the Turks for not taking Smyrna

(Izmir) from the crusaders. Shami wrote of the crusaders, 'None of them paid *djiziya* and *kharaj* to anybody; and forever a door was open to depravity among the Muslims, and no king was able to defeat them during that time . . .'[21]

From this quotation it could be assumed that these two taxes were usually paid in Timur's domains, but this assumption is incorrect. The system of taxation in Timur's empire was complicated, but there are numerous primary sources on the subject of the land-ownership and tax system at this time. This system includes several different taxes, such as the tax from a private land (*ushur*), the tax from gardens (*mol-i-daraht*), the customs duty (*boj*) and various other taxes. The land tax (*haraj*) was paid but was called *mol*. Even the special tax *peshkash*, or 'gifts for officials, who crossed the region territory' is mentioned.[22] *Djiziya* is not mentioned among the taxes existing in Central Asia. We may assume that even if this tax was paid in Timur's domains it was not counted as an obligatory payment by some specific groups of citizens. Perhaps it was paid only in some regions of the empire. Once again it is not completely clear which groups of citizens paid it. In the case of Timur's empire we cannot use the information we have on *djiziya* in order to understand the conditions of Jewish life.

To avoid the danger of jumping to conclusions, several reasons for the sources' disparity can be discussed:

- The numbers of the Jews in Timur's domains were insignificant compared to those of other nations.
- The Jewish influence on the main trend of political, military and economic history of that period was insignificant.
- Both the Muslim and the Christian historians and travellers found it inappropriate to mention the Jews frequently in their writings.

Some additional research is needed. But one fact is certain from the current sources of knowledge, Timur never issued any anti-Jewish orders, laws or restrictions. Timur never oppressed the Jews for being Jews. Also the Uzbek anti-Semitic folklore does not exist.

Let us now take a close look on what the Jews did in the vast Timur's domains.

Part II

THE JEWS AND THE MIGHTY MUSLIM RULER

6

THE JEWS BECOME TIMUR'S CITIZENS

> Here I began to martcht towards *Persea*,
> Along *Armenia* and the Caspian sea,
> And thence unto *Bythinia*, where I tooke
> The Turke and his great Empresse prisoners,
> Then martcht I into *Egypt* and *Arabia*,
> And here not far from *Alexandria*,
>
> . . .
>
> From thence to *Nubia* neere *Borno* Lake,
> And so along the Ethiopian sea,
> Cutting the Tropicke line of *Capricorne*,
> I conquered all as far as *Zanzibar*.
> (Christopher Marlowe, *Tamburlaine the Great*, the second part, 1606)[1]

Marlowe was too generous in his description of Timur's military might, Timur never reached Zanzibar but his Asian domains were more than impressive. Conquering one country after another he accepted more and more Jews as citizens. We do not know how many, but from the previous chapter we know that Jews lived in practically every locality of Asia from Russia to India and from China to Egypt. Alas, the simple question of how many Jews were in Asia in the fourteenth century has no definite answer yet. European sources do not help us much either. To the Europeans, the Jews and Timur did not have the same kind of relationship as did the Jews and Chingiz Khan and the Mongols. Actually, it was even assumed that the Jews were blood-related to Chingiz Khan and the Mongols. First of all, the Europeans of the thirteenth century mistakenly thought that the *Tartares* (Mongols) could be the Jews or, at least, were descendants of King David,[2] and the time had come for these Tataro-Jewish Mongols to take vengeance on the Christians for all their previous humiliations. The Mongols were moving towards Europe so rapidly and victoriously that a rumour appeared about German Jews co-operating with their 'brothers, the long-shut-up tribes of Israel'. The Jews of Germany were accused of undertaking traitorous measures to aid the invading Mongol hordes and subsequently suffered severe persecutions.[3] Local folklore created the fable that the Jews even supplied the Mongols with weapons. The Mongols therefore unintentionally provoked pogroms in Europe in the thirteenth century.[4]

Timur's campaigns did not affect the Jews in this way; his fighting was with the Mongols, Ottoman Turks, and Mamluks, making him, in fact, an ally of Europe. When Ottoman Sultan Bayazet (Bayazid) was badly beaten in 1402, the West was enthusiastic. Timur was the great saviour who had come to destroy the Turks, contain the Mamluks, and succour Constantinople. The French marshal Boucicaut was given the task of contacting Timur and the Castilians and French hurriedly sent off some Franciscans to find him at the end of 1403. The acme of these efforts was the famous Spanish embassy to Tamerlane led by Clavijo in 1403–6. The Jews were not involved in these political affairs and this time they were safe. European Jews were persecuted in the fourteenth century but these troubles had no connection with Timur's achievements. As a result we have no European sources about the fate of the Jews in connection with Timur and we have no European sources on the Jewish population in Asia. From the sources that we do have we can assume that in achieving his objectives, Timur was indeed as ruthless as Chingiz Khan, but despite his cruelty Timur was very far from ideas of genocide, Holocaust, or 'ethnic cleansing'.

Asian sources are also absent. A hundred years ago, in 1897, Elkan Nathan Adler, the Jewish scholar from England, journeyed to Bukhara in search of old Jewish books. 'In Bokhara I had to beg from house to house for a sight of all the books the inhabitants possessed, and then to bid for such as I wanted', he wrote.[5] He found books on astrology, religion, liturgies, medicine, poetry, Kabbala and 'belles-lettres', but no books on history or chronology. Adler gave descriptions of sixty-five books from Bukhara including medical prescriptions in Hebrew, fragments of the Torah and Siddur, astrological charms, the *Cusari* of Jehuda ha Levi, but no books on the real life of the community from the previous centuries.[6]

A hundred years passed. In 1994 M. Nosonovskiy, a scholar of St Petersburg, catalogued all the possessions from the library and archives of the Jewish Museum of Samarkand. There were two hundred and fifty books and twenty manuscripts in the library including 'Arabian Nights' in the local Tajik–Jewish language, and works of Ibn Gabirol in

Hebrew, but again no historical sources. There were thousands of papers in the archives, stored in fifty-three organisers, and almost nothing on the medieval history of the local Jews.[7] Only one Jewish letter written in Central Asia in the fifteenth century has survived and is in the collection of the Ahmad Donish Academy of Sciences of Tajikistan.

Almost the same can be said about the history of the Jewish communities of the fourteenth centuries in other regions of Asia that were in the area of Timur's actions. There is, however, an indirect way to evaluate the size of the Jewish communities in the Muslim world by investigating the amounts of money paid as the poll-tax (*djizya*). This tax had to be paid by both Jews and Christians and by knowing the amount of money paid and knowing the size of a Christian community, if any, we would be able calculate the number of Jews in a certain city.

Alas, this method cannot be used in the case of Timur's empire. It is most probably that there were no traditional Arab Islamic *djizya* in his domains. The uncertain situation connected with this tax in Persia and Central Asia could already be seen in the eighth century AD when Arabs collected it from the Zoroastrians as well. Sometimes even Muslims were obliged to pay *djizya*.[8] During the Mongol occupation of the region, *djizya* was being paid by all the local populations and religion was not being taken into account.[9] During the Sarbadar government of the city Mafia in Samarkand in 1337–81, Muslims did not pay *djizya*, yet there is no direct evidence that Jews and Christians rather than all non-Muslims paid this tax.[10]

The basic tax in Timur's empire was the land tax (*mal* or *kharaj*). Other taxes that seem to have been levied were a per capita tax (*dudi*) and a poll-tax called *sar-shumar*. Another sort of a tax was the *ulagh*, the obligation to provide government couriers with relay horses and also to furnish heavy transport.[11] The Hebrew word used for the poll-tax was *gulgolet*. I have not been able to find any Hebrew document, chronicle, or even letter stating that the Jews paid *gulgolet* to Timur's officials. All these Jewish and Muslim primary sources cannot generally prove the existence of a Jewish tax in Timur's empire.

Only by putting together historical fragments on Jewish life in various Asian cities is it possible to understand to some extent the process of integrating the Jews into Timur's empire. But first some attempt to examine and understand the different periods in the forty-four-year duration of Timur's activities is needed. We can divide this into three periods:

- *First period: 1360–70*. Timur became a ruler of Transoxania (Central Asia) with the exception of Khoresm. The inhabitants of Bukhara,

Samarkand, Kesh (modern Shakhrisabs), Tashkent and Balkh became his citizens.

- *Second period: 1371–87*. Timur conquered Khorezm, territories of modern Afghanistan, Pakistan, Iran, northern Iraq, Azerbaijan and included them in his empire. The inhabitants of Herat, Kabul, Merv, Urgenj, Isfahan, Shiraz, Tabriz, Nishapur and other Persian cities became Timur's citizens.
- *Third period: 1388–1405*. Timur was campaigning in the Golden Horde, territories of modern Russia, Ukraine, Armenia, Georgia, Turkey, Syria, southern Iraq, northern India. These lands were not included in the empire or were occupied for only a short time. Jews of Russia and Eastern Europe, Caucasus, India and the Near East, including the Jews of Damascus, Baghdad, Aleppo, Sarai, Asrakhan and Crimean ports, were in contact with Timur's armies. Some of them presumably were moved to Transoxania with their families.

Plate 2 Djami Mosque of Amir Timur. The south darskhana (lecture hall), Samarkand

We will now examine cities with Jewish communities in Timur's empire according to these three chronological periods. This is a fairly long list and is presented in a concise format geographically.

Cities of the first period

Kesh (Shahrisabs)

Were there any Jews living in the native city of Timur at the time of his childhood? It would be possible to find an indirect indication of this from the existing Jewish cemetery in the city. Tradition states it is 800 years old,[12] and Timur lived 600 years ago.

Samarkand

A clear statement about Jewish inhabitants of Samarkand is found in Benjamin of Tudela's diary. This evidence appeared in the twelfth century, more than 160 years before Timur was born. During these years Samarkand suffered the Mongol invasion and in the Arab chronicle of Ala ad-din Juwayni, there is a description of the Mongols' capture of Samarkand:

> Then all in the citadel were brought out into the open, where the Turks were separated from the Taziks and all divided into groups of ten and a hundred. They shaved the Turks' heads in the Mongol fashion in order to tranquilize them and allay their fears . . . [but at sunset they were all killed]. There were more than thirty thousand Qanqli and Turks.[13]

The Jews are not mentioned. However, if we assume that there was a Jewish community in the city, the Jews could be counted as Tadjiks [Taziks in the text]. Indeed, Turks were nomads, they fought with Mongols and they were killed. Tadjiks were local settled people and had not fought with Mongols before.

There is an indication that the Jews were expelled from Samarkand when it was under Islamic rule, for the city was regarded as sacred.[14] We do not know, however, whether this expulsion occurred before or after Timur took Samarkand in 1366, and then without much of a fight![15]

There are many indications in primary sources that Timur moved numerous craftsmen, doctors, poets, musicians and calligraphers to Samarkand, but there is no direct evidence that Jews were among these displaced families.

Bukhara

Most probably there was a Jewish community in Bukhara in the fourteenth century. Abu Bakr al-Narshakhi, a native of the vicinity of Bukhara, is famous for his *History of Bukhara*, written in Arabic in 943. Describing Bukhara in the middle of the eighth century he wrote, 'Most of the people of Bukhara were *dhimmis* who paid the poll tax'.[16] The size of the community in the thirteenth and fourteenth centuries is unknown. Chingiz Khan fought twelve days at the gate of Bukhara in 1220 before he captured and destroyed it. Timur never fought against this city. Bukhara became his domain automatically, shortly after Samarkand was taken.

Tashkent

We can only speculate on the Jewish presence in this important trade centre on the Silk Route from China. It is possible that Jewish merchants could have visited this city in the fourteenth century but there is no available data about any community.

Timur entered Tashkent peacefully but after his death the city suffered from local civil strife.[17]

Balkh

For centuries before and after the Arab conquest this town in northern Afghanistan was a stronghold of Jewish settlements in the region. It was to Balkh, according to Muslim tradition, that the Prophet Jeremiah fled, and where the Prophet Ezekiel was buried.[18]

There was a significant Jewish community in Balkh before the Mongol period. The Arab historian al-Maqdisi wrote about *bab-i-Yahudan*– the gate of the Jews – in Balkh.[19] In the eleventh century the Jews of the city were forced to maintain the garden of Sultan Mahmud of Ghazna, which he built in Balkh. For that purpose, they were ordered to pay a special tax that the sultan said should not be more than 500 *dirhems*.[20] There is a possibility that this flourishing community suffered during the Mongol invasion,[21] leaving us without knowledge of the exact size of the Jewish community of Balkh in the second half of the fourteenth century.

Timur did not besiege Balkh. There was a battle between him and Sultan Hussein, the Balkh ruler, in the open, in April 1370.[22] Hussein was defeated on the battlefield and his capital was taken without resistance. According to the Jewish tradition, 'at Balkh, the mother of cities, Timur gave them a whole beautiful quarter of their own, with a gate to enclose it'.[23]

Writing about the conditions of the nineteenth century, V. Barthold mentioned, 'Even now, despite the total decline of the commercial importance of Balkh, there is a considerable Jewish colony in the town, located in a special quarter'.[24]

Cities of the second period

Herat

Jews lived in Herat at least since the time of the Arab conquest.[25] The cemetery tombstones of 1115–1215 clearly indicate the presence of a sizeable Jewish community in the city.[26] The Mongols conquered Herat in 1221, and we do not know how many Jews, if any, remained in the city after the Mongol invasion. From that time onward we have no information about the Jews of the city until the eighteenth century.

Timur conquered Herat after a long siege in April 1381.[27] Despite the siege and attacks, when the city surrendered to Timur it was not plundered by his soldiers. Requisitions were made by the officials, some noblemen were transferred to Kesh, the walls and gates of the city were destroyed, but its citizens in general were left unharmed.[28] Herat was not destroyed by Timur and later became a capital of a Timurid state.

Merv

This town in modern Turkmenistan had a sizeable Jewish community at least a thousand years before the time of Timur. The Arabian historian at-Tabari mentioned the Jewish community of Merv under the leadership of 'Akiba, the Jew' in the eighth century.[29] There were Jews in Merv in the eleventh century and some Jews called themselves 'Mervians' even in 1336, after the Mongol invasion.[30]

However, there were two cities called Merv. The old Merv was destroyed by the Mongols in 1221 and all of its citizens were killed with the exception of 400 artisans and some children.[31] In 1340 this Merv was still in ruins.[32] The new Merv replaced the village Mahan and survived until modern times. There was even a time when the local ruler Ali-bek[33] imprisoned young Timur there with Amir Hussein.

By the time of Timur's campaigns in Khorassan, Merv was already destroyed, but the history of the Jewish community in Merv was not over yet. In 1410, five years after Timur's death, his son Shah Rukh gave orders to restore the area. The irrigation system and settlements were then built anew.[34] As a result we have a manuscript of a Judeo-Persian dictionary of 1473 that originated in Merv.[35]

Urghench

Nothing is known about the Jews of Khoresm after the time of Khazars and Biruni. Among the regions of Central Asia, Khorezm suffered most from the Mongol invasion. However, a certain Solomon ben Samuel compiled the Judeo-Persian dictionary, *Sefer Hamelitza*, in Urgench, the capital, in 1339.[36] There is no indication that any Jews lived in Urgench in the second half of the fourteenth century. Timur also destroyed Urgench during his long-lasting wars with the local dynasty. The city was then rebuilt but there is no information on Jewish communities.

Ghazna

There are reliable Jewish and also Arab sources indicating that Jews lived in the city of Ghazna (which is not far from Kabul in Afghanistan) up to the twelfth century.[37] But from the time of Benjamin of Tudela we have no additional sources on the Jews for the next few centuries. Chingiz Khan himself took Ghazna without any resistance in 1221 and its citizens were not killed.

Timur did not attack Ghazna. The city became his automatically after Afghanistan was taken. Perhaps Timur was never in Ghazna himself, yet when he started his Indian campaign, he moved his army to India via Kabul.

Isfahan

Isfahan is a very important city in Jewish history. This Iranian city was more 'Jewish' than any other city in the region and according to a well-established tradition, the Jews founded Isfahan. Tradition states that the city was built by the captives whom Nebuchadnezzar transported thither after he had taken Jerusalem.[38] The Jewish district of the city, *Al-Yahudiyyah* (*Jahudistan* in Persian), despite several incidental anti-Jewish acts of violence, was a large and prosperous community for centuries. In the twelfth century Benjamin of Tudela found fifteen thousand Jews in Isfahan.[39]

Alas, the Jews of the city were under constant terror and humiliation during the century prior to the Mongol invasion. The pressure to embrace Islam was heavy. The Mongols tried to attack Isfahan for the first time in 1227 and failed. The city was taken only in 1231.[40] Isfahan was destroyed and 'hardly anyone was left alive'.[41] The city was then rebuilt and perhaps some Jews returned, but we do not know how many.

In general, the Jews prospered under Mongol rule, especially in the 1280s. In the specific case of Isfahan we have no sources on the size of the Jewish community in the fourteenth century. In general, information available from sources about the Persian Jews of that century is inadequate and scarce.

Timur conquered Isfahan without any resistance in 1387 when the governor of the city surrendered the keys to him. The city was not ruined and its citizens were not killed, yet in 1388 the population of Isfahan attacked the tax collectors and some of Timur's troops were killed in the city. This revolt was ruthlessly suppressed by the ruler of Asia, and many people died. But the city was not destroyed and there were still Jews in Isfahan in the fifteenth century.[42] During the time of the Timurids the Jews did not encounter any trouble, but in the sixteenth century, when the Dynasty of the Timurids was replaced by the Safawid Dynasty, the Jews in Isfahan were persecuted. Under Abbas I (1586–1629) and Abbas II (1642–66) there were widespread forced conversions to Islam.[43]

Shiraz

Shiraz is a big city in the Fars province in the south of Iran. In the twelfth century, the 10,000 strong Jewish community of Shiraz[44] was mentioned by Benjamin Tudela, but the size of the community in the second half of the fourteenth century is unknown.

Timur seized the city in January 1388. Once again there was no resistance because the local rulers paid homage to the conqueror,[45] its citizens paid tribute and the Jewish community was left untouched.

Tabriz

Tabriz was a large trade city in the north-west of Iran, close to Azerbaijan. There was a large colony of Jews living in the city before and after the Mongol invasion. There was a Jewish pogrom in the city in 1291.[46] The Dominican friar Jordan visited Tabriz in 1320. He wrote that there were 'just a few Jews' in this region of Persia.[47]

Tabriz became Timur's domain automatically when he subjugated the Caspian provinces of Persia in the early 1380s. During the Timur–Tokhtamish wars, Tabriz was taken by Tokhtamish, the troops of the Golden Horde captured and plundered the city in the winter 1385–6, and Tokhtamish left the city in ruins. After this disaster Timur had no difficulty in taking the city in the summer of 1386. The inhabitants of Tabriz, still quite prosperous through their trading connections, were forced to pay a heavy tribute, and scholars, artists and craftsmen were deported to Samarkand.[48] Perhaps we can assume that some of those people were Jews, but additional research is needed to prove this assumption. Timur gave orders to restore the ruins of Tabriz.[49]

Derbent

Derbent was a very important port on the Caucasian shore of the Caspian Sea, in Dagestan, north of Azerbaijan. The Jewish population of Derbent probably descends from the military colony of the Persian kings of the sixth century AD.[50] There was a continuous flow of Jews from the Byzantine Empire to Derbent because of the Christian oppression[51] and in the tenth century many Jewish Khazars came to Derbent after they were defeated by the Russians.[52]

During the period of wars between Timur and Tokhtamish, warriors from both sides plundered Derbent several times. Tokhatamish took the city on his way to Iran, but Timur recaptured the city. Derbent suffered severely but was not completely destroyed and has survived until modern times.

Nishapur

Nishapur is a city in Persia, in the province of Khorasan, not far from Turkmenistan. Before the Mongol invasion there were Jewish and Christian communities in the city.[53] There was also a 'warlike Jewish tribe' on the highlands by Nishapur. This tribe numbered 4,000 families, and was governed by a Jewish prince. These Jews believed that they were descendants of the tribes of Dan, Zebulon, Asher and Naphtali.[54]

The Mongols killed all the inhabitants of Nishapur. The soldiers were ordered to leave nothing living, '. . . that the town should be laid waste that the site could be ploughed upon; and that in the exaction of vengeance not even cats and dogs should be left alive'.[55] This catastrophe happened in 1221 and only 400 skilled craftsmen survived. The city, the burial place of Omar Khayyam, was then rebuilt, but we do not know how many Jews came to live in it. Timur conquered Nishapur and made it his domain without any resistance. The Spanish envoy to Timur, R. Gonzalez de Clavijo, visited the city in 1404 and wrote that Nishapur was 'very densely populated, and it is a most delightful place to live in'.[56] There are no sources on the Jews there during this period.

Hamadan

Another Persian city, ancient Ecbatana, famous for the Avicenna's Mausoleum and the tombs of Esther and Mordecai, also contained a large

Jewish community. There are said to have been 50,000 Jews in the city in the twelfth century before the Mongol invasion.[57]

In February 1221 the Mongols entered Hamadan without violence due to the submission of the governor, allowing the inhabitants to survive. Very soon, however, the citizens of Hamadan decided to take action against the occupation and the Mongols returned to the city to put down a revolt.[58]

Timur captured Hamadan during his battle with the local rulers of Kurdistan and Luristan in 1393. This campaign was a part of his long-lasting war with Tokhtamish. Ibn Arabshah wrote that Timur 'made his way to Hamadan and reached the place, its citizens acting with negligence, and disaster befell it by night, the citizens sleeping at midday'.[59] Mujtabi, a local nobleman, made a treaty with the great conqueror and the city survived by paying tribute.

> And when that persecutor [Timur] strove a second time to impose tribute upon them, this true man [Mujtabi] approached him and stood supplicating with the mien of an abject wretch and he accepted his entreaty and granted everything to him.[60]

Cities and lands of the third period

Astrakhan

Astrakhan was an important port on the Volga river and in the fourteenth century Astrakhan was named Haji Turkhan. It was situated not far from Itil, the former capital of the destroyed Khazar Kaganate. The only fact known concerning the Jews of Astrakhan in the post-Khazar period is that Jewish merchants were actively engaged in trade there,[61] yet there is no evidence about a permanent Jewish colony existing in the city.

Timur destroyed Astrakhan in 1395 during his war with the Golden Horde.[62] It was in the strategic interest of Timur to cut the trade routes going through the territory of the Golden Horde and by destroying Astrakhan and Sarai he achieved this goal.

Sarai

Sarai, the capital of the Golden Horde, was a very large city. It was also situated on the Volga riverbanks and was an important trade centre. There is an indication of a possible Jewish presence in Sarai in the middle of the fourteenth century in the Russian *Troitskaya* chronicle.[63]

Timur destroyed Sarai in 1395. The destruction was even more severe than that of Astrakhan. The city did not rise from the ashes again.

Kaffa

The modern town of Feodosiya that lies on the Crimean peninsula is built on the foundations of medieval Kaffa. Kaffa was an important seaport of the Black Sea. Because we have no direct indication of Jewish presence in the city in the fourteenth century, we may surmise that there were at least some Jewish merchants, yet it is doubtful that the number of these merchants was significant. The Jews played a comparatively minor role in the great Mediterranean–Black Sea international trade, and as this trade was an Italian monopoly, the city was involved in the wars that took place between Venice and Genoa.[64]

Timur took Kaffa during the war with the Golden Horde when Timur was continuing his strategic plan of the cutting off of the trade routes. The population suffered from the devastation and loss but Timur saved their lives. Johannes Schiltberger, the German mercenary man who was captured by Timur's soldiers in 1402, described in his memoirs his visit to Kaffa shortly after Timur's death. He called Kaffa 'a populous city' where the Christians live together with the people of 'six other religions'.[65] It is also known that the Jewish physician from Spain, Isaac, visited Kaffa in 1472 on his way to Uzun Hasan, 'the senior of all Persia and Media'. Isaac was chosen as an envoy because he knew Persian.[66]

Tana

Tana was an important port on the river Don in the southern part of Russia and was used by Italian, Armenian, Russian, Arab and Jewish merchants for trade. The Italians were responsible for the water routes and the other nations held the land routes. There is unfortunately a distinct lack of knowledge about a permanent Jewish community in the city during the fourteenth century.

Tana was sacked by Timur in 1395. Although Timur's plundering of Tana made it less valuable to the Italians, this did not hold for long[67] as in 1436 the Italian merchant Josafato Barbaro visited Tana and found it again to be a trade centre.[68]

Tiflis (Tbilisi)

This ancient and beautiful city was the capital of the Kingdom of Georgia. Jews enjoyed an extensive period of living here and the Georgian dynasties of Bagratun and Amatun in the Middle Ages claimed a Jewish ancestry.[69] Marco Polo also mentioned a small Jewish community in the city.[70] In 1399 beautiful Tiflis was severely damaged when conquered by Timur.

Baghdad

Baghdad has a unique place in the history of the Jewish Diaspora. The Jewish community (beginning from the eighth century) flourished from the ninth to the thirteenth century. As the seat of the exilarchate, Baghdad became a centre of Jewish learning. The city was important for the Karaites and the Kabbalists as well.

In contrast with the Jewish communities in other Asian cities, historians have seriously studied the Jewish community in Baghdad. There is even a monograph on the subject written by David Solomon Sassoon.[71] The community had its commercial and cultural peak from the eighth to tenth centuries, then, in 1258, the city was destroyed by the Mongols. Kirakos, an Armenian historian of the thirteenth century and contemporary to the events, described this destruction very vividly:

> [Hulegu] then ordered the troops guarding the walls to descend and kill the inhabitants of the city, great and small. [The Mongols] organised as though harvesting a field and cut down countless, numberless multitudes of men, women, and children. For forty days they did not stop. Then they grew weary and stopped killing. Their hands grew tired; they took the others for sale. They destroyed mercilessly.[72]

Kirakos mentioned that the Christians of Baghdad were not harmed but said nothing about the Jews of the city. The destruction was not complete and the city soon recovered. Sassoon did not find direct evidence that the Jewish community suffered during the siege of Baghdad.[73] Benjamin of Tudela estimated the number of Jews in the city as 40,000.[74] No figures are present for the Mongol and the Timurid period.

Sasson only dedicated two pages to the fourteenth and fifteenth centuries in his book because of the lack of sources. What is known though, is that there was a Jewish community in Baghdad in 1376 under the leadership of David b. Hodayah, a Nasi.[75]

In 1393 Timur approached Baghdad. The citizens, fearing a repetition of the horrors of the Mongol invasion, opened the gates of the city.[76] This act saved them. The learned and prominent men in the arts and sciences were transported to Samarkand and the others had to pay the usual ransom in consideration of having been spared from pillage.

Because of the local unrest within, the city was taken by Timur's enemies twice, forcing Timur to recapture Baghdad both in 1394 and in 1401. The conquest and massacre of the city in 1401 was the most severe. Faraj, the governor of Baghdad, decided to fight Timur's troops and

Timur had little choice but to fight back. After forty days of siege the city was conquered. Timur ordered a general massacre as he counted the citizens of Baghdad as traitors, 'although the sayyids, ulema, and learned persons who could take refuge in Temur's camp and were saved'.[77]

Evidence of Jewish life in Baghdad appeared again in the sixteenth century.

Delhi

The capital of the Delhi Sultanate in the northern part of India was a big city. There are, however, no clear indications that there was a sizeable Jewish community in Delhi in the fourteenth century. In general, the Jews of India settled down in the seaports such as Bombay, Calcutta and Rangoon farther to the south. For example, Friar Odorico Mattaussi di Pardenone, who travelled through India in the 1320s, mentioned the Jewish presence in Flandrin, a seaport not far from Calcutta.[78]

During the so-called 'Indian campaign' Timur defeated the troops of the Delhi Sultanate and the city was taken and plundered. Some craftsmen were sent to Samarkand. All the primary sources, including the main source of Giyyas ad-Din Ali, said nothing about the Jews in the region of the campaign.

Aleppo (Khaleb)

Aleppo was an important trade centre in Syria where both the Venetians and Armenians had a significant silk and cloth trade. The Jews lived in the city for a long time. Bar-Hebraeus, 'son of the Jew' (1226–86), who was a Jacobite bishop of Aleppo when the Mongols came to the city in January 1260,[79] managed to save some of the Christian community of Aleppo, but nearly all the Jews and Muslims were killed during these six days of massacre. 'And there took place in Aleppo a slaughter like unto that of Baghdad, only more terrible', wrote Bar Hebraeus.[80]

There is no evidence that the sizeable Jewish community was restored in Aleppo in the thirteenth and fourteenth centuries. In fact, the Mongols gave the city to the Christian crusader, Bohemund VI, prince of Antioch–Tripoli,[81] and as a rule, the Jews were not permitted to settle in the crusaders' domains.

Timur took Aleppo in October 1400 after a short siege. The Mamluk army did not try to defend the city, and Aleppo was almost completely destroyed. There is some unclear evidence about a Jewish presence in Aleppo during this time; one anonymous medieval Jewish Rabbi mentioned the destruction of the city by Timur in a manuscript. He wrote then that 'during that time the holy man came to Aleppo and some Jews remained to read before him'.[82] He also stated that Timur 'killed old men and children' but it is unclear whether these were Jewish victims, Muslims or Christians. The above-mentioned 'holy man' and his associates were not killed.

A sizeable Jewish community appeared in the city again in 1492 and many Jewish refugees from Spain settled there.

Smyrna (Izmir)

This city was a port in Asia Minor. The Jewish settlement in the city dates back from the second century AD.

By the time of Timur this important seaport of the Turkish coast of the Mediterranean was in hands of the crusaders, which means that there was no Jewish community in the city. In December 1402 Timur drove the Knights of the Hospital out of Smyrna and the crusaders' presence in Asia ended.

Damascus

Being very close to Palestine, Damascus had a large Jewish community for many centuries and was made a tributary by King David. The Jews flourished there under the Fatimids in the tenth century until the crusaders and later the Mongols destroyed the city twice. Nevertheless, the community survived and there is clear evidence that there were Jews living in Damascus in 1375.[83] The size of the community, however, is not known.

At that time Damascus belonged to Mamluks and this is an appropriate moment to say a few words about Jewish life in the Mamluk Empire. In 1354 Sultan Al-Malik Al-Salikh issued the decree against *dhimmis*. Here is just a small fragment from it:

> They [Jews and Christians] may not resemble the Muslims in their dress. They must wear blue and yellow distinguishing costumes. Their women are likewise forbidden from resembling Muslim women. They may not ride on saddles. They are not to wear swords. They are not to ride horses or mules, but only on donkeys, seated sidesaddle on litters. They are not to sell wines.[84]

In addition, it was forbidden for a Jew to be employed by the Mamluk authorities and occupy any position 'which would give him authority over a single Muslim'. In reality this regulation was not very strict and in some periods the Jews were employed as government clerks and soldiers, although the Jews also had to take a humiliating oath and put up with many other restrictions.[85]

This does not, however, necessarily mean that Timur was seen as a liberator. First of all, Timur was a Muslim. Secondly, he was a terrifying warrior.

Approaching Damascus from Baalbek, Timur stopped to pray at the legendary tomb of Noah, and he entered the city in March 1401 after a short and chaotic battle with the troops of Sultan Faraj. Damascus was saved from immediate massacre by a delegation of distinguished men who relinquished the city and begged for mercy. Faraj, though, was unable to defend Damascus and fled the city at night.[86] A few days later Timur plundered and destroyed the city. Ibn Arabshah wrote about Timur's actions afterwards:

> And he took from Damascus learned men and craftsmen and all who excelled in any art, the most skilled weavers, tailors, gem-cutters, carpenters, makers of head-coverings, farriers, painters, bow-makers, falconers, in short, craftsmen of every kind, and collected Ethiopians, as related above. And he divided these companies among the heads of the army and ordered them to lead them to Samarkand.[87]

No Jewish chronicle described this event but, nevertheless, we can assume that some portion of the Jewish community, weavers, gem-cutters, craftsmen were transferred to Samarkand. The revival of Jewish life in the city occurred in 1492 when the Spanish refugees arrived.

Armenia

The Armenian people left us a first-hand *History of Tamerlane and His Successors*, written by T'ovma Metsobets'i (1378–1446), the Armenian Church *vardapet* (Doctor of theology), in the 1440s.[88] Timur's invasions of Armenia of 1387, 1388, 1395, 1401 and 1402 are described as vividly as only an eye-witness can describe them. In his narrative, T'ovma always specifies the religion of the described people – Armenian Orthodox Christians, Catholics, Tachiks (Muslims, Arabs). The account is more detailed for the first three decades of the fifteenth century. The Jews of Armenia are not mentioned in this manuscript, although it is known that Jews had lived in Armenia at least since the first century BC when King Tigranes the Great, who ruled northern Palestine, transferred many

Jews from Palestine to Armenia.[89] We know that in the ninth century AD the Jewish community of Armenia was very large and important. Benjamin of Tudela[90] and Petachia of Ratisbon found Jewish communities there at the end of the twelfth century, but not in large numbers. Rabbi Petachia wrote: 'There are large cities in the land of Ararat. There are few Jews there. In ancient times many Jews lived there'.[91] Kirakos Ganjakets'i (d. 1271–2) described the Mongol invasions of Armenia in the thirteenth century in his *History of Armenia*.[92] He was very specific about the religion of described nations, however he did not mention the Jews of Armenia in his long and detailed book. In October 2000 three experts from the Hebrew University of Jerusalem surveyed an ancient Jewish cemetery in Armenia. The Director of the expedition was the Hebrew University's Professor of Armenian Studies, Michael Stone. The cemetery is in the region of Vayots Dzor, south and west of Erevan, the capital of Armenia. Over forty tombstones were found at this site, and on them were sixteen inscriptions in Hebrew and Aramaic. The find is unprecedented as the inscriptions are dated to the late thirteenth and early fourteenth centuries, the period between invasions of the Mongols and of Timur.[93]

Timur battled against the Armenians several times and they were severely beaten. There is no evidence whether the few Jews who were living in Armenia then were killed or not.

* * *

Do we know how many Jews became Timur's citizens? No exact figures are available. In fact, Benjamin of Tudela's survey of the Jews in the big cities like Baghdad or Isfahan is the only source on the subject, and this we know from Benjamin's travels in the twelfth century. We do not know how the Mongol invasion of the thirteenth century affected these known numbers. If we take into consideration the size of Timur's empire and figures of the world population at that historical time,[94] we may assume that several hundreds of thousands of Jews did become Timur's citizens and later citizens of the Timurid states. Obviously because of the wars in the Timur empire and then the Timurid states, lives of the Jews could have been affected like any other victim of war, yet we only know for certain that there was no mass slaughter of Jews during the period of Timur's wars.

7

THE JEWS IN TIMUR'S EMPIRE

> THE PRINCIPAL JEWS
> And we have manuscripts in peacock styles
> by Ali of Damascus; we have swords
> engraved with storks and apes and crocodiles,
> and heavy beaten necklaces, for Lords.
>
> THE MASTER OF THE CARAVAN
> But you are nothing but a lot of Jews.
>
> THE PRINCIPAL JEWS
> Sir, even dogs have daylight, and we pay.
> (James E. Flecker, *The Golden Journey to Samarkand*, London, Martin Secker, p. 6)

Assuming that there were several hundred thousand Jews in Tamerlane's domains,[1] the following question arises, how did they subsist? The Jews, who for centuries were much in demand for the provision of doctors, interpreters and scholars of various kinds to the Islamic world, were not organised under one authority in the new massive empire of Timur. Also, as is well known, Diaspora Jews, including the Asian Diaspora, were mainly artisans and city-dwellers. Timur's stable empire demonstrated both the humane flexibility and the practical good sense of the Timurid administration in its policies toward the status of its non-Muslim subjects. Under the principle 'the bent head is not to be stricken off', all Muslims were bound to spare the 'Peoples of the Book', provided they agreed to pay *djiziya*, (if indeed this poll-tax survived in the empire in its initial Islamic meaning), and provided they gave no trouble. These religious communities were accorded a surprising degree of autonomy in the conduct of their affairs and it is most probable that each community had its own leader, as there is no direct evidence in regard to the Chief Rabbi, Exilarch, or any other similar Jewish authority in the empire.

Timur fought with the Christians, Muslims and 'pagans' of India, and he was ready to fight with the pagans of China too. At the same time he never issued a law against the *dhimmi* who lived within the borders of his empire. Generally, the affairs of the Christian and Jewish communities were left in the hands of the people who understood them best – their own leaders. This lenience was amply repaid in co-operation and docility, as there is no evidence of any Christian or Jewish revolt against Timur or the Timurids in the fourteenth or fifteenth centuries. Timur's institutions affected Persian and Central Asian Jews in one fundamental respect, as the absence of rigid social hierarchies under the ruling institution meant there was no special categorisation for the Jews, in contrast to the Jews in the Christian West or the Mamluk state. The Jews of Timur's empire could own houses and land; they could be farmers. The need for interest-bearing loans was, perhaps, lower than in Europe and the Mamluk Sultanate because of the continual inflow of military contributions and loot. Legality of these loans prevented money lending from being a particularly Jewish occupation as it was in the West. Such stigmas or concepts were meaningless in Timur's international empire, with its numerous religious minorities, and the Jews were allowed to follow many different occupations, some of which will be discussed in context of their various historical events.

Jewish professional orientation continued to be generally the same as it was during the time of the Arab caliphates. The Jews were still involved in trade, medicine and translation. They worked as dyers, cobblers, farmers, and there was no lack of variety in occupation and economic position except in the areas of administrative, fiscal, judicial and military positions. Many of them were bilingual – Persian/Turkic – and those specialising in medicine, mathematics and the chemical sciences were accustomed to using Arabic as their medium of broader education. However, some changes did occur over time and it is worth examining the professional status of the Jews under Timur.

Jewish merchants

Any story of mediaeval trade would be incomplete without the Jewish merchants! The Arab Empire had erected a mighty arc-shaped barrier around all Christian lands extending from Spain to the Crimea. Since the victorious advances of Islam, Central Europe had been cut off from both Africa and Asia and the once-lively trade across the Mediterranean had almost come to a halt, bringing the stream of goods from the Orient also to a slow cessation.

The Jews were still in a position to mediate between Christian Europe and the Muslim East, as Jews lived everywhere in the realm of Islam, and European Jews could turn to them for aid in negotiation and travel.[2] During the period between the eighth and the eleventh centuries the Jews acted almost exclusively as a commercial people and only they could trade freely with both the areas of Europe and the Muslim East. Ibn Khurradadhbeh relates that Jewish merchants from the south of France crossed the sea to Egypt, traversed on foot the isthmus of Suez, and travelled by ship to India; others went overland from Ceuta to Egypt, and from Syria to the Indus. They often visited Constantinople too.[3] Another great trade route that was entirely overland lay farther north, and proceeded through the difficult terrain of Russia towards China. From Prague it passed through the lands of the Slavs, through the kingdom of the Jewish Khazars, which was an important Jewish trade stronghold right in the middle of Asia, and on across the Caspian Sea, the Oxus, and the mountain range of Central Asia up to the Chinese borders.

Many historians mention the prosperity of Jewish trade, but they do not define the timeframes of this prosperity. We should not extrapolate these bright perspectives from the tenth to the fourteenth centuries because between the eleventh and the fifteenth centuries there was a gradual decline in Jewish trade. In the eleventh century the Crusades once more made the Mediterranean a busy centre of trade, but this really only benefited the cities of the Italian peninsula. The Christian Italian cities became the great distributing centre for commerce with Asia and Africa, and the Jews found themselves pushed out of a leading role. In the meantime, the troops of Russian principalities destroyed Jewish Khazaria, the immense empire of the Eurasion steppe. This large state, which was very friendly towards the Jews, was completely annihilated and several Jewish trade routes were cut off.

After the Crusades had come to an end, these same Italian cities remained the distribution centres for Oriental goods, which the people of Europe had come to depend on during the time they had been in the Near East. Then, in the thirteenth century, the destructive Mongols appeared and the East–West trade came to a standstill for a decade or two. But once their supremacy was established, the Mongol rulers efficiently organised roads and trade extending from the borders of Hungary to the Sea of Japan.

So the Jewish merchants survived. There is clear evidence that they remained in Russia in 1288 despite the fact that the Russian city of Kiev was destroyed by the Mongols in 1240.[4] Before that, the Armenians and the Jews had used Kiev as a main trade city in Russia. The Jewish merchants were responsible for the trade between the Anatolian Turks of

Asia Minor and the Oghuz Turks of Inner Asia. It is interesting to note that the word *bazirganlar*, which means 'the Jewish merchants',[5] was assimilated from Persian into the Turkish language.

At the same time the Jews faced bitter competition from the Germans, Venetians, Greeks and Armenians, the Russians from Novgorod and, of course, the Muslim caravan traders.[6]

From the time of Chingiz Khan the Muslim traders supported the Mongols. In return, the Mongols gave them many privileges. As a result, the caravan trade reached its acme in the thirteenth century.[7] The Christian influence on the Mongols was also significant and the Christian merchants were welcomed in the Mongol domains.

The decline of the Jewish Mediterranean and Black Sea trade is clearly demonstrated in the comprehensive three volume work of W. Heyd, *Histoire du commerce du Levant au Moyen-Âge*. Armenians, Greeks and Italians were the main traders at the beginning of the fourteenth century.[8] Heyd mentions the Jewish glassmakers of Tyre but says nothing about the Jewish traders.[9]

Prior to the time of Timur, the northern Asian trade routes to Europe were more important than the southern ones because of the post-Il-Khanid civil wars in Persia.[10] Timur tried to change this by conquering Persia and bringing about political stability. Then he defeated the Golden Horde and destroyed the northern trade cities, as shown in Chapter 6. Therefore, at the very beginning of the fifteenth century the main trade routes again passed through Persia.

Also at the beginning of the fifteenth century, G. de Clavijo reported on the comparative prosperity prevalent in many parts of Persia and Central Asia through which he travelled whilst on embassy to Timur. In Arzinjan he noticed 'many opulent merchants' and 'many caravans carrying much merchandise [that] journey on their way, coming hither from Syria and bound for Turkey'.[11] He wrote about Sultaniyya that 'it is a more important centre of exchange for merchants and their goods'.[12] Describing Tabriz, Clavijo mentioned 'goods of all kinds, such as silk stuffs and cotton clothes, crapes, taffetas, raw silk and jewellery, for these shops wares of every kind may be found. There is indeed an immense concourse of merchants and merchandise here.'[13] Once again no Jews were mentioned.

Timur tried to make trading as safe as possible. Generally he succeeded. Khwandamir wrote in the 1520s:

> His [Timur's] punishment was indeed so effective that if during his glorious days a woman were to put a pot filled with gold on her head and go from the east to the west, no one would have

> dared molest her. For this reason merchants sailing the seas and traders from every land brought precious wares and goods from every place, making great profits and realizing much gain.[14]

Jewish merchants, subject to the same conditions as other merchants, lost their market. Why? The reasons are due to events occurring outside Timur's empire. In the fourteenth century, due to the official acts of Jewish expulsion in both England and France, Jewish history was terminated. The German Jews suffered several diabolic persecutions at the same time and at the end of the fourteenth century the first persecution of the Jews began in Spain. The Jews of the Mamluk Empire were oppressed and humiliated, so the Persian and Central Asian Jews lost many of their ties with the other Jewish communities in Europe and the Near East.

Yet Jewish trade survived more or less intact in Crimea. Here the Karaites were more active than the Rabbinical Jews. The Black Sea stronghold of Karaites, Chufuth-Kale, 'The Jewish Castle', survived until the sixteenth century. The Karaites supported the Mongols and the 'Tartars'. When the Lithuanian Prince Witold (Vitovt in Russian sources), was trapped between Poland, the Russian principalities and the Golden Horde, and was also completely defeated by the Mongols at the battle of Worskla in 1399, the Karaites used this situation to their own advantage. The modern Polish historian Jan Tyszkiewicz called it 'the Oriental colonisation of the Lithuanian Principality by the Karaites, Jews and Armenians'.[15] But this local Jewish triumph in Eastern Europe did not permit them to organise trade with the Jews of Central Asia because of the almost permanent state of war between Timur and the Golden Horde.

There were, no doubt, Jewish merchants in the empire of Timur, but their influence decreased owing to the above-mentioned sad circumstances. Thus, Jewish trade remained local, with many Jews having to call at the homes of Muslim, Shamanist, Christian or Zoroastrian peoples to offer their services as traders.

The last stage of decline in Jewish trade in Asia occurred in the fifteenth century after the great sea trade routes were established. The Jews were ostracised from these new opportunities. In Europe they were expelled from Spain and Portugal and locked in ghettos in Italy and Germany. In Asia they had more freedom but the Great Silk Route had disappeared and the merchants were reduced to the status of local tradesmen. These Jewish tradesmen survived in Iran until modern times. All their previous greatness had gone and their life was simple:

> The occupation of the Jews in our city was as follows: some of them used to go to sell mercery goods in the villages, and sleep

> there the night also. They used to know the people at whose house they used to sleep, and used to give them strings, needles and wax for nothing; the latter on their part, used to give the Jews in the morning milk, curds, cheese and bread. Other Jews used to buy fabric from the merchants in the city and take it to the village. The lord of the village used to give them a place; sometimes he used to give a house to the peddler where he could live. When his business was slack – as it would happen at times – the peddler used to take his bundle, put his goods on his back and go to other villages.[16]

A simple and ingenuous story of the decline of the great Jewish Asian trade.

Jewish physicians

Throughout the ages the Jews have shown a remarkable predilection for medicine, and in all epochs their skills have been recognised. In the Middle Ages half of the best-known Jewish scholars, philosophers, historians and statesmen – men like S'ad ad-Daulah, Moses Maimonides, Jehuda ha-Levi, Rashid ad-Din – were physicians by profession, a striking illustration of the respect with which that calling was generally held.

The earliest medical figures in the history of Islamic Persia were Christians and Jews. Among the Jews, Hunain b. Ishaq was the most outstanding, and we are in debt to him for the best translations of the Hippocratic and Galenic corpus into Persian and also major independent treatises on medicine. The physicians of the caliphs continued to be Christians and Jews until the time of the caliph al-Mu'tadid (AD 892–902), who had a Persian Muslim physician.[17] In the next hundred years Central Asia produced the greatest Muslim physician, Abu Ali Ibn Sina.

The Mongol invasion of Persia brought about a short period of decline in medicinal affairs but later produced several prominent Jewish doctors. Two of them sustained wonderful careers and became prominent statesmen because of the Asiatic system of patronage.

Patronage was a widespread social institution of the Middle East and Central Asia in the Middle Ages, and one which is still very powerful in this region today. During the Mongol and Timurid periods patronage was a fundamental form of social binding and hierarchical organisation. It was of vital importance for physicians, scholars, poets and historians. For physicians, patronage ties were considered honour-bound rather than being dictated by economic rationality. Consequently, they were viewed as voluntary. For the Jews in Asia, patronage was more than an economic exchange, it was a statement of status, identity and credibility. It was a process of self-fashioning.

Personal patronage relationships developed when the physician ceased being a visitor and became a courtier. A Jewish doctor, Sa'd al-Daula of Baghdad, created such a career for himself at the court of the Mongol khan Arghun, who ruled Persia from 1284–91. Arghun chose as his personal physicians Sa'd al-Daula and Amin ul-Doula, whose nickname was Khwaja or 'The Eunuch'. Sa'd al-Daula soon abandoned medicine for politics and became so accomplished at this that Arghun appointed him *vizier* (prime minister).

Then Sa'd al-Daula became a patron himself and favoured a Muslim doctor named Qutb-ul-Din. In return, Qutb-ul-Din dedicated his commentaries on the *Canon* of Ibn Sina to him, a work which he entitled *Tuhfat-ul-Sa'diyya* or *The Present to Sa'd*.[18] These commentaries were in use for the next several centuries in Iran and Central Asia.[19]

Another example of how this system of patronage could be put to good use is demonstrated by Rashid ad-Din, a Jewish physician from the Persian city of Hamadan. Rashid ad-Din converted to Islam, became a physician and almost immediately *vizier* of another Mongol khan of Persia, Ghazan, in 1295, and held this post for twenty-two years. He founded colleges, hospitals and libraries. One whole quarter of Tabriz was named after him.[20]

What really brought him fame was his well-known history of the Mongols, the famous chronicles *Jami-ul-Tawarikh*, or *Collection of Dates*. Among his written works are a few volumes on medical subjects that are so completely overshadowed by his great historical work that up till now they have received no notice. However, he was a good health-care manager and built several big hospitals in Persia. There are existing letters from Rashid ad-Din addressed to his son and other people ordering them to furnish large quantities of drugs for use in these hospitals.[21]

Bar Hebraeus – Son of a Jew, *Ibn ul-Ibri* – was another Persian physician with an unusual career. He was born in 1226 and his father Aaron was also a physician and his first teacher. Bar Hebraeus was baptised under the name of Abu ul-Faraj Gregory and completed his medical studies in Damascus. He commented on Hippocrates, Galen and Ibn Sina; and he is said to have prepared, but never completed, a translation into Syriac of the *Canon* of Ibn Sina.[22] Bar Hebraeus enjoyed a wonderful religious career under the Mongols. He was a Jacobite bishop of Aleppo and then became Primate of the Eastern Jacobites in 1264. He died in 1286 in Persia.

After a hundred years, when Islam firmly established itself in Persia and Central Asia for the second time, opportunities for Jewish doctors for such unusual 'medical' careers were limited. There were still many Jewish doctors in Iran, Iraq and Afghanistan, especially in Herat and in other parts of the empire of Timur, but their efforts were limited to local means. No one became a courtier like Sa'd ad-Daula or Rashid ad-Din. In addition to religious complications, Timur was a difficult person to seek patronage from as his first preference were the peoples of his native Barlas tribe. Because Timur was always on the move his court moved with him and he visited his capital Samarkand rarely and then only for short periods of time. The settled Persian Jews, whether converted or not, including doctors, had almost no opportunities to be under his patronage.

Furthermore, Jewish medical influence reached its acme in the tenth and twelfth centuries. There still were many skilled Jewish physicians in the fourteenth and fifteenth centuries in the Muslim world, but this period did not produce such geniuses as Isaac Israeli (Isaac Judaeus, *c.* 855–955) or Maimonides (Rabbi Moses ben Maimon, 1135–1204).

There are 181 Oriental medical manuscripts in the collection of the Oriental manuscripts of the Academy of Sciences of the Republic of Uzbekistan.[23] No work of Isaac Israeli, Maimonides or, for example, Ahmed Ibn al-Djezzar is present. This collection shows that the main medical authorities in Timur's empire, in addition to world famous Avicenna and Razes, were Muslim doctors like Muhammad b. Yusuf al-Ilaki, Qutb-ul-Din ash-Shirazi, Ibn an-Nafis, Muhammad b. Yusuf and others.

Jewish translators, interpreters and envoys

The contribution of Jewish translators to the development of international medieval thought is very well recognised.[24] A large proportion of Arab writings reached Europe through the medium of Jewish translators, although Persian and Turkic works were translated in smaller proportions. During the thirteenth century the rate at which translations come to the Latin West was greatly accelerated, as their preparation became an almost recognised profession. Enlightened European rulers were specially associated with the work and Spain, Italy and Sicily became centres of Jewish translations from Arabic into Latin.

How about translations from Latin or other European languages into Arabic, Persian and Old Turkic? We may assume that the Jews were also active in that field but the information is scanty, as for the area of Persia, Central and Inner Asia in the late fourteenth century, we have no information at all.

Timur, no doubt, used interpreters during his campaigns to translate from Arabic, Armenian or, for example, Georgian. Could some of them have been Jews? Perhaps. But no one became so famous as to be mentioned in the chronicles.

There is documentation that Timur sent letters to European kings.[25] However, these letters were written in Persian and were translated into European languages when they arrived in Europe.[26] In return, the European rulers sent letters to Timur, but we have no records as to the identity of the translators. The Spanish ambassador to Timur, Gonzales de Clavijo, did not mention any Jewish interpreters or translators at the court of Timur. It is most probable though, that Christian friars, who at the time of the Mongols were numerous in Persia, had learned the local languages, and wrote the translations.

Another career opportunity for the Jews was that of being an envoy. Indeed, this employment had a long tradition. Ibrahin Ibn Yacoub Ha-Israeli was a member of an embassy sent by the caliph of Cordova to eastern Germany in AD 970 of which he wrote an account in Arabic.[27] Another Jew, Isaac by name, was one of the members of the embassy of Caliph Harun ar-Rashid to Charlemane in AD 802.[28] It is true that sometimes ambassadors were killed, but if they survived, they would then be in great favour.

We have no direct indications that Timur used the Jews as his envoys. There is, however, a letter written by Timur in May 1402 to 'Brother Francesco', the regent of Constantinople, concerning co-operative efforts in the struggle against Ottoman Sultan Bayazet. A certain Isaac is mentioned in this letter as Timur's envoy[29] but he is not identified. Isaac, of course, could have been a Christian. However, he was not called 'brother', 'father', 'friar', 'monk', 'nobleman' or by any other title usual for Christians, to indicate his position.

I do not think that Timur used Jewish envoys in his diplomacy. In the late fourteenth century and the beginning of the fifteenth century it was a humiliating act to send a Jew as an envoy to a Christian king or regent. It was much more convenient to use Christian monks for this purpose. In return, the Spanish king would send Timur an embassy led by a Christian nobleman. The only possibility for a Jew to become a member of an embassy was if he held the position of an interpreter. Once again, the Christian monastic competition was high. The fourteenth century was not the best time for a Jew to make a court career in a Muslim country.

In general, the Jews of Timur's empire remained quiet and humble artisans, local merchants and doctors, who obediently paid taxes, lived simply, and died naturally. None of them became famous. None of them was killed in a court plot as Sa'd al-Daula or Rashid ad-Din of the previous epoch. Neither did Timur show special attention to this group of citizens during his thirty-five year rule. Neither did he issue any regulations, negative or positive, concerning the Jews in particular.

It is true that some Jews, those who were skilful artisans or prominent in another field, could have been transferred to Samarkand and other places in Central Asia, without becoming slaves. There is no clear evidence about Jewish transfer but there is enough evidence about the Muslim 'replaced persons' that shows how they fared and their good fortune. For example, Abdallah b. al-Djazari ash-Shafi'i (d. 1429) was a prominent theologian in Damascus. When Timur captured Damascus, this Muslim *kazi* (a judge) was moved to Samarkand where he lived very well and continued his religious writings. After Timur's death he moved freely to Shiraz where he was appointed a *kazi* again.[30] Another prominent Muslim, *Mirza* Bahadur-Hojja b. Hussein Hojja-ii Pirmesti, was moved by Timur from his town of Abiverda in Khorassan to Bukhara where he received seventy-five *tanaps* of tax-free land. He settled down in Bukhara and his descendants continued to live there until the beginning of the twentieth century.[31]

The Jews were not that lucky, but the important factor was that the Jewish population of Central Asia was able to increase due to Timur's policy of relocation within his empire. Timur used his Jewish subjects mainly as taxpayers and skilful artisans. They were an integral part of the economy, though their actual contribution is difficult to assess for the same reason that it is difficult to accurately estimate their numbers, the existing documentation is spasmodic and only for isolated periods. It was clearly inadvisable to withdraw the protection of the state from any community that was able to contribute to the economy. The continuation of Timur's protection of the Jews meant that their social relations, no less than their juridical status, remained unchanged. They continued to participate in the public life of the Timur's empire and to mingle freely with their fellow citizens.

8

THE LAST TRIP OF THE PROPHET DANIEL AND THE LIFE AND CULTURE OF THE JEWS OF CENTRAL ASIA

> You, O king, the king of kings – to whom the God of heaven has given the kingdom, the power, the might, and the glory, into whose hand he has given human beings, wherever they live, the wild animals of the field, and the birds of the air, and whom he has established as ruler over them all – you are the head of gold.
>
> (Daniel 2:37–38)

> Look 'round thee now on Samarcand! –
> Is she not queen of Earth? her pride
> Above all cities? in her hand
> Their destinies?
>
> (Edgar Allan Poe, 'Tamerlane')[1]

There is a legend that when Timur conquered Persia, he was shown the tomb of the Prophet Daniel. As a result, there are now two tombs of Daniel, one in Iran and the second in Samarkand, Uzbekistan. We do not know who wrote the Book of Daniel, a canonical book of the Old Testament. Some researchers argue that Daniel seems to be a legendary literary creation rather than a historical figure like King David or King Solomon.[2] However, the mausoleum of the Prophet is located in the modern Iranian town of Shush, ancient Susa. The conical white sugared-loaf shrine stands on the east bank of the river Shaur. When the Arabs first reached Susa in the seventh century, they found Daniel's coffin in the city citadel.[3]

Despite the fact that Daniel is not mentioned in the Koran,[4] Muslim pilgrims have for centuries regarded the Prophet's remains as having miraculous powers, particularly in preventing drought, and pilgrims still continue to visit Shush. There was also an intensive Jewish pilgrimage to the tomb, and in the twelfth century, according to Benjamin of Tudela,[5] a synagogue stood near the sepulchre of Daniel.

We do not know exactly when the mausoleum was built. According to a beautiful legend written by Benjamin of Tudela and retold by H. Graetz,[6] during the time of Sultan Sanjar the coffin was hung on chains over the river in order to stop the quarrels between the inhabitants of Susa concerning the place of its burial. In the nineteenth century a beautiful mosque stood near the tomb instead of the synagogue.[7]

It is also not perfectly clear when the Samarkand tomb of Daniel was built. The building wherein the tomb is located is perched on a high cliff overlooking the bank of the small river Siab in the north-western part of

Plate 3 The tomb of the Prophet Daniel in Samarkand. According to the legend, ashes of the biblical Prophet were brought to Samarkand by Tamerlane

Samarkand where there is a spring with water considered to have healing properties. The building itself is twelve metres long and six metres wide and is devoid of any external or internal decorations. In its present form it has existed since the nineteenth century and was last restored in the twentieth century. The interior is very simple and the few arches and cupolas on the ceiling provide the Oriental beauty.

The tomb itself is ten metres long and occupies nearly the whole of the interior. White cloths without inscriptions or decorations cover it. At the head of the tomb there are several fragments of an imbedded tombstone and these fragments have incomplete Arabic and Persian (or Tajik) inscriptions. The Arabic phrases (in fragments) represent the Koranic verses and the fragment of the Persian inscription has these three words: *Allahi charikor mardoni* that can be translated as 'Oh, Allah, a day-labourer, some men . . .'.

Uzbekistan became an independent state in 1991. Since that time some additional effort has been made to renovate this historical site including the new road leading to the brick building, as pregnant women from Samarkand and women wishing to conceive make a pilgrimage to the tomb and to the spring.

According to legend, the Prophet, after his burial, continued growing inside the tomb, and the tomb, therefore, continued to grow with him, hence the unusual length of the tomb. In 1912 the Russian administration of occupied Turkestan ordered the local Muslim authorities 'to stop' the growth of the deceased. Since that time the 'growth' has stopped.[8] Since 1946 this *mazar* (a tomb of a Muslim saint) was not counted as a historical site and was neglected by tourist authorities. It was only in 1992 that the tomb became a historical heritage once again.

There are two legends about the appearance of Daniel's tomb in Samarkand in connection with Timur. The first legend was described by E.N. Adler a hundred years ago:

> Tradition has it that Tamerlane had seen the tomb at Susa in Persia, with a warning inscribed thereon, that none should open its door; and so he broke it open from behind, and found it written that Nebi Daniel was there buried. The impetuous conqueror had the sarcophagus removed with all reverence, and carried it with him to his own capital to be its palladium. The sarcophagus is over twenty yards long as beseems a prophet's stature. It has been recently covered by a brick chapel with three cupolas, but photographs of the ancient structure can be had in Samarkand. It is grandly placed at the edge of a cliff overhanging the rapid river Seop. The local Jews do not believe the

> story, nor do they quite disbelieve it, for I went with two who prayed there at the grave of the righteous.[9]

V. Barthold also visited Samarkand with an archaeological expedition at approximately the same time as Adler. He describes the tomb, as a sepulchre of Daniyar-Ata.[10] According to the current local Uzbek legend, Timur did not remove the whole sarcophagus. Only a handful of ash was taken and sent to Samarkand with a special caravan.

After Barthold and Adler, the Austrian traveller Gustav Krist visited Daniel's tomb in Samarkand in the 1930s:

> A low sarcophagus, some nine feet six inches long, lay there in the desert sand. According to legend Daniel's body is steadily growing longer, and when it reaches a certain size he is to rise again. Behind the grave the ground fell away abruptly and in the loess cliff there was built a niche with shallow stone basins in which pious pilgrims place food for the dead saint. At the head of the grave, which is turned towards the west, there stand high poles with black horse-tails, at the foot is a bronze tablet with a Kufic inscription, while loose stones lie round about, which are displaced as Daniel grows. These roughly hewn stones enclose a rectangle of about fourteen feet by three feet six inches . . .
>
> The mulla told me that Daniel grows half an inch or so every year, and every year the rectangle of stones has to be slightly enlarged.[11]

How old is the Samarkand tomb? Russian novelist Sergey Borodin mentioned the tomb of 'Ho-Daniyar at Siab' in his novel *Stars above Samarkand* dedicated to the last years of Timur's reign.[12] Borodin does not adhere to the legend and rightly so, as the tomb (*mazar*) of Daniel is at least 300 years older than sites built by Timur in Samarkand. This was also first mentioned by imam Abu-l-Fazl Muhammad as-Samarkandi in his book *The Smaller Kandiya* (*al-Kand or Ta'rikh-i kand*) in the twelfth century.[13]

Despite the fact that the present local name of the tomb is 'Hojja Daniyar,' this name is a corruption of Daniel. *The Smaller Kandiya* clearly called the tomb 'the mazar of the Prophet Daniyal'.[14] Daniel was called a Prophet, not a saint or hojja. It means that the tomb belongs to a biblical personage and not to a local saint. The legend about Daniel and Timur does seem indeed to be just that, a legend.

The historical background of Timur's campaigns was very favourable to the creation of such legends. Timur's efforts to collect the most valuable things in the world and bring them to his capital were described in every detail by his court historians and other chroniclers. His Muslim piety was also glorified. These biographies, however, said nothing about any transfer of the ashes of Daniel or any other saint or prophet to Samarkand.

It was natural, however, for the citizens of Samarkand, Muslims and Jews alike, to connect Daniel with Timur, their beloved fellow-citizen. Somehow the Prophet Daniel remained an extremely popular biblical character among the Bukharian Jews and at the beginning of the seventeenth century the Jewish poet Khwaje of Bukhara (*c.* 1606) wrote a long poem entitled 'Daniyal-Name'. Thanks to the copyist Elyahu Eshaq ben Mordekhai, the British Museum now holds the manuscript. The poem was written in the Persian language in Hebrew characters presumably in Bukhara. The main part of this poem is a verification of the Book of Daniel, developed, paraphrased and expanded by the author. In one place Daniel is described as *nazok-chashm*, 'narrow-eyed', the kind of beauty admired in the author's native land, Central Asia.[15] Till modern times, legendary stories about Daniel survived in the folklore of the Bukharian Jews.

This devoted attachment to Daniel was not the only cultural peculiarity of the Central Asian (Bukharian) Jews, but also of the Persian Jews to whom they were related, both sharing much of the same uniqueness because of the political and cultural climate. These two large communities did not see themselves as part of the framework of the Hellenistic and Roman, and then of the Christian and Mediterranean Islamic worlds. As such, they were impervious to the impact of the assimilatory nature of Mediterranean culture, and instead thrived in a much more Oriental environment, wherein the wide variety of ethnic communities were granted a major degree not only of political self-rule but of cultural autonomy as well.

We have no rich written sources dealing only with Jewish cultural life in Central Asia in the fourteenth and fifteenth centuries; what is available, though, including several manuscript collections, is kept in various institutions, in Uzbekistan and Tajikistan, the Ben Zvi Institute collection and the National Library collection in Israel, and the Cairo Genizah Collection of Cambridge University. Analysing these sources, we may assume that the vast majority of Timur's Jewish subjects were Persian-speaking, despite the level of their Hebrew knowledge. Only in post-Timurid time, mainly during the sixteenth and seventeenth centuries, was the classic Persian language slowly being divided into *dari*, *farsi* and the Tajik languages. At the same time, the language of the Central Asian Jews was evolving from the Judeo-Persian to the Bukharian through the Judeo-Tajik. The Bukharian language, a peculiar mixture of

Persian, Hebrew, Arabic, Tajik and Uzbek words, is cemented by Persian grammar.[16] The Karaites were Jews who wrote in the Judeo-Persian dialect instead of Persian itself. The Prophet Daniel was of their particular veneration and respect too. Two Karaite commentaries on Daniel, written in Judeo-Persian, survived in Cairo Genizah.[17] Although this book is not concerned with the linguistic problems of the times, I do want to point out that in the case of the Timurid period, most Jewish written sources are not in Judeo-Persian, but are written in a precise Persian with Hebraisms.[18] Similar to modern English with Gallicisms, for example.

Timur was bilingual Persian–Turkic. The Timurid nobility and officials also spoke Persian in addition to their native tongue, usually the Chagatay Turk language, and there was no language barrier between them and their Jewish subjects.

It must now be asked how Timur's statesmanship affected the internal life of the Jewish community, its customs and its level of Jewish learning. These are particularly important areas when we look at the opposing tendencies prevalent at that time concerning Central Asian Jewry. Benjamin of Tudela in Persia observed that there were general favourable conditions that benefited the growth of such a strongly built well-organised community. Yet the absence of rigid social or economic barriers between the Jews, Muslims, Christians and Zoroastrians was equally likely to cause a weakening of this communal bond. This weakening created apathy towards Judaism, and a progressive assimilation into the dominant culture. It is in the light of these opposing tendencies that the internal life of the Central Asian community must be approached; it is by an estimate of their relative strength that the position of Jews in medieval Central Asia can finally be assessed. Unfortunately, it is precisely in the area of their internal community that information is disappointingly inadequate. There is little documentation and the sources are often fragmentary, making it risky to generalise in comparison to the documented sources dealing with the attitude of the Timurid's administration to the community. The Jews of the empire of Timur and the Timurid states did not write any specific treatise about their own culture. Our main tools with which to study Jewish life therefore are from archaeological evidence and the local Jewish folklore.

Archaeological discoveries help us to understand festival customs, burial customs, religious cults and everyday life patterns. In the case of Central Asian Jewry, archaeological evidence is fragmentary.[19] Putting these fragments together, we can clarify only some details and aspects of the cultural and spiritual life of the community. We know that the main Jewish community in Central Asia during the Second Temple Period (sixth century BC–first century AD) was the community of the city of

Merv. We know there were synagogues in several Central Asian cities and *migbe* (Mikveh, Jewish ritual bath) at these synagogues. Also there were specific places for ritual washing (*tushnuk* or *tashnav*) in the houses of the Jews. This place could be outside in the courtyard or inside the house, in a corridor. Copper jugs (*oftoba*) and copper washbasins (*tashtak*) were used for this procedure. The earliest Jewish *oftoba* and *tashtaks* that survived were made in the seventeenth century. The Jews' habit was to sign their utensils in black Indian ink and archaeologists have been able to identify several kitchen utensils as Jewish from these inscriptions. The Jews used ossuaries to bury their dead. The oldest ossuaries found are from the fourth and fifth centuries AD, and the oldest tombstones are from the middle of the eighth century. They were discovered not far from Herat, in Afghanistan, and have inscriptions both in Hebrew and in Persian.[20] Jewish ossuaries were also found in different parts of Central Asia including Margilan city in the Ferghana Valley, at the east of modern Uzbekistan, not far from Kyrghizia. These ossuaries were decorated with stone rosettes and columns similar to Jewish ossuaries from other lands. The oldest Jewish document found in Central Asia, in eastern Turkestan (Dandan settlement), was written in the eighth century. The document was prepared by Jewish merchants from Persia, and was written in Hebrew. These merchants reached Dandan by the way of Sogd, Chach (modern Tashkent), and the Ferghana settlements.[21] This is about the only archaeological evidence there is to tell us about the patterns of everyday Jewish life.

The folklore of Bukharian (Central Asian) Jews was first studied only at the end of the nineteenth century. Some serious research was accomplished during the twentieth century,[22] and in addition to folklore sources, the family names and nicknames of the local Jews were also studied. For centuries, the main types of this folklore were songs (*ashula*), folk sayings (*zarb-ul-masal*), fairy tales (*afsona*), jokes (*latifa*), and historical legends and family traditions (*khikoya*). Among the large collection of these literary sources, now kept in the Central State Archives of Uzbekistan, there are two short stories in Judeo-Tajik, dedicated to Timur. The stories are *Zikhronom le-vet Taimuri* (Recollections about Timur) and *Khikoyati Timur* (A Story about Timur).[23] The first story is almost a replica from the legend about Timur's benevolence to the Jews of Herat, heard and retold by Joseph Wolff in 1846. Another one is a legendary story about the Jewish minister and advisor to Timur, David ha-Tsadik. The story narrates that Muslim advisors to Timur became jealous and tried to charge David with undermining the security of the empire. David was called to the audience hall of Timur along with seven Muslim *ulema* who brought charges against him. The story continues with,

'Speak, David,' said Timur.

'May I ask to bring pens and paper?' said David.

Paper and pens were brought.

'Give them to your advisors, and let them separately write an answer to this question. What is bread?' said David.

This was done. The papers then were given to Timur, who read the answers.

The first wrote, 'Bread is a food'.

The second, 'Bread is flour mixed with water'.

The third, 'A gift from Allah'.

The fourth, 'A nutritious substance'.

The fifth, 'Baked dough'.

The sixth, 'Nobody knows for sure'.

The seventh, 'The wealth of your Majesty'.

'Let the wise men first decide what bread is, and then they can press charges against me,' said David ha-Tsadik. From then on Timur kept David close to him as his finest adviser.[24]

There are two uncertainties about this story. This legend is very similar to a story about legendary Middle Eastern folklore personage Hojja Nasreddin, and its primary origin is not clear. Secondly, the century of its creation is not known either. In either case, the folklore stories present Timur as a wise ruler, tolerant and benevolent to the local Jews.

Only folklore sources and no other documented sources tell us that there were numerous synagogues in Central Asian cities during the time of Timur and the Timurids. Each synagogue had a *gabboy*, a responsible elder, to run the place. *Shulchan Aruch*, the code of Jewish law compiled by Rabby Joseph Caro in 1555, was known in Central Asia and was used as the main standard authority for Jewish religious practice. Jewish festivals were observed, and Passover was the most important of them. It was the custom with the Bukharian Jews to have many families gather in the house of a learned man who knew enough Hebrew to explain the Haggadah in the Judeo-Persian language. Among the other festivals, Sukkoth, Hanukkah and Purim were also observed.

Family names and nicknames of the local Jews are also helpful for us to learn about their history. Timur, as it is well known, transferred many skilled workers with their families to Central Asia, and some of the family names of Bukharian Jews indicate their place of origin:

Balkhiev – (born in Balkh city)
Gurjiev – (born in Georgia)
Hirotov – (born in Herat)

Koptiev – (born in Egypt)
Plishtiev – (born in Palestine).

Some nicknames indicate Jewish professional orientation. The examples are numerous, *burranda* – tailor, *buekchi* – dyer, *bazzoz* – manufacture merchant, *zargar* – gold jeweller, *hammomi* – public bath servant, and even *zakotchi* – tax collector (from *zyaket*, an Arabic term for the special Muslim tax collected from the rich to feed the poor).

Up until the seventeenth and the nineteenth centuries, when Central Asian Jews were forced to convert to Islam, they had preserved their national identity without any trouble. Their assimilation was generally limited to language change and garment adjustments. The time of Timur and the Timurids brought positive changes to their social life. Jewish families from numerous conquered lands were moved to Central Asia. They brought their religious and cultural knowledge with them to enrich the local communities. This was the last period of such an inflow of new Jewish blood to the region. When the Timurids were replaced by the nomadic dynasty of Sheibanids in the sixteenth century, Central Asia became a semi-isolated land. Only later, in the nineteenth century, when Russia occupied Central Asia, did Ashkenazi Jews from the Russian Empire come to Turkestan and change the face of the local Jewish community.

9

WHY TIMUR CONQUERED DAMASCUS BUT DID NOT CONQUER JERUSALEM

Tis all a Chequer-board of Nights and Days
Where Destiny with Men for Pieces plays:
Hither and thither moves, and mates, and slays,
And one by one back in the Closet lays.
(*Rubáiyát of Omar Khayyám*)

Medieval history has witnessed three different armies march from Central Asia towards Jerusalem. The Khoresmian warriors of 1244 were first, then for the next hundred years Jerusalem lived under the constant fear and dread of the Mongols, and finally, in 1401, the army of Timur approached the boarders of the Holy Land. The Khoresmians and Mongols destroyed Jerusalem. Timur did not. Why? Let us have a closer look at these three invasions.

The Khorezmians in Jerusalem

The distance between Jerusalem and Khorezm is 2,000 kilometres for Europeans, though, this distance was not considered great. Plano Carpini described Khorezm and its borders in 1247 'To the south of it lies Jerusalem'.[1]

The Khorezmian attack upon Jerusalem in 1244 was by accident, as the Khoresmians did not pre-plan the invasion. Their military presence in the Near East was due to the Mongol invasion of their own country. Chingiz Khan had defeated Khorezm completely and this huge state ceased to exist. However, Jalal ad-Din, the son of the last Khorezmshah, had managed to salvage some cavalry and moved toward the west; his small band of troopers joining the mercenaries of the Egyptian Sultan Salikh.

Meanwhile, the crusaders had gained control over Jerusalem for the second time, and Salikh, too weak to fight them, ordered Jalal ad-Din and his Khorezmian troops to counterattack. In his book *Jerusalem*, F.E. Peters wrote that the Muslims repossessed Jerusalem in 1239 and faced the Khorezmians a few years later.[2] There is, however, a great deal of evidence that Jerusalem was under Christian control in 1244.

V. Barthold credited the Khorezmians for the second expulsion of the crusaders from Jerusalem[3] and some medieval European histories and chronicles support this point of view.[4] In 1245 a Minorite, Simon de Saint-Quentin, joined the papal mission to the Mongols; fortunately his notes survived and we have a first-hand account of the event:

> And so Khwaresmians have fled persecution avoiding them [the Mongols] and have poured forth to the borders of Persia. . . .
>
> After that, indeed invited and gathered together by the Sultan of Babylon lord of Egypt, those coming into the kingdom of Jerusalem and subduing the Christians before the city of Gaza have destroyed a great multitude of Franks, who surrendered themselves unto the Lord, and have torn down the holy sepulchre of our Lord; and so, within and without the sacred city they have killed as many Christians as possible in the year of the Lord 1244 'as told later in the place itself'.[5]

There are several other medieval European chronicles with similar descriptions.[6] In general, the Khorezmian troops, defeated by the Mongols, destroyed Christian Jerusalem in 1244. The troopers of Jalal ad-Din paused only long enough to conquer and besiege the Holy City, burn down its churches, and reduce Jerusalem to a smoking ruin. The Jews, who were out of the city, were not massacred, but a short while later the Mongols appeared on the scene to conquer the Holy Land themselves.

It is well known that there were no Jews in the crusaders' Jerusalem, as the Christians did not tolerate Jews in the Holy City, unlike the Muslims, who usually allowed Jews to continue to live there. The Jews, therefore, did not suffer from siege and devastation when the Christians repossessed the city.

The Mongols in Jerusalem

The Mongol invasion of the Holy Land was not by accident, it was part of their general strategy. In the middle of the thirteenth century there was only one power in Asia able to resist the Mongol hordes, that of the Mamluk Sultanate of Egypt. It was therefore a must for the Mongols to annihilate this power.

These two powerful forces were on a war footing for a long time. In January 1260 the Mongol army conquered Aleppo in Syria. A few weeks later the invaders entered Damascus. This invasion of Syria was a direct aggression against the Mamluks and the war began. Despite all the Mongol military experience the Mamluks defeated them in the decisive battle of 'Ayn Jalut' (Fountain of Goliath) in Galilee on 3 September 1260.

The Jewish historical sources state that Jerusalem was taken by the Mongols in 1260 and that the city Jews 'had either been slain or scattered.'[7] The main evidence of this, is in the letter of Moses b. Nahman (Nahmanides, Ramban) who visited Jerusalem in 1267. In this famous and frequently-cited letter he wrote:

> Jerusalem is more desolate than the rest of the country; Judea more than Galilee. But even in this destruction it is a blessed land. It [Jerusalem] has about 2,000 inhabitants, about 300 Christians live there who escaped the sword of the sultan. There are no Jews. For since the arrival of the Tartars [Mongols], some fled, others died by the sword. There are only two brothers, dyers by trade, who have to buy their ingredients from the government. . . . we succeeded in finding a vacant house built on pillars of marble and with a beautiful arch. That we took for a synagogue. For the town is without a master and whoever will take possession of ruins can do so. . . . We have sent already to Shechem [Nablus] to fetch some scrolls of the Law from there which had been brought thither from Jerusalem at the invasion of the Tartars.[8]

Some modern historians of the Crusades period challenge the statement that the Mongols destroyed Jerusalem in 1260. According to their sources, during the campaign of 1260 the Mongols occupied Nablus and Gaza, though they did not reach Jerusalem itself.[9] It is possible, therefore, that the Jews of Jerusalem fled from the city in fear of the Mongol invasion and were therefore not killed.

How many Jews settled in Jerusalem between 1244 and 1260? Why did the Jews hide the Holy Scrolls of Jerusalem in Nablus, the city taken by the Mongols? Who told Nachmanides, who had spent all his life in Spain and only came to Palestine in 1266, about the local events of the previous years? Did 73-year-old Nachmanides understand everything correctly?

We still have no direct answers to these questions.

According to Graetz, the energetic Mongol invasion was even linked by the Jews to their hopes of the coming of the Messiah. ‘The hateful, deformed men of the East, who had subdued both the oppressors of Israel, the followers of Jesus and Mahomet, might perhaps bring near unto Israel the hour of redemption.’[10]

Defeated by Mamluks, the Mongols did not give up their struggle for Syria and Palestine. They established themselves firmly in Persia and watching the Mamluks closely tried their hand at secret activities in several Mamluk cities including Jerusalem. This war of espionage lasted for decades. In the case of Jerusalem, however, the Mongols used local Christians rather than Jews as their spies.[11]

In 1289–91 the last crusaders made a treaty with the Mongols of Persia proposing a joint campaign against the Mamluks. The Mongols agreed to cede Jerusalem to the Christians if the Mamluks were defeated, but once again the Mongols were beaten and Jerusalem remained in the hands of the Muslims.[12]

The last and the most successful Mongol penetration into Syria and Palestine occurred in 1308. This was when Jerusalem was finally taken. The Mongols did not occupy the city for a long time, but presumably looted as much as they could.[13] Unfortunately, there was no one like Nachmanides to describe the event. It was not until 1334, when Isaac ben Joseph visited the city, that the situation, events and general atmosphere were recorded in his recollections and the picture of Jewish life in Jerusalem at that time appeared to be pleasant:

> The Jewish community in Jerusalem, God be gracious to her, is quite numerous. It is composed of fathers of families from all parts of the world, principally from France. . . . They live there in happiness and tranquility, each according to his condition and fortune, for the royal authority is just and great. . . . Among the different members of the holy congregation at Jerusalem are many who are engaged in handicrafts such as dyers, tailors, shoemakers, etc. Others carry on a rich commerce in all sorts of things and have fine shops. Some are devoted to science, such as medicine, astronomy, and mathematics.[14]

In sixty-six years the heavy foot of Timur would appear in Syria. Meanwhile Jewish life in Jerusalem was still idyllic.

Timur and Mamluks

Timur was never preoccupied with the Mongol idea to conquer and occupy the Sultanate of Egypt. Being trapped between the Mamluks and Ottoman Turks, Timur tried to negotiate in order to avoid fighting.[15] The 10-year-old Sultan in Cairo and the dull-witted local authorities in Mamluk Syria spoiled the deal. The Mamluks of the fourteenth century were weak but they put up a front beyond their military capabilities. Timur, though, saw through this and his soldiers devastated Syria.

At that time Jerusalem was just a big village without a city wall.[16] It was not a capital. The local authorities of this *sanjak*, the region of the Mamluk Empire, were in Damascus. Somehow, Russian medieval chronicles included Jerusalem in a list of Timur's possessions, along with 'Great Armenia, Damascus, and Sarai'.[17] However, this was a monastic understanding of history.

It is most probable that Timur himself did not visit any places in the Holy Land. The anonymous author of the appendix to the chronicles of Bar Hebraeus wrote that campaigning 'towards the country of Palestine', the troops of Timur attacked Rish Aina and Amid.[18] These settlements are not identified. Ibn Khaldun in his autobiography wrote about his trip to Damascus in 1400:

> We reached Gaza; here we rested for several days awaiting news. Then we set out for Damascus in order to forestall the Tatars, encamped at Shaqhab, and then set out at night, arriving at Damascus in the morning. Emir Timur and his army by this time had left Baalbek, also on their way to Damascus.[19]

Shaqhab was a Syrian town south of Damascus close to the Golan Heights. Timur himself had an observation post above Qubbat Yalbugha with a view to Mount Hermon.[20] However, one portion of Timur's army ravaged the Syrian coast as far south as Acre (Akko), which is not far from today's modern Israeli Haifa. Why did he not penetrate farther south into Palestine? Why did he not capture Jerusalem? There is another legend on this subject that a Russian chronicler wrote about in the fourteenth century:

> Temir was moving south towards Egypt passing aside the whole Greece. When he had captured the walls of Damascus, he wanted to move towards Jerusalem. He however realized that each person who dared to trouble Jerusalem was punished by God. That is why he did not move towards Jerusalem and turned east.[21]

The real reasons were political and not religious. After the heavy defeat in Syria the Mamluks decided to negotiate peace with the victorious *kurakan*. The special ambassador, Baisaq ash-Shaikhi by name, was sent to Timur. Timur managed to achieve his goal, and the Mamluks declared him their sovereign and promised to pay yearly tribute. After that Timur turned his armies sharply north and went to fight Bajazid.

Timur did not conquer Jerusalem!

Sharaf ad-Din, the court historian of Timur, mentioned that his patron seized the granary in Damascus, and the corn inside, collected as a tribute for Mecca and Medina, was sold by Timur and the sum dispatched via Jerusalem to the holy cities. Sharaf ad-Din indicates clearly that Timur did invade Palestine, which he called *Kan'an* (i.e. Canaan) in his *Zafar-nama*,[22] but did not take Jerusalem, although expensive gifts were sent to 'the holy town of al-Kuds' (Jerusalem) itself.[23] That seems to be the only connection between Timur and Jerusalem. Hojja Muhammad Parsa from Bukhara [d.1420] compiled a historical and topographical description of Jerusalem in Timur's time in a manuscript called 'The History of Mecca'. There, he describes the mosques and tombs of Jerusalem calling the town *Bait al-Mukaddas*.[24] Two copies of this manuscript have survived in Tashkent until today.

The reaction of the Jews of Jerusalem, Mamluk citizens, to the approach of Tamerlane's army, is not known. It is not hard, however, to imagine how the Jews of Palestine would have interpreted the events of the war between Timur and the Mamluks. For the Palestinian Jews, Timur's campaign was just another 'Persian' invasion. The Jews, in their sacred writings, kept the saying of Rabbi Shimon b. Yohai, the notable second-century Palestinian wise man, who said, 'If you see a Persian horse tied to graves in Eretz Israel, wait for the feet of the King, the Messiah'.[25] At that time, however, the 'Persian' king was a Muslim, and in reality this was just another war between two Muslim powers.

The Palestine episode shows that Timur, as a warrior, was very practical. Jerusalem was of no military and strategic interest to the Timur–Mamluk war and that is why the city was not taken. We may only assume that in the case of continued Mamluk resistance, Timur might have marched farther south towards Egypt[26] and possibly would have taken small, defenceless Jerusalem on his way to Gaza, the main Palestinian city of that time. But Timur decided otherwise; he did not destroy the Mamluk state, and after the Mongol invasion, Jerusalem enjoyed several centuries of peace and quiet.

10

THE ATTITUDE OF TIMUR AND THE TIMURIDS TO THE JEWS

> *Tam[erlane]:*
> In vaine I see men worship *Mahomet.*
> My sword hath sent millions of Turks to hell,
> Slew all his Priests, his kinsmen, and his friends,
> And yet I liue untoucht by *Mahomet.*
> (Christopher Marlowe, *Tamburlaine the Great*,
> the second part, 1606)[1]

As a ruler, Timur had two examples of statesmanship he could use as a model, the Mongol and the Muslim. Timur was a Muslim, but he also was an admirer of Chingiz Khan. He had a charismatic personality and independent viewpoints on the craft of governing. His attitude to the Jews was made up of these three components, the Mongol, the Muslim, and his personal beliefs.

The Muslim attitude

The empire of Timur was a Muslim empire, the court historians were Muslims, the sons and grandsons of Timur were Muslims and their court historians were Muslims too. Ibn Arabshah, also a Muslim, hated Timur and when he wrote Timur's biography he conveyed these feelings accordingly. All these historians, however, said nothing definite about Timur's attitude to the Jews. No one had written that Timur behaved toward the Jews as a true Muslim or that there were any unusual deviations in this behaviour.

Two hundred years ago Edward Gibbon wrote of Timur:

> In his religion, he was a zealous, though not perhaps an orthodox, Musulman; but his sound understanding may tempt us

> to believe that a superstitious reverence for omens and prophecies, for saints and astrologers, was only affected as an instrument of policy.[2]

Gibbon had cause to write this as he used Ibn Arabshah's writings as his main primary source. Arabshah reproved the impiety of Timur and 'the Moguls', who mostly preferred the *Yasa* (Law of Chingiz Khan) to the Koran. Describing Central Asian states at the time of Timur's rise to power, Arabshah wrote that 'religion, which is called the law of Jenghis Khan, was spread through the whole of both states'.[3] Writing about Timur's occupation of Iraq, Arabshah mentioned that Timur's purpose 'was to let its buildings remain and to extend his authority there, in the manner that the religion of Jenghiskhan required'.[4]

This viewpoint was completely opposed by the Timurid court historians who praised Timur's Muslim piety. Unfortunately, except for Giyyas ad-Din Ali's *Diary of the Indian Campaign* and Shami's *Zafar-nama*, all the historical works allegedly produced in Timur's lifetime have vanished. Recent research on the Timurid historiography shows that we cannot rely entirely on the works of the Timurid court historians.[5]

In trying to understand Islam at the end of the fourteenth century we need to remember that Islam was not conceived as a political and religious unity as it had been four or five centuries earlier. This unity had already been shattered prior to the Crusades. Even more harmful was the effect of the Crusades on the spirit of Islam. Being intolerant of idolaters, the Muslims were, in general, tolerant towards the 'People of the Book', the Jews and the Christians. Mohammed himself considered that Jews and Christians had received a partial revelation and were therefore not to be persecuted. The savage intolerance shown by the crusaders was reciprocated by the growing intolerance among the Muslims, and by the time of the Mamluks, the Muslims had become as narrow-minded as the Christians.

Ibn al-Fuwati (d. 1323), a historian, cited Ibn Fadlan (d. 1233), an inspector of the finances of the *dhimmis*, who wrote in the thirteenth century:

> Their homes were not to be of the same height as those of Muslims. . . . They were not allowed to have a horse as a mount, but only a mule, or an ass without a pack or a saddle, which they were not allowed to ride astride, but on one side only. Although all this has been abandoned, no increase of tax has been enacted, whereas in most [Muslim] countries they are still forced to wear [distinctive] badges and are admitted to none but the most

> humiliating employment. Thus, for example, in Bukhara and Samarkand [!] the *dhimmis* clean out the lavatories and sewers and carry away the rubbish and refuse.[6]

Except in Persia, with its own disquieting Shia heretical traditions, the Muslims enclosed themselves behind the curtain of their faith and developed an intolerant attitude towards all peoples of different faiths.

This intolerance was not, however, nation-wide. Even the Mamluks employed Jews as soldiers or government officials during some periods. The Ottoman Turks at the time of Bayazet (Bayazid) and his father Murad were also religiously tolerant, even though this was in sharp contrast to the intolerant Byzantine Empire with whom they were at war.[7]

Timur, being a Muslim, was fighting other Muslims in most of his campaigns, even destroying mosques occasionally.[8] At the same time, as shown in previous chapters, he respected Muslim theologians and religious leaders. The Persian historian Khwandamir wrote about the destruction of Baghdad by Timur:

> although the sayyids, ulema, and learned persons who could took refuge in Temur's camp and were saved. When the massacre was over, the buildings and houses of the city were razed to the ground – except for mosques, madrasas, and khanaqahs, which were excepted.[9]

Let us now take a closer look at Mignanelli's story mentioned in the prologue about Timur's cruelty towards the Jews of Aleppo. Walter Fischel, of the University of California, tried to prove that this story, which had appeared in a Christian source, was pure legend.[10]

First, he paid attention to the fact that a story with a similar plot was told by the Dominican monk Jean of Sultaniya in 1403, not about Aleppo but about Brusa in Turkey. This story then migrated to the *Chronographia Regum Francorum*. Second, Fischel noted that J. Schiltberger told the same story not about the Jews of Aleppo but about the Christians of Damascus. According to Schiltberger, Timur ordered the priests in Damascus, together with their wives and children, to gather in the temple for protection. Schiltberger wrote about the fantastic figure of 30,000 people in that one building. Timur then gave orders that when the temple was full they should be shut up in the building. This was done and 'wood was placed around the temple and he ordered it to be ignited and they all perished in the temple'.[11]

Another anonymous medieval German chronicle contains the story with similar motifs pertaining, however, not to Aleppo but to Damascus and not to the Jews but to the Yezidis.[12]

All those facts persuaded Fischel to consider this story to be a legend and not historical evidence. I would also like to add that no Muslim historical work, whether Arabian, Persian or Turkish, contains a similar story. On the contrary, the Arab historian, Abou'l Feda, wrote that when the Mongols entered Aleppo the Jews collaborated with them against the Muslims (which is very doubtful), destroying and pillaging mosques. According to Feda, 'the Jewish temple in Aleppo was one of the few secure places where people sought shelter from massacres'.[13] This brings us to consider this legend as having Christian roots and showing a Christian attitude toward the Jews.

Timur never persecuted the Jews because they were *dhimmis*. His mentally unstable son Miranshah, however, ordered the tomb of the great historian Rashid ad-Din in Tabriz to be destroyed and his bones buried in the Jewish cemetery.[14] When Timur learned about Miranshah's deed he was displeased; the prince was punished by being deposed, and the counsellors and companions of his dissolute life were executed. The authority Miranshah had misused was transferred to his son Abu Bakr.

In general, the Muslim component of Timur's attitude to the Jews was not dangerous to them, as Timur was not a Muslim fanatic who was intolerant of the *dhimmis*. The Timurids did not persecute Jews in Persia or in Central Asia, but in the seventeenth century, when the new Safavid dynasty of Persian rulers replaced the already weak Timurids, they designed a religious policy to impose Shi'a Islam as the sole denomination in Persia. Naturally this situation created a good deal of bad blood because of the forcible conversion of Zoroastrians, Jews and Christians and all kinds of coercive measures and underhand practices were then employed to convert the Jews to Islam.[15]

The Mongol attitude

Many historians count Timur's wars as the last strike of the Mongol fist. They argue that Timur tried to repeat the great achievements of Chingiz Khan, making the life of Chingiz a glorious example for himself.

Ibn Arabshah was very straight about Timur's preference, 'He clung to the laws of Jenghizkhan, which are like branches of law from the faith of Islam, and he observed them in preference to the law of Islam'.[16] As far as his religious attitudes were concerned, Timur perhaps remained strongly attached to the Mongol traditions. After his death his followers felt constrained to design his burial-place according to Mongol custom and in defiance of Muslim beliefs.[17] Later, during the rule of Timur's children and grandchildren, some Muslim decorations were added to the tomb.

The rules laid down by Chingiz Khan are known as the *Yasa*. Timur was a Muslim, but as far as politics and administration were concerned he mostly followed in the footsteps of his hero, Chingiz Khan, and adhered to the *Yasa* Code. This is true to some extent for the whole period of the Timurids. In the sixteenth century, Babur Mirza, a distant descendant of Timur and the founder of the Empire of Great Moguls in India, wrote in his memoirs:

> In former times our fathers and forefathers meticulously observed the Chenghisid Code. In assemblies and court, at banquets and dinners, in sitting and serving, nothing was allowed to go counter to the code.[18]

Babur was very sincere in what he said in his memoirs. If he wrote this in the sixteenth century, it meant that Timur assuredly followed the 'Chenghisid Code', the *Yasa*. This Code has several laws, which are important for our study. The first law states, 'It is laid down that people should believe in only one Lord of the Heaven and the Earth. It is He who gives life and death, poverty and riches.'[19] This sounds as if it were received on Mount Sinai. The second law states, 'Religious leaders, advisers, priests, keepers of mosques, doctors, and those who bathe corpses, should be given free food by the state.'[20] This is a clear indication of religious tolerance.

Some of the laws of *Yasa* contradict the laws of the Torah. For example, 'It is permitted to eat the entrails of the animal and drink its blood.' Some other laws are in concord with it, 'It is forbidden to marry within the family, or those in the first or second degree of consanguinity.'[21]

This religious tolerance of the Mongols permitted the Franciscans to send their missions to the Mongol courts and permitted the Nestorian Christians of the thirteenth century to maintain their communities throughout the whole Asian continent from China to Jerusalem. In 1281, for example, there was a Nestorian metropolitan of Samarkand, Mar James.[22]

The Mongols did not affect Jewish life. The new rulers of Asia even ordered *djiziya* to be paid by all the settled people, Muslims and non-Muslims alike.[23] This regulation did not make Jewish life easy but at least it made the Jews equal to their fellow Muslims in taxation.

Edward Gibbon described an idyllic religious situation in the Mongol empire:

> The Tartars and Moguls were addicted to the idols of their peculiar tribes; and many of them had been converted by the

> foreign missionaries to the religion of Moses [!], of Mahomet, and of Christ. These various systems in freedom and concord were taught and practised within the precincts of the same camp; and the Bonze, the Imam, the Rabbi [!], the Nestorian, and the Latin priest enjoyed the same honourable exemption from service and tribute.[24]

It would be difficult for us to imagine a soldier in the Mongl army reciting the prayer *Shema Israel*, but in fact Jewish soldiers did serve in the army of Chingiz Khan.[25] We need to remember that the Mongols repeatedly attacked the Mamluks in Syria and Palestine during the second half of the thirteenth century and at the beginning of the fourteenth century. For these Mongol soldiers who prayed, the phrase 'next year in Jerusalem' was very topical.

Gibbon bases his words about the Mongols being followers of 'the religion of Moses', on archaeological evidence discovered in Iran. There is a small town, Touisserkan, in modern Iran, where a pleasant Mongol tomb–tower with a typical fluted conical roof, stands in a field on the western side of the town. This mausoleum contains a tombstone with an inscription in Hebrew.[26]

There was, however, one incident in 1251, described by Bar Hebraeus and Mirkhwand, that concerned the above-mentioned tax exemption, *djiziya*, for religious leaders. In occupied Persia, Mungka Khan commanded that the Christian priests and monks and the learned men and scribes of the Muslims should be free from taxation. Only the Jewish rabbis were deprived of this benefit.[27] There is a simple explanation for this fact: the Jews had no mediators and protectors in the Horde of the Khan.[28] Meanwhile, the Christians, Muslims and Buddhists were properly introduced by Mungka court officials.

As previously mentioned, Jewish prosperity in Mongol Persia reached its acme in the 1280s when Arghun became Khan. Like many other Mongols, Arghun was religiously eclectic. His own sympathies were for Buddhism, but his vizier, Sa'd ad-Daula, was a Jew, and his best friend was the Nestorian Christian, Mar Yahbhallaha. This Jewish doctor took a first step in building his brilliant future career whilst living in Persia, where he learned both Turkish and the Mongol languages.

Sa'd ad-Daula had first won the Khan's confidence as a financial administrator when he was sent to Baghdad to restore the economy after the large-scale speculations of the previous vizier. He performed the job brilliantly and soon became vizier himself. The rule of a Jew over a predominantly Muslim country must of itself have caused widespread resentment. Such resentment was naturally aggravated by his practising the usual nepotism of his age and time and distributing the key posts in the administration amongst his relatives and other Jews.[29]

The situation, indeed, was unusual. 'Well might the Jews fancy that their Messiah had arrived, when they saw one of their long-despised race treated as an equal by the princes and noyans [Mongol noblemen], and even by the Ilkhan himself', Henry Howorth, the author of the *History of Mongols*, wrote this in the nineteenth century.[30] In 1291 Arghun died, Sa'd ad-Daula was killed in the court plot and the period of Jewish prosperity was cut short.

Rashid ad-Din, another Persian Jew who converted to Islam, had an almost parallel career. He was also a physician, also became a prominent administrator, was also in favour at the Mongol court, and was also killed afterwards by his Muslim enemies.[31]

These two examples, no matter how vivid they are, do not illustrate the whole picture of Jewish life within the Mongol domains. In general, we can divide the Mongol period into two sub-periods – pre-Islamic and post-Islamic. The Mongols of the first sub-period were religiously tolerant. The Mongols of the second sub-period were less tolerant but, however, more tolerant than nations that had accepted Islam earlier. This difference in tolerance appeared because of the simultaneous use of the laws of the *Yasa* and the Koran by the newly converted Mongols.

The Mongols in China, who were not under direct Islamic influence, remained religiously tolerant without any fluctuations. At the same time, with Arghun Khan in Persia, the Chinese Jews enjoyed complete freedom of faith under the Mongol Khan of China, Kublai.[32]

The personal attitude

It is not my intention to psychoanalyse Timur. Different life models, however, influenced his early social education. He accepted the laws and ethics of the Koran, he accepted the rules and spirit of the *Yasa*, and he also accepted the natural way of life of his family. Timur was born into a semi-nomadic family and nearly all his life was spent as a nomad. It is true that Samarkand was the capital of his empire. But how much time did he spend within its walls? Being forever involved in three-year, five-year and seven-year campaigns, he never remained in Samarkand for longer than several months at a time. His court and wives travelled with him. Campaigning in Asia Minor, he preferred to spend the winters in Karabakh because of its good pastures for horses and cattle. Even after having occupied a big city he usually kept his headquarters in the open countryside.

This nomadic way of life, so similar to the way of life of Chingiz Khan, was pleasing for Timur. But was he a true nomad?

The real nomads had their own institutions, their own structure of everyday life. These obligatory institutions are *the tribe*, *blood-vengeance*, *hospitality* and *asylum*.

Timur belonged to the Barlas tribe. Rashid ad-Din briefly mentioned this tribe in his history and there is no doubt that the tribe was of Mongol and not of Turkish origin.[33] The Barlas controlled the region of Kesh, which apparently constituted a *tumen*. The organisation of the tribe was by families and clans. The basic unit of social organisation was the family. Timur's father, Amir Taragay, was obviously the head of a family that included plural wives, sons and their wives and children, unmarried daughters, and slaves of both sexes. The father as undisputed head of this extended family possessed the power of life and death over the children.

Families related by blood ties comprise a *clan*, which is nothing more than a collection of families. Sustaining this unity was the strong tie of blood kinship characteristic of both the Mongols and the Turks.

When Timur distributed land and power among the Barlas after his acquisition of power, he bestowed the top administrative positions upon his immediate family and also favoured Cheku, his closest military assistant, although Cheku descended from another clan of the Barlas.[34]

Heads of families, all related to one another by blood, formed a kind of council at the clan level. The council at the level of tribes was called *kurultai*. It was at such a meeting of that *kurultai* that Timur was officially proclaimed the sole ruler of Transoxania.

Blood-vengeance was an institution which represented personal security for a Mongol. It stemmed directly from the nomadic way of life where the tribe was the permanent element, while the individual was incidental. Given this situation, an aggressive act by an outsider to one member of a family or clan was an affront to the tribe itself. Murder, of course, was the worst affront.

We see numerous acts of blood-vengeance during Timur's wars. The most vivid examples took place in some of Timur's occupied cities, such as Isphahan or Baghdad, where the citizens tried to revolt against Timur's garrisons and killed small detachments of his troops while Timur himself was somewhere else. Timur treated these citizens as traitors and murderers and acted against them according to the code of blood-vengeance. His cruel methods of warfare were not unique to him, but corresponded to the almost inconceivably harsh practices of the period, as we have seen from those symbols of terror, the pyramids of skulls, invented by Chingiz Khan. When citizens of a city did not engage in hostilities against Timur or fought only to protect themselves, Timur did not usually retaliate by killing them. What happened in Damascus is a good example: the citizens surrendered, paid heavy military contributions, but were not hurt.[35]

Hospitality came out of nomadic necessity too. Each nomad might during his journey become sick or suffer an adversity of some sort. Since the host himself might be in need of hospitality one day, he gave it to the stranger automatically. History has many examples of Timur's hospitality. As stated previously, Khwandamir wrote very clearly about 'the sayyids, ulema "Muslim religious leaders" and learned persons who took refuge in Temur's camp'. Timur saved their lives during the massacre of Baghdad.[36] In Damascus Timur gave hospitality to the famous historian Ibn Khaldun, even though he was a Mamluk protege. Timur also hosted the Mongol prince Tokhtamish who was driven from the Golden Horde. Tokhtamish then betrayed Timur and *sahibkiran* fought against him bitterly.

Ibn Khaldun, in his writings, addressed Timur's army as the nomadic army with the soldiers who 'follow the custom of the Bedouin Arabs'.[37]

Despite the often-discussed antagonism between nomads and settled people, Timur, who had deep nomadic roots, was tolerant of the Jews. First of all, he was free of the settled peoples' stereotypical views of the Jews. Secondly, as a rule, nomads are much more religiously tolerant compared to settled nations.

Comparing Timur with Chingiz Khan, Edward Browne wrote in his famous *Literary History of Persia*:

> The invasion of Timur the Tartar, horrible as it was, was not so terrible in its effects as this [the Mongol invasion], for Timur was professedly a Muslim, and had some considerations for mosques, libraries, and men of learning; but Chingiz and Hulagu were blood-thirsty heathens.[38]

As I have tried to show, the Muslim versus non-Muslim approach to Timur appears narrow. In general, Timur's empire was a society of law and order, a centralised state where decisions were likely to be carried out by a loyal cadre of local administrators. In such a society, legislative action was more likely to give results than the decrees of contemporary European Christian rulers, which often remained mere expressions of personal intention. Timurid legislation was closer to modern institutions, a reflection of commonly held attitudes and an application, usually effective, of commands or prohibitions inspired by Islamic religious and Mongol moral axioms.

The body of legislation completed by the Timurids,[39] which assigned the Jews a place in society, was Muslim (Jews are *dhimmi*) as well as Mongol (religious tolerance). According to this legislation, the civil status of the Jews, their right to the protection of the law, became identical with that of every other race and nation ruled by Timur. They did not lose this right after the death of Timur nor during the whole period of the Timurid dynasty. This legislation did not contrast Jews to the other nations, and did not single out their religion. Indeed, Christians and Zoroastrians can also be *dhimmis*. The Code did not disable Jews from performing public functions. We do not know, however, any Jews who held administrative position in the empire of Timur. We do know that the Jews had to seek the protection of the holders of political power. No primary sources, however, indicate that Central Asian Jews were the 'king's serfs' of the Timurids, as with the kings in medieval Europe. Timur was the protector of the Jews, but he was not the 'owner' of this community.

We see therefore that Timur, who grew up with this mixture of Islamic, Mongol and nomadic values of life and behaviour, and also because of his personality, was very remote from any religious fanaticism and intolerance. He probably could not, for example, understand the concept behind the Spanish Inquisition. This attitude undoubtedly benefited the Jews in Persia, Central Asia, and other domains of this World conqueror. Jews were assigned to a position of mild inferiority, but were protected in daily life. In contrast with the Persian rulers of the seventeenth century and with the Uzbek *khans* of the eighteenth century, the Jews, during the time of the Timurids, were not forced to desecrate their Sabbath or their festivals. Judaism remained an explicitly permitted religion.

11

TIMUR AND THE JEWS IN THE TWENTIETH CENTURY

> The Ball no Question makes of Ayes and Noes,
> But Right or Left as strikes the Player goes,
> And He that tossed thee down into the Field,
> *He* knows about it all – HE knows – HE knows!
>
> (*Rubáiyát of Omar Khayyám*)

The long coexistence of the Jews and the nations of Central and Inner Asia produced an anthropological 'Mongoloid type of Jew'. In 1911, when anthropological studies were in fashion, Maurice Fishberg published his book *The Jews: A Study of Race and Environment*. He wrote the following about the Mongoloid Jews:

> The most curious is the *Mongoloid type* of Jews, often seen in Russia, Poland, and Germany, especially among women and children. Their chief characteristics are long, smooth, black hair, which is very thick. It grows very long on the head, but only sparingly on the body and face. In fact the Mongolian beard is often seen among Jews. The most distinguished trait, however, is the Mongolian eye . . . In general the face of these people is square or lozenge-shaped, and the nose small, short, slightly depressed at its upper half, while broad at its lower half. Many Jewesses of this type are easily taken for Japanese, and in Russia for Tartars.[1]

Fishberg placed several convincing photographic pictures to illustrate the subject. Indeed, in Poland and Lithuania the Jews, mainly the *Karaimi* (Karaites), were called 'Tatars' from the fourteenth century onward.[2]

Central Asian Jews have maintained a close connection with Persian Jews throughout their history. Despite frequent political upheavals, during the next few centuries after Timur's death, Jewish life continued fairly smoothly in Persia. A definite change for the worse occurred in the seventeenth century, when the Muslim clergy of the sect of Shiites gained the upper hand. The Shiite clergy forced the Persian government to adopt a law whereby a convert to Islam became the sole heir to the property of all his Jewish relatives. Physical attacks also became more frequent. At the same time, though, the Uzbek khanates of Central Asia remained tolerant of the Jews. That is why a significant number of Jewish families moved from Persia to Central Asia to enlarge the existing community.

The Jewish communities have survived in Central Asia until the present day. They were in a miserable semi-isolated state in the eighteenth and nineteenth centuries until the Russians occupied the whole area in the 1860s and 1870s. But already, during the time of Peter the Great, at the beginning of the eighteenth century, the first Russian envoys to the Central Asian states made reports about the Jews. Florio Beneveni, the Russian ambassador to the Emirate of Bukhara in 1718–25, reported to the Ministry of Foreign Affairs in 1724:

> In this Bukhara land, there is a special type of tree with worms located in a steppe. An expensive dye of kermez, called *coush-enina* [cochineal] in German, can be derived from this tree. This dye costs eight roubles a pound in Russia. There is plenty of this dye in Bukhara. The Bukharians, however, do not know the secret of manufacturing this dye. They only collect worms and sell a lot of them to the Jews. And the Jews [*zhidy*] use those worms to produce the dye, which they mix with the German dye afterwards.[3]

It seems that the Jews specialised in being professional dyers for centuries.

Under Russian rule, these 'Bukharian Jews', so-called because they were citizens of the Bukhara Emirate, proved their abilities as traders. They monopolised the cotton trade with Russia. Once again, as was the case five centuries earlier, they were able to travel abroad through Russia. Even the famous French neurologist Jean Martin Charcot was curious to meet a patient who was a Bukharian Jew.

The Jews from Russia moved in the opposite direction. They settled in Russian Turkestan, met the local Jews, and formed a uniquely mixed European–Oriental community, which would also exist in Israel fifty years later, on a much broader scale. At the same time, the Bukharian Jews were able to move out from Uzbekistan and some of them immigrated to Turkish Palestine. They formed the Bukharian quarter in Jerusalem.

The Jews from Europe were able to visit Central Asia for scientific purposes. The most famous of them was Aurel Stein from Budapest, the 'pioneer of the Silk Road'.[4] The West hailed Stein as the first and greatest of Silk Road archaeologists.

The last major wave of Jews into Uzbekistan came at the beginning of the Second World War, when the country absorbed more than 180,000 Jewish refugees from Russia, the Ukraine, Byelorussia, Moldavia and even Poland. This fact was realised only in the 1990s, and the Jewish Bnai Brith world organisation honoured the Uzbek ambassador to Israel with a special award on behalf of the Uzbek nation in 1999.

History once again became interesting and a new period of scientific research on the subject of Timur began. In the twentieth century, Soviet Russian scientists, including Jews, contributed significantly to the study of history during the time of Timur. They used Marxism in their methodology, and their attitude to the great Oriental ruler was negative. The personality of Timur was described as a vivid specimen of cruel feudalism, absolutism and militarism. There was, however, another reason why Moscow painted Timur in such a negative light. Timur was an Oriental hero. He was the national pride of the Uzbeks. The Soviet goal was to erode the national self-consciousness out of the Uzbek soul in order to make the people lose their feeling of national pride and to become reconciled with their dependence and subjugation.

In 1941 the tomb of Timur in Samarkand was opened and the body investigated. Unfortunately the tomb was opened not by an archaeologist but by a sculptor. The Soviet sculptor M. Gerasimov had become famous by reconstructing images of dead persons by using their actual skulls for the measurements and proportions. He reconstructed images of medieval Russian princes and then turned to Timur and the Timurids.

The skulls of Timur, his son Shah Rukh and his grandson Ulugh Bek were taken out, measured, and the sculptural portraits were made.[5] Malik Kaumov, who was the first Uzbek documentary film-maker, was a cameraman during these tomb excavations. I met and interviewed him in Tashkent in 1997 when he already was in his eighties.[6] He had constantly filmed the process and 5,000 metres of film were used. Gerasimov, having no special skills in archaeology, was interested primarily in the skulls, Kaumov said. He was not careful in his movements and disconnected the skulls from the bodies in an unprofessional manner.

Malik Kaumov's recollections about this event are indeed unique. 'We worked at Gur Emir (the mausoleum of Timur and Timurids) from 1 June to 22 June 1941,' he told me. 'Three old men approached the mausoleum on 17 June. I went out into the open to drink some tea and they asked me if we had opened the tomb of Timur himself. We opened the tomb of Shah

Plate 4 General view of the Medrese of Ulugh Bek, built 1417–20, Registan Square, Samarkand

Rukh, the father of Ulugh Bek, first. Then we opened the tomb of Ulugh Bek. Only after that did we start to work with the tomb of Timur. We had no suitable devices for that and the tombstone was very heavy, up to twenty tons. I told the old men that we had not yet touched it. They asked me not to open the tomb because it could start another war. I went downstairs and reported these words to Kary-Niyazov (a member of the Uzbek Academy of Sciences), to Academic Semenov, and to Sadriddin Ainy, a Samarkand writer. All three of them went out. Ainy began to speak with the elders in the Tajik language, grabbed a stick and ordered them to leave. These old men showed me a book saying that the tomb of Timur should not be opened, otherwise a war could be provoked. I was young at that time and not too wise. I did not pay too much attention to this event. On 21 June we removed the skull of Timur and Gerasimov was there. He remained in Tashkent then and worked with the skulls of Timur, Shah Rukh, and Ulugh Bek. Then, on the 22 June the war with the Germans began.'

The order was given to send all the material filmed directly to Moscow and Uzbekistan lost the negative of this unique film. The excavations were aborted in June 1941 when the German troops attacked the USSR. Timur's skull and body were re-buried only in 1942.

> After five centuries it is clear to us that he [Timur] was the last of the great conquerors. Napoleon and Bismarck are secure in their niches; we know the details of their lives. But the one died a failure, and the other triumphed in the political leadership of a single empire. Tamerlane created an empire, and was successful in every campaign he undertook; he died on the march toward the last power strong enough to oppose him.[7]

In these words Harold Lamb expressed his respect for Timur. Ibn Khaldun, who met Timur personally, kept his opinion short, 'This king Timur is one of the greatest and mightiest of kings'.[8] During the Soviet period of the history of Central Asia, however, Timur became an anti-hero. He was considered a tyrant, a ruthless warrior, and not at all a humanitarian. The history of his rule was studied and several works were published, but negative appraisals appeared even in high-school history textbooks.

Gustav Krist, an Austrian prisoner of war in the Second World War, spent some time in a camp in Central Asia. When he was released after the war, he returned to Austria. However, he soon became 'homesick' for his prisoners' camp and visited Central Asia as a tourist in the 1930s. He wrote in his travel diary:

> Not far from the prison I saw a Turkoman woman who was wearing an exceptionally valuable breast ornament, while at work in a field of cotton. I was told that she was Niya Qurban Neppez, and was said to be the veritable last descendant of Timur.[9]

This was the reality of the 1930s in the Soviet Union. For Uzbekistan the Soviet domination revealed itself in three 'anti's': anti-Islamism– mosques were closed and women's veils removed; anti-Semitism – the cultural life and national education of the Bukharian Jews was suppressed; and anti-Timurism. The great film director Sergey Eisenstein, world-famous for his *Battleship Potemkin*, planned to start his picture *The Fergana Canal* with the scene of a tower built by Timur, who used living bodies instead of bricks. The pencil sketches of this scene were displayed at the exhibition of Eisenstein's drawings in the Pushkin Art Museum in Moscow in March 1998. The film was never made.

'But to the men of Asia he is still *The* Lord', Harold Lamb wrote in 1928.[10] In 1991 things changed dramatically. In that year Gorbachev resigned, the Soviet Union broke up, and Uzbekistan became an independent state. Almost immediately anti-Islamism, anti-Semitism and anti-Timurism disappeared. Mosques and Koranic schools, *medrese*, were reopened, Jewish cemeteries were reconstructed and Jewish centres and schools established, and Timur was proclaimed Father of the Nation. The Order of Amir Timur was established, Monuments to Timur were erected, historical textbooks were rewritten, the magnificent Memorial Museum of Timur was built in the centre of Tashkent, and even the Amir Temur Charity Foundation was organised. Numerous new books, though not scientific ones, were written about Timur both in Uzbek and in Russian.[11] These books tried to describe Amir Timur as a wise ruler, clever statesman, brave warrior full of chivalry, and a patron of the sciences. In this way the authors tried to overcome the negative Soviet approach to Timur's character. They tried to explain that Timur was not at all a ruthless bloody and narrow-minded vandal as he was sometimes described in the past. In fact, this modern Uzbek attitude to Tamerlane is more balanced and more correct. The only problem with the modern Uzbek historiography on Timur is an almost complete lack of academic works on the subject with proper notes, a scientific usage of primary sources, a proper bibliography, and an index.

In Samarkand a monument to Timur was erected and the tomb of Daniel was restored at the same time. Freedom of religion, any religion, was proclaimed. It was pointed out that Timur was a great statesman and a religiously tolerant person. Freedom of faith, of course, had been declared in the Soviet Union too, but in reality there was freedom for only one religion – atheism. Sentiments for 'the good old days' have a special meaning for modern Uzbeks. For them, it amounts to maintaining their own pre-Soviet traditions. For example, there are numerous folklore stories of the national character Nasreddin in which Timur appears.

With independence some Uzbeks turned to wearing Muslim clothes, including white shawls for girls, but without the old-fashioned veils. Architects began using vivid national motifs in new buildings, borrowing heavily from the Timurid style. Some earlier holidays like Navruz and Ramadan are celebrated anew. Biruni, Ibn Sina, Navoi and Ulugh Bek were glorified. Uzbeks are largely Sunni Muslims and as a group have no use for Muslim fundamentalism, which is prevalent mainly among Shiites. Religion is welcome in Uzbekistan, nonetheless. It is not an exaggeration to say that thousands of mosques and schools, as well as some new synagogues and churches, have been erected based on Koranic principle. President Karimov was even awarded the St Vladimir Order of the Russian Orthodox Church. At the government level, however, politicians don't allow religious considerations to interfere with policy.

Jews, both Bukharian and European, were free to emigrate and many of them moved to the USA or to Israel. Those who remained realised to their surprise that they had the opportunity to learn Hebrew in Tashkent and Samarkand as well as in Tel-Aviv.

Despite its geographical remoteness, Israel has established extensive relations with Uzbekistan, offering technical assistance in agriculture and aviation, as well as political assistance in Uzbek to resist Islamic fundamentalism. In 1992, Israel was the third country to recognise the new state of Uzbekistan, following the United States and Turkey. Uzbek leaders have realised that Israel is valuable as a conduit to the West. They view good relations with Israel as important as their ability to develop ties with the Western world, especially with the United States. In addition, the Uzbekistan president, Islam Karimov, shares Israel's concerns about Islamic radicalism. During a visit to Tashkent in 1994, Israel's foreign minister in the Rabin government, Shimon Peres, warned him about Iran and its regional intentions.[12] Meanwhile, beginning in 1988, more than 200,000 Central Asian Jews, from both Ashkenazi and Bukharian backgrounds, arrived in Israel. The newly erected Tashkent monument of Timur waved them good-bye with its extended arm.

This continuous flow of Uzbek Jews to Israel made the Israeli Embassy in Tashkent and the Uzbekistan consulate in Tel-Aviv quite busy. Israelis from all walks of life, journalists, specialists in Islamic art, photographers and tourists visited the new country. Slowly but steadily, business relationships between the two countries grew. The then Israeli Prime Minister, Benjamin Netanyahu, returning from a visit to China, made a short visit to Tashkent in early 1998. The trade minister of Netanyahu's government, Natan Sharansky, a native Russian speaker, visited Tashkent in June 1998, further securing ties between the countries.

'Let the spirit of creation and co-operation, which was inherited so brightly from the Amir Temur's times, serve us the good example today,' Karimov said and went himself to Israel in September 1998.[13] Before becoming president, Islam Karimov, who holds a PhD in economics, held the posts of finance minister and deputy prime minister in Soviet Uzbekistan. Analysts consider him both wise and tough, and he has foresight – all-important qualities for a statesman – yet the task that lies before him is formidable, and he will need to rely on his aids to achieve his goals.[14] Karimov was born and grew up in Samarkand. Seeing Timur's prominent buildings every day, he had, perhaps, some personal feelings for his great predecessor.

Karimov's visit to Israel was heavily packed with meetings and negotiations. Dripping irrigation, new sorts of cotton, usage of an aviation plant in Tashkent, and a dozen other questions were on the list. He found time to visit the Jerusalem Al-Aksa mosque to pray, to get information about the Wailing Wall, to turn the local Uzbek consulate into an embassy, and to meet the community of Bukharian Jews. At his meeting with Israeli businessmen in the King David Hotel, Karimov spoke not only about 'trade turnover' and 'mutually beneficial co-operation' but also about 28,000 Jewish citizens of Uzbekistan, sixteen synagogues, the Chief Rabbinate in Tashkent and the Central Asian Theological Seminary, Ahei Tmimim.[15]

When Karimov returned to Tashkent an interesting official document appeared. It was entitled 'The Measures for Further Development of Co-operation with the State of Israel'. It would have been absolutely impossible for such a document to appear in Uzbekistan ten years earlier. It was indeed a very brave document for a Muslim country. The Cabinet of Ministers of Uzbekistan decided to try dairy mini-factories packed with Israeli technologies and new Israeli types of cotton and methods of turkey breeding, and also 'to investigate the historical aspects of relationships between the Uzbek and the Jewish people and their states, and to consider the pilgrimage to Jerusalem'.[16] The above-mentioned Amir Temur Charity Foundation was called upon to take care of personal belongings of Uzbek pilgrims to Jerusalem.

Political results of the visit were important but not spoken about much. Karimov always kept in mind the needs and reactions of not only Israeli but also American Jewry. However, his main endeavour was to find a partner to resist Islamic radicalism. Upon his arrival back in Tashkent he intensified his struggle against the local partisans of fundamentalism and partially succeeded. This struggle reached its acme in February 1999. One sunny, early spring day, six blasts shook Tashkent. Six cars exploded on the route of the presidential cortege and sixteen people were killed. Karimov was not hurt. The arrested terrorists appeared to be Islamic fundamentalists. For some time after that Tashkent looked like Tel-Aviv, with security personnel searching private bags at the entrances of public buildings. The necessities of political life made Israeli–Uzbek relations tighter.

Today, relations between the two countries are warm and there is good contact between the Muslims and the Jews. Several positive articles about Uzbekistan appeared in Israeli magazines.[17] History has repeated itself. Timur was very remote from medieval European anti-Semitism and modern Uzbeks feel the same way as their 'Father of the Nation' felt.

Previously I wrote how Biruni studied the basic foundations of Judaism. Central Asian philosophers, who are known among the Eastern Arab-speaking Jewish thinkers, also contributed to Jewish philosophy. There is a rare article on this subject, written by Erwin Rosenthal, entitled *Avicenna's influence on Jewish thought*,[18] which traces the development of Avicenna's philosophical ideas up to Maimonides' writings. Influence is always mutual. For today's Jewish–Uzbek relations this is true, as it was true for the times of Ibn Sina (called Avicenna in Europe) and Timur (also called Tamerlane in Europe). There is also a poetical symbol of this unusual Jewish–Muslim friendship. In 1941, an Uzbek poet, Gafur Gulyam, wrote a poem entitled *I am a Jew*, reflecting the unbelievable cruelty of the Holocaust:

> I am a Jew!
> Do not say my name, you, a vampire!
> Ask your great-grandmother about my ancestry!
> . . .
> Millions of books will tell about my ancestors.
> A bitter smoke of expulsion is in my eyes . . .
> I am a Jew.[19]

CONCLUSION

The fourteenth century was a century of endless opportunities in Asia. If one was brave and smart one could become a demi-god. Timur's actions proved this. He built a state based on a Turco-Mongol government with military organisation, and combined them with Muslim culture and Islamic faith from which the legacy of Islam derives its culture. In the state of Timur, this Muslim culture also had a Persian flavour. Historians have explained very clearly that the process of the replacement of Mongol traditions by Islamic values was very slow both in Persia and Central Asia.[1] The fourteenth century was the era during which this gradual process was unfolding. The people of Central Asia had already lost contact with Chinese materialism and it was Timur who led them to accept Islam, not merely as a religion, for that was already accomplished, but as a basis for their social institutions.

For the Asiatic Jews this situation was, in general, convenient. They lived in a society with different religious orientations. In addition to Muslims there were Nestorian Christians, Buddhists, Shamanists, Zoroastrians and Magi. Also there were different sects such as, for example, the *Daoodee*, 'a people who believe in the divinity of David'.[2] The Jews in Europe had no such favourable environment. For Europe in the fourteenth century was a place where a person could be a Christian or not a Christian, with few other alternatives.

When William of Rubruck and other Christian missionaries came to Asia to preach to the Mongols and Turks, nobody killed them. William of Rubruck tried to convert the Great Khan Mungka himself to Christianity but failed and said naïvely, 'If I had had the power of working miracles like Moses, he might have humbled himself'.[3] William wrote about the Muslims, 'I wonder what devil carried the law of Mohammed there'.[4] Imagine now what would have happened if a Jew or a Muslim had come to preach in France or Germany.

We can look at the predominant features of the Tamerlane–Jewish relations in this way: better off than in the Christian West, better off than in the Mamluk Sultanate, and worse off than under the Mongol rulers of China! The Jews, usually secure, potentially receptive to the culture around them, but still a very long way from assimilation, did enjoy a legal but inferior status. The Jews of the empire of Timur constituted in various ways and in their various communities at once a link and a dividing line between the Mediterranean world and the Orient, and between the medieval and the modern world – just as, in a different way, did Tamerlane himself.

The Jews, as all other nations, have always lived better in large stable states than in small crumbling states fighting each other. Timur, by founding an empire, delivered Central Asia from the last of the Mongols and brought the nations of Transoxania within the orbit of Persian civilisation. The Central Asian Jews absorbed this spirit and preserved it in their language and culture until modern times.

Alas, with the exception of Shah Rukh, Timur's son, and Babur, who conquered India, the Timurids sacrificed public security to private ambitions. After Timur's death they undid his glorious work and destroyed themselves. The Timurids recognised no law of succession and forever fought each other. One after another they drunk themselves to death. Timur's descendants, in diverting the flow of Persian culture to their own enjoyment, were only concerned with the pleasures of this world, not of the next. The meaning and purpose of life was left to the saints and theologians, whom they endowed in life and commemorated in death. But the practice of it, within the Muslim framework, was conducted according to the Timurids own common sense, without prejudice or sentiment except in favour of a rational intelligence. Therefore no synagogues were destroyed, no expulsion, inquisition, or forced conversion faced the local Jews.

The Timurids exhausted themselves in wars until another dynasty, the Sheibanids, replaced them in the sixteenth century. Finally, Central Asia became isolated, weak, disintegrated and defenceless until occupied by the Russians. When the Russians came they found the local Jews in a state of decline and isolation and they did not bother themselves with scholarly investigation of the local Jewish community. They preferred speculation. There was a book, for example, published in Russia in 1912, in which the author tried to prove that all the biblical stories about Solomon originated in Central Asia. Central Asian epic folklore has a story about the Star Tsolmon (Venus). Therefore, 'Solomon is just the Westernised pronunciation of Tsolmon'.[5] Jewish semi-scientific historiography, on the other hand, developed into two major trends. First, it concentrated on Jewish achievements in different spheres, and books entitled, for example, *The Jewish Contribution to Civilisation or The Legacy of Israel* were published. Second, it concentrated on the bloody series of Jewish persecutions throughout the ages, as in *The Valley of Tears*. In this book I have demonstrated that there was a third way too. The Asiatic Jews in the time of Timur did not contribute much in the way of science, philosophy, medicine and literature but at the same time were not persecuted at all.

There were several major conflicts in the fourteenth century. The main conflict between the West and the East originated itself in a long struggle between the Christians and Muslims. In Asia, the main conflict was in the struggle between the Far Eastern and the Near Eastern peoples. Within the Islamic countries there was a conflict between Sunni and Shi'a Muslims. These conflicts were so wide and strong that Asia simply forgot about the Jews for some time. They paid their taxes the same as other people, they suffered from the wars the same as other people, they prayed to their own God the same as other people prayed to theirs, and they lived among other peoples and co-operated with them.

Timur was wise enough to pay no specific attention to the Jews. This policy was the best he could maintain. If he had appointed a Jewish vizier as Arghun Khan did in the thirteenth century in Persia, he would have possibly provoked another anti-Jewish pogrom. If he had forced the Jews to convert to Islam, he would have installed fear into many other subjects in his multi-national empire, with a dozen different religions. Not harming the Jews was a policy for stability.

Timur and the medieval Asiatic Jews are too remote for most people to romance over. It has become a pleasant habit of our time to speak patronisingly of the benighted people of the Middle Ages, who, as we all know, lived in utter darkness. In the case of the Central Asian Jews, their relations with the mighty Muslim ruler present a positive example of Jewish–Muslim coexistence. This example of coexistence is indeed a very promising paradigm in view of the current political changes taking place in the Middle East.

CHRONOLOGICAL TABLE

c. 586 BC	Kingdom of Judah and Jerusalem Temple are destroyed by Babylonian invaders. King Nebuhadnezzar forcibly resettles prominent Jews in Babylonia. The Babylonian captivity begins.
538 BC	Persian conquest of Babylonia ends captivity. Jews begin to return to Israel and disperse throughout the Persian Empire.The first Jewish encounters with the people of Central Asia.
AD 70	The Second Temple of Jerusalem is destroyed by Romans during the First Jewish Revolt (AD 66–73) against Roman rule.
***c.* AD 135–500**	Jews disperse from the land of Israel. Beginning of Rabbinic Judaism.
600–1050	Gaonate Period. Heads of Jewish academies in Persia expand the influence of Talmud.
632	Muhammad, Islamic prophet, dies. By this time he has unified much of Arabia, thus forming a nucleus for the Muslim Empire.
773	Imam al-Bukhari is born in Bukhara. His famous collection of the Hadith, *Al Jame' as-Sahih*, is considered to be the second most holy book in Islam after the Koran.
738	An Arab merchant colony is in China. It is soon followed by the Jewish colony. Jewish merchants investigate the Great Silk Route.
980–1037	Abu Ali Ibn Sina (Avicenna), famous Muslim philosopher and physician.

1030	Biruni, scientist, philosopher and traveller, writes *Description of India*.
1165–73	Rabbi Benjamin of Tudela travels to Asia.
1220	Chingiz Khan appears in Central Asia. The Mongol period begins.
1290	The Jews are expelled from England.
1312	Partial conversion of the Golden Horde into Islam.
1336	Timur (Tamerlane) is born on 8 April.
1360–70	Timur tries to reunify Central Asian principalities.
1370	The beginning of Timur's rule in Central Asia. Timur chooses Samarkand as a capital of his kingdom.
1371–79	Timur successfully fights the Khorezm amd Moghulistan and becomes the supreme power in Central Asia.
1372	Disintegration of the Golden Horde.
1378	Timur helped Tokhtamish to ascend the throne of the Golden Horde.
1379	Khorezm becomes a part of Timur's state.
1380	The Russians defeated the Mongols at the battle of Kulikovo Pole.
1382	Timur conquers Afghanistan.
1383	Timur conquers northern Persia.
1383–95	Timur fights Tokhtamish.
1388	Timur conquers Iran.
1389–1402	The rule of the Ottoman Turk Sultan Bayazet I Yildirim.
1392	Jews are expelled from France.
1393	Timur seizes Baghdad. Invasion of Iraq, Georgia and Fars.
1394	The birth of Ulugh Bek, Shah Rukh's son, Timur's grandson.
1395	Timur's victory over Tokhtamish. The capital of the Golden Horde, Sarai, is destroyed.

1396	Timur in Samarkand.
1397	Timur's pilgrimage to the tomb of Hojja Ahmad Yassavi.
1398	The beginning of Timur's campaign in India. Timur wins the battle against Mahmud Sultan of the Delhi Sultanate.
1399	The beginnig of Timur's seven-year campaign in the Near East.
1400	Aleppo is taken.
1401	Damascus is taken, Baghdad is recaptured. Timur at the gates of the Holy Land.
1402	Battle near Ankara and defeat of the Bayazet's army. Seizure of Izmir fortress and end of the crusaders' presence in Asia.
1403	Timur campains in Caucasus, wintering in Karabagh.
1404	Timur returns to Samarkand. Arrival of the Spanish envoy Ruy Gonzales de Clavijo at Samarkand.
1405	Timur's death on 18 February.
1409–49	The rule of Timur's grandson Mirzo Ulugh Bek in Central Asia. The development of mathematics and astronomy in Samarkand.
1441–1501	Mir Alisher Navoi, a prominent statesman, the founder of the Uzbek literary language and Uzbek literature.
1483–1530	The years of life of Zahiriddin Babur, Timur's descendant, the founder of the Great Moghul Empire of India.
1492	The Jews are expelled from Spain. Spanish inquisition.
1507	Fall of the Timurid dynasty in Central Asia and Persia.
1517	The Turkish Sultan Selim I conquers Jerusalem. More opportunities for Bukharian Jews to visit the Land of Israel.
1616	Osman bek al-Bukhari al-Sufi settles in Jerusalem and builds the first Uzbek hospice (*hanka*) for the Naqshbandi dervishes. The beginning of a permanent Uzbek presence in the Holy Land.

1740	Nadir Shah of Iran invades Bukhara. Contact between the Persian and Bukharian Jews is interrupted.
1865	Tashkent is taken by the Russian troops. Contact between the Bukharian Jews and those of the Russian Empire.
1920	The end of the Bukhara Emirate. Central Asia under Soviet domination. Jews emigrate from Uzbekistan and many of them go to British Palestine. The Bukharian Quarter is built in Jerusalem.
1991	Uzbekistan becomes an independent republic. Massive Jewish immigration to Israel and the USA. Timur is proclaimed the Father of the Nation in Uzbekistan.
1992	The Uzbek consulate is established in Tel-Aviv. The citizens of Uzbekistan are permitted to visit Israel and vice versa. First Israeli tourists visit Samarkand and Bukhara.
1998	The first president of the Republic of Uzbekistan Islam Karimov visits Israel and meets representatives of the former-Uzbek Jewish community of Israel.
2000	The Uzbek Cultural Center is established in Jerusalem as an official representation of the Uzbek nation. Permanent Jewish–Uzbek cultural contacts.

NOTES

INTRODUCTION

1 Some examples of plays and novels on Timur are (in chronological order): Luis Velez de Guevara (1642) *La nueva ira de Diois, y Gran Tamerlan de Persia*, Valladolid o. J; Jean Magnon (1647) *Le grand Tamerlan ou la mort de Bajazet*, Paris; Ser Wouters (1657) *Den grooten Tamerlan met de Doobt van Bayaset de I Turks Keizer*, Amsterdam; Anonymous (1675) *Asterie ou Tamerlam*, Paris; Nicolas Pradon (1675) *Tamerlan ou la mort de Bajazet*, Paris; Charles Saunders (1681) *Tamerlane the Great, a tragedy*, London; Francis Fane (1686) *The Sacrifice, a tragedy*, London; Nicholas Rowe (1702) *Tamerlane, a tragedy*, London: L. Smith; Mademoiselle de la Roche-Guilhem (1710) *Tamerlan (Histories galantes)*, Amsterdam; William Popple (1732) *Tamerlan the Beneficent, a tragedy*, London; Sergey Borodin (1961) *Zvezdy nad Samarkandom* [Stars above Samarkand], Moscow: Sovetskiy Pisatel; Evgeniy Berezikov (1994) *Velikiy Timur* [Timur the Great], Tashkent: Ukituvchi.

2 Christopher Marlowe (1590) *Tamburlaine the Great*, London: Richard Jhones and (1606) *Tamburlaine the Great, the second part*, London: Ed. White.

3 Edgar Allan Poe (1827) 'Tamerlane', Boston. Contents of the poem have nothing to do with history.

4 Händel wrote 'Tamerlano' in July 1724. The opera was first performed in the theatre of the Royal Academy of Music in London on the 31 October of the same year. The words are by Nicola Haym. Tamerlano, 'Imperator de' Tartari', sings in alto. Händel, G.F., *Tamerlan*, Klavierauszug mit Text, Herman Roth (1876), Leipzig: Edition Breitkopf. Perhaps the first opera on Tamerlane was written in Italy: Marc Anton Ziani (1689) *Il Gran Tamerlano*, Opera seria, Venezia. Some others that followed: Johann Philipp Förtsch (1690) *Bajazet und Tamerlane*, Hamburg; Étienne Morel de Chefdeville (1786) *Tamerlan*, music by Johann Friedrich Reichardt, Paris; Matthew Gregory Lewis (1811) *Timour the Tartar, A Romantic Drama, in two acts*, music by P. King, London.

5 Beck, R.B., Black, L. *et al.* (1999) *World History*, Evanston – Boston – Dallas: McDougal Littell, pp. 443–4.

6 Barthold, W. (1984) *An Historical Geography of Iran*, ed. C.E. Bosworth, trans. S. Soucek, Princeton: Princeton University Press.

7 Ghiyas ad-Din Ali (1399) *Diary of Timur's Campaign in India*, ed. L. Zimin (1958), trans. A.A. Semenov, Moscow: Izdatelstvo Vostochnoy Literatury.
8 Ahmed Ibn Arabshah (1936)*Tamerlane or Timur the Great Amir*, trans. J.H. Sanders, London: Luzac & Co., p. 102.
9 Van Loon, H.W. (1930) *The Life and Times of Rembrandt*, New York: Liveright, p. 214.
10 Law, D.A. (1992) *From Samaria to Samarkand: The Ten Lost Tribes of Israel*, Lanham: University Press of America.
11 John of Plano Carpini described Karaites, or Karanites, in his *History of Mongols* in 1248: John of Plano Carpini (1966) 'History of the Mongols', in Dawson, C., ed., *Mission to Asia*, New York: Harper & Row, pp. 21, 41. See also: Hambly, G. *et al.* (1969) *Central Asia*, London: Weidenfeld and Nicolson, pp. 86, 90–1.
12 Hambly, p. 245. For details of Dayan's long reign (1470–1543) see: Grousset, R. (1970) *The Empire of the Steppes. A History of Central Asia*, trans. from the French by N. Walford, New Brunswick: Rutgers University Press, pp. 508–13.
13 Fischel, W.J. (1945) 'The Jews of Central Asia (Khorasan) in Medieval Hebrew and Islamic Literature', *Historia Judaica*, vol. 7: 29–50. On Rabbinic and Karaitic Jews, see pp. 45–6.
14 Shterenshis, M. (2000) 'Approach to Tamerlane: Tradition and Innovation. Ending 600 Years of Historiography of Timur', *Central Asia and Caucasus* 2: 193–200.

1 THE FOURTEENTH CENTURY IN ASIA

1 Komroff, M. ed. (1973) *Contemporaries of Marco Polo, Consisting of the Travel Records to the Eastern Parts of the World of William of Rubruck 1253–1255; The Journey of John Pian de Carpini 1245–1247; The Journal of Friar Odoric 1318–1330 and the Oriental Travels of Rabbi Benjamin of Tudela 1160–1173*, New York: Liveright Publishing Corp. Dawson, C., ed. (1966) *Mission to Asia. Narratives and letters of the Franciscan missionaries in Mongolia and China in the 13th and 14th centuries*, New York: Harper & Row. Willem van Ruysbroek (1900) *The Journey of William Rubruck to the Eastern Parts of the World, 1253–55, as Narrated by himself with Two Accounts of the Earlier Journey of John of Pian de Carpine*, trans. and ed. W.W. Rockwill, London: Hakluyt Society.
2 Benjamin of Tudela (1840) *The Itinerary of Rabbi Benjamin of Tudela*, trans. and ed. A. Asher, 2 vols, New York: Hakesheth Publ. Co.
3 Ben Jacob Pethahiah (1861) *Travels of Rabbi Petachia, of Ratisbon, who in the latter end of the twelfth century visited Poland, Russia, Little Tartary, the Crimea, Armenia, Assyria, Syria, the Holy Land and Greece*, trans. A. Benisch , London: Longman and Co.
4 Yule, H. (1866) *Cathay and the Way Thither*, 2 vols, London: Hakluyt Society. Jordanus de Severac (1863) *Mirabilia Descripta, The Wonders of the East by Friar Jordanus*, trans. H. Yule, London: Hakluyt Society.
5 Power, E. (1926) 'The Opening of the Land Routes to Cathay', in Newton, A.P., ed., *Travel and Travellers of the Middle Ages*, New York: Alfred A. Knopf, p. 136.

6 Wilson, A.T. (1926) 'Early Spanish and Portuguese Travellers in Persia, *The Asiatic Review* 22: 641.
7 Lamb, H. (1955) *Tamerlane*, New York: Bantam Books, p. 3.
8 Eubel, C. (1913) *Hierarchia Catholica Medii Aevy I*, Monasterii, vol. I, p. 457.
9 Loenertz, Fr. R., O.P. (1937) *La Société des Frères Pérégrinants: Étude sur l'Orient Dominicain*, Rome, p. 172; also Lockhart, L. (1986) 'European Contacts with Persia, 1350–1736', in Jackson, P. and Lockhart, L., eds (1986) *The Cambridge History of Iran*, Cambridge: Cambridge University Press, vol. 6, p. 375; Moranvillé, H., ed. (1894) 'Mémoire sur Tamerlan et sa Cour par un Dominicain, en 1403', in *Bibl. De l'École des Chartres*, Paris, vol. 55: 433–64; De Sacy (1882) 'Mémoire sur une correspondance inédite de Tamerlan avec Charles VI (1403)', in *Mémoires de l'Académie des Inscriptions*, Paris, vol. 6: 470–522.
10 Ellis, H., ed. (1846) *Original Letters illustrative of English History*, 3rd series, London, vol. I, pp. 54–8.
11 Loenertz, p. 171; Lockhart, p. 375.
12 Carpini, P. *History of the Mongols*, in Dawson, C. (1966), p. 33.
13 Marco Polo (1926) *The Travels of Marco Polo, the Venetian*, revised from Marsden's translation and edited with an Introduction by Manuel Komroff, New York: Horace Liveright.
14 Seymour, M.C., ed. (1967) *Mandeville's Travels*, Oxford: Clarendon Press, pp. 178–9.
15 Gibbon, E. (1914) *The Decline and Fall of the Roman Empire*, ed. J.B. Bury, London: Methuen, vol. 7, p. 24.
16 For detailed enumeration of these items see: Sodikova, N. (1998) 'Cultural and Historical Heritage of the Period of Timur and Timurids', *Bulletin of SCST*, 2: 64–73.

2 THE JEWS IN ASIA PRIOR TO TIMUR

1 *The Mishna*, Shebiith 6:1, Shekalim 3:4, Nedarim 5:4–5, Kiddushin 4:1, Yadaim 4:3. Graetz, H. (1894) *History of the Jews*, Philadelphia: the Jewish Publication Society of America, vol. 2, pp. 503–30; Keller, W. (1971) *Diaspora: The Post-Biblical History of the Jews*, trans. R. and C. Winston, London: Pitman, pp. 76–80, 106, 146–9. Connections between ancient Persia and Central Asia are very well described in: Ghirshman, R. (1954) *Iran*, London: Penguin Books, pp. 21, 23, 46, 52, 182, 222, 249, 339, 353–5.
2 Wiesehüfer, J. (1996) *Ancient Persia from 550 BC to 650 AD*, trans. A. Azodi, London and New York: I.B. Tauris, p. 143.
3 Matheson, S.A. (1972) *Persia: An Archaeological Guide*, London: Faber and Faber, p. 186.
4 Wiesehüfer, J. (1996), p. 143. See also: Fischel, W.J. (1945) 'The Jews of Central Asia (Khorasan) in Medieval Hebrew and Islamic Literature', *Historia Judaica*, vol. VII: 29–50.
5 Primary sources were translated and published in: Porten, B. (1968) *Archives from Elephantine*, Los Angeles: University of California Press, pp. 35, 47, 94, 243. See also: Tolstov, S.P. (1948) *Po sledam drevnekhoresmiyskoy tsivilizatsii* [Tracing the Ancient Khoresmian Civilization], Moscow – Leningrad: Izd. Akademii Nauk SSSR, p. 108.

6 Ghirshman, R. (1954), p. 298; Matheson, S.A. (1972), p. 111. The previous period is described in detail in: Neusner, J. (1969) *A History of the Jews in Babylonia: The Parthian Period*, Leiden: E.J. Brill. See also: www.babylonjewry.org.il

7 Baron, S.W. (1957) *A Social and Religious History of the Jews*, Philadelphia: The Jewish Publication Society of America, vol. III, p. 55.

8 The Persian Jews served in the Persian army during this campaign. Commanders gave them the same consideration they gave to other sects, even to avoid fighting on their holy days. See also: Zachariah of Mityline (1899) *The Syrian Chronicle*, trans. F.J. Hamilton and E.W. Brooks, London, IX: 4. [Antiochus Strategos] Conybear, F. (1910) 'Antiochus Strategos' Account of the Sack of Jerusalem in A.D. 614', *English Historical Review* 25: 502–16. Peters, F.E. (1985) *Jerusalem*, Princeton, NJ: Princeton University Press, pp. 170–3.

9 Lazard, G. (1975) 'The Rise of the New Persian Language', in Frye, R.N., ed., *The Cambridge History of Iran*, Cambridge: Cambridge University Press, vol. 4, pp. 606–7. *Dari* was spoken in Bukhara up to the tenth century. After that it remained in Bukhara as a language of the minority. There are numerous *dari* language manuscripts of Bukharian origin kept now in the Collection of Oriental Manuscripts of the Academy of Sciences of Uzbekistan. See also: Tolstov, S.P., *et al.*, eds (1955) *Istoriya Uzbekskoy SSR* [History of the Uzbek SSR], Tashkent: Izd. Akademii Nauk UzSSR, vol. I, 1: 224.

10 Bevan, E.R. and Singer, C., eds (1953) *The Legacy of Israel*, Oxford: Clarendon Press, pp. 129–70. Baron, S.W. (1957), vol. III, p. 99.

11 Ibn Khurdādhbih, 'Ubaidallāh ibn 'Abdallāh (*c.* 870) *Kitāb al-masālik wa' l-mamālik.* Goeje, M.J. de, ed. (1889) *Bibliotheca Geographorum Arabicorum*, Leiden, vol. 6, pp. 169, 188. See also: Kramers, J.H. (1965) 'Geography and Commerce', in Arnold, T. and Guillaume, A., eds, *The Legacy of Islam*, London: Oxford University Press, pp. 102–3.

12 On jizya see: Al-Bukhari. Sahih Al-Bukhari. vol. 4, 21: 251; Ahadith nos. 384, 385, 386. Dennett, D.C. Jr. (1950) *Conversion and the Poll Tax in Early Islam*, Cambridge, Mass.: Harvard University Press. Goitein, S.D. (1955) *Jews and Arabs*, New York: Schoken. Lewis, B. (1981) *The Jews of Islam*, Princeton: Princeton University Press, pp. 14–16, 31, 65–6, 152. Vajda, G. (1937) 'Juifs et musulmans selon le hadith', *Journal Asiatique* 29: 57–127.

13 Abd al-Husain Zarrinkub (1975) 'The Arab Conquest of Iran and its Aftermath', in Frye, R.N. (1975), vol. 4, p. 31.

14 Archaeological excavations of 1940s (Tolstov, S.P.) and of 1970s and 1980s (Rtveladze, E.V. *et al.*) confirmed coexistence of temples, prayer houses, and altars of different religions in Bukhara during this period. See: Tolstov, S.P. *et al.* (1955), pp. 111–12. Rtveladze, E. (1999) *Velikiy shelkovyi put'* [The Great Silk Route], Tashkent: Uzbekiston millii entsiklopediyasi, pp. 73–90.

15 Menasce, J. De (1975) *Zoroastrian Literature After the Muslim Conquest.* In: Frye, R.N., ed. (1975), vol. 4, pp. 560–1.

16 Keller, W. (1971).

17 Lewis, B. (1981).

18 Vyshenskaya, T., ed. (1995) *Evrei v Sredney Asii, proshloe i nastoyashee* [Central Asia Jews in Past and Present: Expeditions, Researches, Publications, Collected Articles], St Petersburg: St Petersburg Jewish University.

19 at-Tabari (1879–1901) *Annales quos scripsit Abu-Djafar . . . at-Tabari.* Edited and published by M.J. De Goeje, Séries I–III. Lugd. Batavorum. For a Russian translation of a fragment see: Volin, S.L., *et al.*, eds (1939) *Meterialy po istorii turkmen i Turkmenii* [Materials on the History of Turmen and Turkmeniya. Arab and Persian sources], Moscow – Leningrad: Izdatelstvo Akademii Nauk SSSR, vol. I, pp. 86–143.
20 Tolstov, S.P. (1948), pp. 224–6.
21 at-Tabari (1879–1901) *Annales quos scripsit Abu-Djafar . . . at-Tabari.* Cum aliis editit M.J. de Goeje, Séries I–III. Lugd. Batavorum, pp. 1321–7, 1332. [Narshakhī] Frye, R.N. (1954) *The History of Bukhara*, translated from a Persian abridgment of the Arabic original by Narshakhī, Cambridge, Mass.: The Medieval Academy of America, pp. 10–11, 1–18, 30–32. Hitti, P.K. (1957) *History of Syria*, London: Macmillan & Co., p. 460.
22 Tolstov, S. P. (1948), pp. 226–9.
23 Dunlop, D.M. (1967) *The History of the Jewish Khazars*, New York: Schoken Books. Koestler, A. (1976) *The Thirteenth Tribe: The Khazar Empire and its Heritage*, London: Hutchinson. See also: www.khazaria.com
24 Carpini, J.P. *History of the Mongols*, in Dawson, C., ed. (1966) *Mission to Asia*, New York: Harper & Row, p. 41: 'The names of the countries and races they [Mongols] have conquered are as follows: . . . Brutachi who are Jews, . . .'; p. 58: '. . . the Brutachi who are said to be Jews and shave their heads . . .'
25 Tolstov, S. (1944) 'In the Deserts of Khwarizm', *Asiatic Review* 40: 408–14.
26 Altman, V. (1947) 'Ancient Khorezmians Civilization in the Light of the Latest Archeological Discoveries [1937–1945]. *JAOS* 2: 67.
27 The letter of Rabbi Hasdai, son of Isaac ibn Shaprut, to the king of the Chazars (about AD 960) and the reply of Joseph the King, son of Aaron the King are published in Marcus, J.R. (1961) *The Jew in the Medieval World. A Source Book: 315–1791*, New York: Meridian Books, pp. 227–32.
28 Tolstov, S.P. (1948), p. 228. V.V. Barthold also supported the idea of tight Khorezm-Khazaria relations in pre-Islamic and post-Islamic periods. He, however, stressed the role of Khorezm in Muslim influence among the nations of Khazaria. See: Barthold, V.V. (1996) *Mesto prikaspiyskikh oblastey v istorii musulmanskogo mira* [The Place of Caspian areas in the History of the Muslim World] in Kurkchi, A.I., ed., *Kaspiysky Transit*, Moscow: Tanais, vol. 1, pp. 284–5.
29 Dunlop, D.M. (1967), pp. 260–1.
30 Ibn al-Athir, *Al-kāmil fi'l ta'rīkh.* Tornberg, C.J., ed. (1867–1871) Leiden, vol. 7. Grousset, R. (1970) *The Empire of the Steppes*, trans. N. Walford, New Brunswick: Rutgers University Press, p. 149.
31 Bar Hebraeus (1286) *The Chronography of Gregory Abû'l-Faraj*, trans. E.A. Wallis Budge (1932; 2nd ed., 1976), Amsterdam: Apa-Philo Press, p. 195.
32 Baron, S.W. (1957), pp. 114–15.
33 al-Biruni (1956) *Hronologiya drevnikh narodov* [Chronology of Ancient Nations], trans. A. Abdollaev, Tashkent: Fan, pp. 345–49, 357. For Soviet reflection see: Tolstov, S.P. *et al.*, eds (1955), pp. 266–7. Together with Ibn Sina (Avicenna), al-Biruni was respected in the USSR mostly as a scientist and less as a philosopher. His works on comparative religion were almost neglected. For the Western approach see: Jeffery, A. (1951) 'Al-Biruni's

contribution to comparative religion', in *Al-Biruni Commemoration Volume, A.H. 362 – A.H. 1362*, Calcutta: Iran Society, pp. 137–8, 152–3.

34 Soubiran, A. (1935) *Avicenne, Prince des Medicins*, Paris.

35 al-Mukaddasi (1939) 'Ahsan at-Takasim fi Ma'rifat al-Akalim', in Volin, S.L., *et al.*, eds (1939), vol. I, p. 194.

36 Ibid. p. 201; and Fischel, W.J. (1945), p. 35.

37 Nosonovskiy, M. (1995) 'Biblioteka i archiv tuzemno-evreiskogo muzeya v Samarkande' [The library and archives of the local Jewish Museum in Samarkand], in Vyshenskaya, T., ed. (1995), p. 216.

38 Amitin-Shapiro, Z.L. (1928) 'Predanie o postroike pervoy sinagogi v Bukhare' [The tradition on the building of the first synagogue in Bukhara], in *Sbornik Nauchnogo Kruzhka pri Vostochnom Fakultete SAGU*, Tashkent: SAGU, vol. I, pp. 6–7.

39 Lambton, A.K.S. (1968) 'The Internal Structure of the Saljuq Empire', in Boyle, J.A., ed. (1968) *The Cambridge History of Iran*, Cambridge: Cambridge University Press, vol. 5, p. 275.

40 Bausani, A. (1968) 'Religion in the Saljuq Period', in Boyle, J.A. op cit., p. 289.

41 Bosworth, C.E. (1968) 'The Political and Dynastic History of the Iranian World (AD 1000–1217)', in Boyle, J.A. op cit., p. 74; Lambton, A.K.S., in Boyle, J.A. op cit., p. 245.

42 Tolstov, S.P., *et al.* (1955), p. 148.

43 [Narshakhī] Frye, R.N. (1954) *The History of Bukhara*, translated from a Persian abridgment of the Arabic original, Cambridge, Mass.: The Medieval Academy of America, p. 59. Tolstov, S.P. *et al.* (1955), pp. 143, 145, 151–2.

44 Shapiro, S., ed. (1984) *Jews in Old China*, New York: Hippocrene Books, pp. x, xiii–xiv.

45 The diary of Benjamin of Tudela was published twice in English: Benjamin of Tudela (1840): Asher, A. *The Itinerary of Rabbi Benjamin of Tudela*, trans. and ed. A. Asher, 2 vols. Reprint: New York, Hakesheth Publ., 1966; Benjamin of Tudela (1907): Adler, M.N. *The Itinerary of Benjamin of Tudela*, critical text, translation, and commentary M.N. Adler. Reprint: New York, Philipp Feldheim, 1965.

46 Benjamin of Tudela (1840), pp. 128–9.

47 Benjamin of Tudela (1907), pp. 58–9.

48 The same number of 40,000 Jews is given also in Sassoon, D.S. (1949) *A History of the Jews in Baghdad*, Letchworth, S.D. Sassoon Publ., p. 89, but it seems that David Solomon Sassoon used nothing else but Benjamin's writings.

49 Abu Takhir Hoja. *Kandiya Malaya* [Minor Kandiya], trans. V.L. Vyatkin, (1906), in: *Spravochnaya kniga Samarkandskoy oblasti*, Samarkand, Issue 8.

50 General books on the subject are: *The History and Life of Chinggiz Khan* (The Secret History of the Mongols), trans. U. Onon (1990), Leiden: E.J. Brill. Martin, D. (1950) *The Rise of Chinggiz Khan and his Conquest of North China*, Baltimore: Johns Hopkins University Press. Hartog, L. de. (1989) *Genghis Khan Conqueror of the World*, London: I.B. Tauris & Co. Vernadsky, G. (1953) *The Mongols and Russia*, New Haven: Yale University Press and Oxford University Press. Chinggis Khan (1993) *The Golden History of the Mongols*, trans. U. Onon, London: The Folio Society. Spuler,

B. (1969) *The Mongol Period*, Leiden: E.J. Brill. It is a generally accepted historical fact that the conquest of Persia by the Mongols of Hulegu Khan, in the thirteenth century, changed the conditions that the Jews of Persia had been living under very much for the better. See, for example: Grayzel, S. *A History of the Jews*, New York: Mentor Books, 1968, p. 632.

51 Shapiro, S., ed. (1984), p. x.
52 Chen Yuan (1984) 'A Study of the Israelite religion in Kaifeng', ibid. p. 39.
53 Pan Guandan (1984) 'Jews in Ancient China – A Historical Survey', ibid. p. 54.
54 Ibid. pp. 76, 79, 82.
55 Marco Polo (1926) *The Travels of Marco Polo, the Venetian*, ed. M. Komroff, New York: Horace Liveright, pp. 120–1.
56 William of Rubruck (1966) 'The journey of William Rubruck', in Dawson, C., ed., *Mission to Asia*, New York: Harper & Row, p. 211.
57 Ibid. p. 237.
58 Marco Polo (1926), p. 28.
59 Grekov, B.D. and Yakubovskiy, A.U. (1950) *Zolotaya Orda i ee Padenie* [The Golden Horde and its Fall], Moscow – Leningrad: Izdatelstvo Akademii Nauk SSSR, p. 189, 416.
60 Bacher, W. (1900) *Ein Hebräisch-Persisches Würterbuch aus dem 14 Jahrundert*, Strassburg.
61 Seymour, M.C., ed. (1967) *Mandeville's Travels*. Oxford: Clarendon Press, pp. 191–4.
62 Lockhart, L. (1986) 'European Contacts with Persia, 1350–1736', in Jackson, P. and Lockhart, L., eds (1986) *The Cambridge History of Iran*, Cambridge: Cambridge University Press, vol. 6, p. 379.
63 Abu Omar . . . al-din al-Jauzjani (1941) *Tabakat-i Nasiri*, in Tizengauzen, V.G., ed. *The Collection of Materials Concerning the History of the Golden Horde*, Moscow – Leningrad: Izdatelstvo Akademii Nauk SSSR, vol. 2, p. 18 [Russian].
64 Bar Hebraeus (1976), pp. 475–6.
65 Ibid. p. 477.
66 Boyle, J.A. (1968) 'Dynastic and Political History of the Il-Khans', in Boyle, J.A., ed. (1968), p. 372.
67 Bar Hebraeus (1976), pp. 505–7; Howorth, H.H. (1888) *History of the Mongols from the 9th to the 19th Century, Part III, The Mongols of Persia*, London, pp. 395–6; Grousset, R. (1970), pp. 378–9.
68 Bar Hebraeus (1976), p. 507.
69 Howorth, H.H. (1888), p. 396. See also: Lichtenstadter, I. (1943) 'The Distinctive Dress of Non-Muslims in Islamic Countries', *Historia Judaica* 5: 35–52. Zayat, H. (1949) 'The Distinctive Signs of the Christians and Jews in Islam', *Al-Machriq* 43: 2: 161–252 [Arabic].
70 Browne, E.G. (1928) *A Literary History of Persia*, Cambridge: Cambridge University Press, vol. 2, p. 321.

3 TIMUR (TAMERLANE): THE BRIGHTEST PERSONALITY OF THE FOURTEENTH CENTURY

1 Galton, F. (1892) *Hereditary Genius. An Inquiry into Its Laws and Consequences*, London: Macmillan and Co., p. 142.

2 Pool, J.J. (1892) *Studies in Mohammedanism, Historical and Doctrinal*, Westminster: Archibald Constable and Co., p. 184.
3 We possess several primary sources on Timur's life. Among them are: Ghiyas ad-Din Ali (1399) *Ruz-nama gazawat Hindustan* [Diary of Timur's Campaign in India], Ms 1520/II of the Collection of Oriental Manuscripts of the Academy of Sciences of Uzbekistan [for a Russian translation see: Ghiyas ad-Din Ali. *Diary of Timur's Campaign in India (1399)*, ed. L. Zimin (1915), trans. into Russian by A.A. Semenov (1958), Moscow: Izdatelstvo Vostochnoy Literatury]; Nizam ad-din Shami (1937[1956]) *Zafar-nama par Nizamuddin Sami avec des additions critique par Felix Tauer*, Prague; Yazdi, Sharaf ad-din Ali (1425) *Zafar-Nama Taimuri*, ed. M.M. Ilahdad (1887), Calcutta: Bibliotheca Indica, partially reprinted in Elliot, H.M., ed. (1952) *The History of India as told by Its Own Historians*, Calcutta: Susil Gupta; Ibn Arabshah, Ahmad ibn Muhammad (1936) *Tamerlane, or Timur the Great Amir*, trans. J.H. Sanders, London: Luzac & Co; [Timur??] *Tuzuk Taimuri* [The Code of Timur], Ms. 38 of the Collection of the Oriental Manuscripts of the Academy of Sciences of Uzbekistan, Tashkent. Translations: [Timur ??] 'Malfuzat-i Timuri or Tuzak-i Timuri', in Elliot, Sir H.M. (1871) *The History of India as Told by Its Own Historians.* Reprint: (1952) Calcutta: Susil Gupta Ltd; *Temur tuzuklari – Institutes of Timur – Les instituts de Temur*, Persian text translated into Uzbek by A. Soguniy and H. Karomatov, into English by M. Davy, and into French by L. Langle, Tashkent, 1996. Nearly all the other biographies are secondary.
4 Dawson, C. (1966), p. 245.
5 Ibn Arabshah (1936), p. 4.
6 Ayalon, D. (1988) *The Great Yasa of Chingiz Khan*, in Ayalon, D., *Outsiders in the Lands of Islam: Mamluks, Mongols and Eunuchs*, London: Variorum Reprints, IVc, p. 153.
7 Grekov, B.D. and Yakubovsky, A.U. (1950) *Zolotaya Orda i ee Padenie* [The Golden Horde and its Fall], Moscow – Leningrad: Izdatelstvo Akademii Nauk, p. 86. The usual misspelling of 'kurakan' is 'gurgan', which could be a corruption of the Mongol title 'ghurkhan'; however, this has another meaning .
8 Khwandamir (1994) *Habibu's-Siyar*, vol. 3, trans. and ed. W.M. Thackston, Harvard University Press, p. 227.
9 Ibn Arabshah (1936), p. 295.
10 Ghiyas ad-Din Ali (1958), p. 8 (introduction by A.A. Semenov).
11 Brion, M. (1963) *Tamerlan*, Paris: Albin Michel.
12 In addition to the above-mentioned primary sources, the story of Timur's life has been described in several modern works which can be of interest to those readers who would like a broader biographical account. In addition to M. Brion we have: Hookham, H. (1962) *Tamburlaine the Conqueror*, London: Hodder and Stoughton; Lamb, H. (1928) *Tamerlane*, London: McBride & Co, reprint: New York: Bantam Books, 1955; Manz, B.F. (1989) *The Rise and Rule of Tamerlane*, Cambridge: Cambridge University Press; Champdor, A. (1957) *Tamerlan*, Paris; Roux J.-P. (1991) *Tamerlan*, Paris: Fayard; Iriskulov, A., *et al.*, eds (1996) *Amir Temur in World History* (collective Uzbek-French work), Tashkent: Sharq.
13 Pool, J.J. (1892), p. 184.
14 Voltaire (1905) *Tamerlane*, in *Ancient and Modern History. The Works of*

Voltaire, a contemporary version, trans. W.F. Fleming, Akron: Werner Co., vol. XXVI, p. 94.

15 Prawdin, M. (1967) *The Mongol Empire: Its Rise and Legacy*, New York: The Free Press, p. 438.

16 Iriskulov, A., *et al.* (1996), p. 38.

17 Evidence of this can be seen from a letter sent by Mu'in al-Dīn Jāmī, the vizier of Sultan Mu'izz al-Dīn Hussein (1331–1370), in which Timur was openly invited to invade Khorassan. This situation is described in detail in Roemer, H.R. (1986) 'Tīmūr in Iran', in Jackson, P. and Lockhart, L., eds (1986) *The Cambridge History of Iran*, Cambridge: Cambridge University Press, vol. 6, pp. 46–57.

18 There are several basic Russian sources on the subject of the Mongol yoke and the struggle between Timur and Tokhtamish: Grekov, I.B. (1963) *Ocherki po istorii mezhdunarodnych otnosheniy vostochnoy Evropy XIV–XVI vv* [Sketches on the history of international relations of the Eastern Europe in XIV–XVI centuries], Moscow: Izdatelstvo vostochrnoy literatury; Grekov, I.B. (1975) *Vostochnaya Evropa i upadok zolotoy ordy* [The Eastern Europe and the Fall of the Golden Horde] Moscow: Nauka; Grekov, B.D. and Yakubovskiy, A.U. (1950) *Zolotaya orda i ee padenie* [The Golden Horde and her Fall] Moscow – Leningrad: Izdatelstvo Akademii Nauk SSSR; Safargaliev, M.G. (1960) *Raspad Zolotoy Ordy* [Disintegration of the Golden Horde], Saransk: Mordovskoe Knizhnoe izdatelstvo.

19 For the original Slavic text see: 'Patriarshaya ili Nikonovskaya Letopis', in *Polnoe Sobranie Russkikh Letopisey* [Complete Collection of Russian Chronicles], Moscow: Nauka, 1965, vols 11–12, pp. 158–61. For a modern Russian version see: 'Povest' o Temir Aksake' [Story on Temir Aksak], in *Pamyatniki Literatury Drevney Rusi: XIV – seredina XV veka*, Moscow, 1981, pp. 230–41. See also: 'Povest' o Temir Aksake', in Rakhmanaliev, R., ed. (1992) *Tamerlane*, Moscow: Gurash, pp. 352–8.

20 'Patriarshaya ili Nikonovskaya letopis', 1965, p. 160.

21 For details see: Grekov, I.B. (1975), pp. 382–3, 399; Tyszkiewicz, J. (1989) *Tatarzy na Litwie i w Polsce. Studia z dziejów XIII–XVIII w.*, Warszawa: Panstwowe Wydawnictwo Naukowe, pp. 123–9.

22 Priselkov, M.D. (1950) *Troitskaya letopis'. Rekonstruktsiya teksta* [the text reconstruction], Moscow – Leningrad: Izdatelstvo Akademii Nauk, pp. 448, 454, 456.

23 Wolff, J. (1860) *Travels and Adventures of the Rev. Joseph Wolff, D.D., LL.D.*, London: Saunders, Otley, and Co., vol. 2, p. 421.

24 Ibn Arabshah (1936), p. 120.

25 Ibid.

26 In addition to the sources mentioned above see: Creasy, E.S. (1878) *History of the Ottoman Turks: From the Beginning of their Empire to the Present Time*, London, pp. 44–51; Gibbon, E. (1914), vol. VII, pp. 60–8.

27 Bradford, E. (1972) *The Shield and the Sword: The Knights of St. John, Jerusalem, Rhodes and Malta*, New York: E.P. Dutton & Co., p. 70; Runciman, S. (1975) *A History of the Crusades, Vol. 3: The Kingdom of Acre and the Later Crusades*, Cambridge: Cambridge University Press, pp. 452, 463–4.

28 Gibbon, E. (1914), vol. VII, p. 68.

29 Shami (1956), pp. 29, 34, 45–6; Yazdi (1887), pp. 63, 167, 178–9. See also: Roemer, H.R. (1986), p. 54.

30 Atiya, A.S. (1938) *The Crusade in the Later Middle Ages*, London, pp. 345–69. Hill, G. (1948) *History of Cyprus*, Cambridge: Cambridge University Press, vol. II, pp. 331–4.
31 Temur tuzuklari (1996), pp. 78–9. See also: Roemer, H.R. (1986), p. 54.
32 Barthold, V.V. (1958) *Four Studies on the History of Central Asia*, Vol. II: Ulugh-Beg, trans. V. and T. Minorsky, Leiden: E.J. Brill, p. 22.
33 Ibid. p. 23.
34 Mirabile, P. (n.d.) *The Book of the Oghuz Peoples or Legends Told and Sung by Dede Korkut*, Voies Itinerantes, pp. 250–1.
35 Giyas ad-Din Ali (1399), 1958, pp. 8, 14, 19; Ibn Arabshah (1936), pp. 45, 67, 99, 122.
36 Iriskulov, A. (1996), p. 5.

4 TIMUR IN JEWISH SOURCES

1 Dimont, M.I. (1962) *Jews, God, and History*, New York: Simon and Schuster, pp. 195–6.
2 Bar Hebraeus (1976) *The Chronography of Gregory Abu'l-Faraj, 1225–1286 . . . commonly known as Bar Hebraeus*, trans. E.A.W. Budge (1976) Amsterdam: Apa-Philo Press, p. xlv.
3 See details in Chapters 3 and 7; see also: Sassoon, D.S. (1949) *A History of the Jews in Baghdad*, Letchworth: S.D. Sassoon, pp. 91–2.
4 Iskhakov, P. (1996) *Kistorii bukharsko-evreiskogo etnosa* [To the History of the Bukhara Jews Ethnos], New York, pp. 97–101.
5 This legend was recorded in 1605 by Father Matteo Ricci, a Jesuit living in China, when he visited the city of Kaifeng. The first synagogue in Kaifeng, however, was built in the twelfth century. See critical discussion of the legend in: Pan Guandan (1953, revised 1983) 'Jews in Ancient China – A Historical Survey', in Shapiro, S. (1984) *Jews in Old China*, New York: Hippocrene Books, p. 72; Keller, W. (1971) *Diaspora*, London: Pitman, pp. 155–6.
6 Wolff, J. (1860), vol. 2, p. 424.
7 Ibid. pp. 424–5.
8 It is not entirely clear why the number nine is so emphasised in this tradition (except for Kabbalistic reasons). Compared to other numbers, nine has no particular symbolism in the Bible, neither from a Jewish nor from a Christian point of view. For favourite numbers and their symbolism in the Bible see: Hastings, J., ed. (1963) *Dictionary of the Bible*, 2nd edn, Edinburgh: T. & T. Clark, p. 703.
9 Wolff, J. (1860), vol. 2, p. 19.
10 For example, nothing is said about Timur, Bayazet, Bukhara, Samarkand, the Mongols, etc. in: Solomon ibn Verga (1991) *La vara de Yehudah (Sefer Sheveth Yehudah)*, trans. M.J. Cano, Barcelona: Riopiedas Educationes (this book was completed in the sixteenth century and is of more value as folklore than as history); Yaacob Ben Isjak Huerin (Yechiel Heilprin) (reprint. 1993) *Kisur Seder Hadarot*, Mexico: Editorial Jerusalem de Mexico; Isaacum Vivam (Isaac Haim Cantarini) (1681) *Vindex Sanguinis. Vindiciae secundum viritatem, quibus Judaei ab infanticidiis & victima humana*, Amstelodami: Adami Jongbloet.
11 Joseph ben Joshua Ha-Kohen (1885) *The Chronicles of Rabbi Joseph ben*

Joshua ben Meir, the Spharadi, trans. and ed. C.H.F. Bialloblotsky, London, vol. 1, pp. 255–6.

12 Joseph Ha-Kohen (1981) *Sefer 'Emeq ha-Bakha, with the chronicle of the anonymous Corrector*, the Hebrew text with a critical edition and comments by K. Almbladh, Upsala; Joseph Ha-Cohen (1980) *La Vallée des pleurs*, trans. J. Sée, Paris.

13 Abraham Zacuto (1580) *Sefer Yujasin (Libro de las genealogias)*, Cracovia. See also: Estrada, F.L. (1943) *Embajada a Tamorlan*, Madrid, p. xxxi; Burgos, F.C. (n.d.) *Abraham Zacut*, Madrid: M. Aguilar, pp. 42–3.

14 The Arabic colophon by an anonymous Jewish Rabbi of an Arabic manuscript by Bahya b. Joseph ibn Pakuda, in Neubauer, A. (1886) *Catalogue of Hebrew Manuscripts in the Bodleian Library*, Oxford: Ms. 1225, p. 433.

15 The Classic Persian language was divided into Farsi, Dari, and Tajik languages during the sixteenth and seventeenth centuries. Sometimes, when a document in Persian is found in the territory of Central Asia, local historians define the language as Tajik or old Tajik. If the document was written in the fifteenth century, the language should be defined as Persian. Currently Farsi is spoken in Iran, Dari is spoken in Afghanistan, and Tajik is spoken in Tajikistan.

16 The letter is kept in the collection of the Ahmad Donish Institute of History, Archaeology, and Ethnography of the Tajik Academy of Sciences, Dushanbe, Tadjikistan, section: 'Oriental letters and deeds'.

5 THE JEWS IN HISTORICAL WORKS ON TIMUR

1 Brooke, C.F.T., ed. (1975) *The Works of Christopher Marlowe*, Oxford: Clarendon Press, p. 99.

2 Lamb, H. (1955) *Tamerlane*, New York: Bantam Books, pp. 7, 128. Being originally written in 1928, this book went through ten reprints to the year 1955. This is a popular biography and has no notes, sources or bibliography.

3 Hookham, H. (1962) *Tamburlaine the Conqueror*, London: Hodder and Stoughton, pp. 7, 227.

4 Clavijo, G. De (1928) *Embassy to Tamerlane, 1403–1406*, trans. from the Spanish by G. le Strange, New York – London: Harper and Brothers, p. 256. Clavijo's knowledge about India was very uncertain. He wrote that 'the people of Greater India are Christians for the most part', and that the Jews 'live here in subjection to the Christians'.

5 Ibid. p. 288. See also in another translation: Clavijo, R.G. de (1859) *Narrative of the Embassy of Ruy Gonzalez de Clavijo to the Court of Timour at Samarcand A.D. 1403–6*, trans. C.R. Markham. Reprint: New York: Burt Franklin, 1970, p. 171.

6 Ibn Khaldun (1952) 'Autobiography', in Fischel, W.J., *Ibn Khaldun and Tamerlane*, Berkeley and Los Angeles: University of California Press, p. 37.

7 Ahmed ibn Arabshah (1936) *Tamerlane, or Timur the Great Amir*, trans. J.H. Sanders, London: Luzac & Co., pp. 53, 149, 181, 267.

8 Ibid. p. 149.

9 Ibid. p. 295.

10 See: Exodus 17:14: 'I will utterly blot out the remembrance of Amalek from

under heaven'; Exodus 17:16: 'The Lord will have war with Amalek from generation to generation'; Numbers 15:6: 'Then the Amelekites and the Canaanites who lived in that hill country came down and defeated them [Jews, M.Sh.], pursuing them as far as Hormah'. See also Jude 6:3; 1 Samuel 27:8, 30:1; 2 Samuel 1:1.

11 Poliakova, E.A. (1984) 'The Development of a Literary Canon in Medieval Persian Chronicles: The Triumph of Etiquette', *Iranian Studies* 17, 2: 237–56; Polyakova, E.A. (1988) 'Timur as Described by the 15th Century Court Historiographers', *Iranian Studies* 21, 1–2: 31–44.

12 *Makktubat Taimuriya*, Mss. 2278 of the Collection of Oriental Manuscripts of the Uzbek Academy of Sciences, p. 168.

13 Ibid. p. 146.

14 Mirza Rumuz (1712) *Taimur-nama*, Mss. 1526 of the Collection of Oriental Manuscripts of the Uzbek Academy of Sciences, p. 341.

15 Schiltberger, J. (1859) *Reisen des Johannes Schiltberger aus München in Europa, Asia und Africa von 1394 bis 1427*, ed. K.F. Reumann, München, p. 106.

16 Moranvillé, H. (1897) *Chronographia Regum Francorum*, Paris: Librairie Renouard, vol. 3 (1380–1405), pp. 222–3.

17 Ibid. p. 223: 'Et hec de Timur Bey dicta sufficient'.

18 Idries Shah (1966) *The Exploits of the Incomparable Mulla Nasrudin*, London: Jonathan Cape; *Anecdotes about Hojja Nasreddin*, trans. from Turkic by V.A. Gordlevskiy (1957), Moscow: Izdatelstvo Vostochnoy Literatury; *Anecdotes of Molla Nasreddin*, trans. from Azerbaijan by U. Granin (1962), Moscow: Gos. Izd. Hudozhestvennoy literatury; *Molla Nasreddin*, trans. from Persian by N. Osmanov (1970), Moscow: Nauka; Kharitonov, M.S., ed. (1978) *Dvadtsat' tri Nasreddina* [23 Nasreddins], Moscow: Nauka.

19 Kharitonov (1978), pp. 342–3.

20 Kharitonov (1978), pp. 417–19, 469–70; [Gordlevskiy, V.A.], 1957, pp. 35–7.

21 Nizam ad-din Ali Shami (1937) *Zafar-nama*, ed. F. Tauer, Prague, vol. 1, p. 267. For a similar idea that 'they never paid djizya and kharaj to any Padishah . . .', but in a somewhat different version, see: Sharaf ad-din Ali Yazdi (1957[1336]) *Zafar-nama*, ed. M. Abbasi, Tehran. Ed. A. Urunbaev (1972), Tashkent: Fan, vol. 2, p. 336.

22 In addition to the above-mentioned *Zafar-nama* of Shami and Yazdi, see also: *Tuzuk Taimuri* [Code of Timur] (1381), Mss. 38 of the Collection of Oriental Manuscripts of the Uzbek Academy of Sciences, pp. 164–7, 189–94.

6 THE JEWS BECOME TIMUR'S CITIZENS

1 Brooke, C.F.T., ed. (1975) *The Works of Christopher Marlowe*, Oxford: Clarendon Press, p. 135.

2 Sinor, D. (1997) 'Le Mongol vu par l'Occident', in Sinor, D. *Studies in Medieval Inner Asia*, Ashgate: Variorum, IX: 64. Sinor used medieval chronicles of *Annales de Marbach* and *Annales de Truves* of 1222–41 in his studies.

3 Paris, M. (1872–83) *Chronica majora*, ed. H.R. Luard, London, vol. IV, pp. 77, 131ff. Bresslau, H. (1887) 'Juden und Mongolen', *Zeitschrift für die Geschichte der Juden in Deutschland* 1: 99–102; Trachtenberg, J. (1961) *The Devil and the Jews*, New York: Meridian Books, p. 40.

4 Roth, C. (1941) *A History of the Jews in England*, Oxford: Clarendon Press, p. 61; Trachtenberg, J. (1961), p. 185.
5 Adler, E.N. (1898?) *The Persian Jews: Their Books and Ritual*, Oxford: Horace Hart, p. 3.
6 Ibid. pp. 6–17.
7 Nosonovskiy, M. (1995) 'Biblioteka i Archiv tuzemno-evreiskogo muzeya v Samarkande. Opis materialov' [The Library and archives of the Local Jewish Museum in Samarkand. A catalog], in Vyshenskaya, T., ed., *Central Asia Jews in Past and Present*, St Petersburg: St Petersburg Jewish University, pp. 188–247. There are also forty-two Jewish books and two manuscripts in the Bukhara State Museum of Architecture and Arts written in Hebrew, Yiddish and Jewish-Tadjik. They contain nothing historical. There are only two Jewish books dated from 1912 in the local Kokand Museum and ten books in the Fergana Local Museum. Among them are prayer-books, the Holy Scriptures, poetical works, but nothing historical. See: Vyshenskaya, T., ed. (1995), pp. 43–4.
8 Muslims paid *djizya* already in the Omeyyad Khaliphate. Abbasids used this situation in their struggle for the throne. They promised to change taxation and release Muslims from paying *djizya*. See: Tolstov, S.P., *et al.*, eds (1955) *The History of Uzbek SSR*, Tashkent: Fan, vol. 1, pp. 154–6.
9 Ibid. p. 327.
10 Ibid. p. 315.
11 *Tuzuk Taimuri* [The Codex of Timur], Mss. 38 of the Oriental Manuscripts Collection of the Uzbek Academy of Sciences. pp. 24, 34–6, 57; Ashrafyan, K.Z. (1988) 'Central Asia under Timur from 1370 to the Early Fifteenth Century', in Asimov, M.S. and Bosworth, C.E., eds (1988) *History of Civilizations of Central Asia*, UNESCO Publ., vol. IV, pp. 175–7. *Djizya* was mentioned several times both in 'Zafar-nama' of Nizam ad-din Shami and in 'Zafar-nama' of Sharaf ad-din Yazdi in the meaning of the special tax for 'non-believers'. However, it is not clear from the texts which particular non-Muslims paid it. See: Yazdi, Sharaf ad-din (1425) *Zafar-nama*, the Persian text, Tashkent: Fan, 1972, pp. 337a, 361b, 403a, 419b, 422a, 424b, 425b, 436a, 441b, 442a, 449a. Shami is very unclear about *djizya*. He wrote, for example, that after Timur defeated Ottoman Sultan Bayazid in 1402, the inhabitants of Constantinople agreed to pay *djizya* to him. This is indeed a fantasy. See: Shami, *Zafar-nama*, Tauer, F. (1956), vol. 2, pp. 258–9.
12 Vyshenskaya, T. (1995), p. 62.
13 Ala ad-din Ata-Melik Juwayni (1912) *Tarikh-i Jehangusha*, GMS XVI, Leyden. For an English translation (Boyle's translation, I, p. 121) and comments see: Ayalon, D. (1988) 'The Great Yasa of Chingiz Khan. A Re-examination', in Ayalon, D. *Outsiders in the Lands of Islam: Mamluks, Mongols and Eunuchs*, London: Variorum Reprints, IVd, p. 151.
14 'Samarkand', in the *Jewish Encyclopedia*, New York & London: Funk & Wagnalls, 1905, vol. 10, pp. 666–7.
15 Ibn Arabshah (1936), pp. 15–16; Iriskulov, A., *et al.*, eds (1996), p. 35.
16 Narshakhi, Abu Bakr Muhammad b. Jafa'r-i. *Tahqīq al-vilāyet* [Precise research of the land (of Bukhara)], Mss. 2110, 4355/III, 4289, 5056/II, 1862/I of the Collection of Oriental Manuscripts of the Academy of Sciences of Uzbekistan. English translation: Narshakhi (1954) *The History of Bukhara*, trans. Richard N. Frye, Cambridge: The Medieval Academy of America,

p. 59. See also: 'Bokhara', in the *Jewish Encyclopedia* (1902), vol. 3, p. 293; and 'Bukhara', in the *Encyclopaedia Judaica*, Jerusalem: Keter, 1971, vol. 4, p. 1470.

17 Ibn Arabshah (1936), pp. 275–6.

18 'Balkh', in the *Encyclopaedia Judaica* (1971), vol. 4, p. 137; Fischel, W.J. (1945) 'The Jews of Central Asia (Khorasan) in Medieval Hebrew and Islamic Literature', *Historia Judaica* 7: 37–8.

19 al-Maqdisi (1877) *Ahsan at-Takasim fi-Ma'rifat al-Akalim*, ed. M.J. de Goeje, BGA, III, Leiden, p. 302.

20 Barthold, V.V. (1900) 'Turkestan v epochu mongolskogo nashestviya' [Turkestan at the epoch of the Mongol conquest], in Barthold, V.V. (1963–66) *Sochineniya* [writings], Moscow: Izd. Vostochnoy Literatury, vol. 1, p. 350–1.

21 'Balkh', in the *Encyclopaedia Judaica* (1971), vol. 4, p. 138.

22 Ibn Arabshah (1936), p. 12; Irirskulov, A., *et al.*, eds (1996), p. 53.

23 Wolff, J. (1861) *Travels and Adventures of the Rev. Joseph Wolff, D.D., LL.D.*, London: Saunders, Otley, and Co., vol. II, p. 13.

24 Barthold, V.V. (1984) *An Historical Geography of Iran*, trans. S. Soucek, Princeton: Princton University Press, pp. 13–14.

25 Fischel, W.J. (1945), pp. 40–2.

26 'Herat', in the *Encyclopaedia Judaica* (1971), vol. 8, p. 340.

27 Shami, Nizam ad-din (1425) 'Zafar-nama', in Volin, S.L., *et al.*, eds (1939) *Materials for the History of Turkmen and Turkmenia*, Moscow – Leningrad: Izdatelstvo Akademii Nauk SSSR, vol. 1, p. 519.

28 Ibn Arabshah (1936), pp. 20–3; Khwandamir (1994) *Habibu's-Siyar, Vol. 3: The Reign of the Mongol and the Turk*, trans. and ed. W.M. Thackston, Deptartment of Near Eastern Languages and Civilizations, Harvard University, pp. 245–6.

29 at-Tabari (1885–9) *Tarikh ar-Rusul va-l-Muluk*, ed. M.J. de Goeje (Annales quos scripsit Abu-Djafar Mohammed ibn Djarir at Tabari), Leyden, vol. 2, p. 1688.

30 Goode, A.D. (1940) 'The Exilarchate in the Eastern Caliphate', *JQR* 31: 149–71; Fischel, W.J. (1945), pp. 35–7.

31 Boyle, J.A. (1968) 'Dynastic and Political History of the Il-Khans', in Boyle, J.A., ed., *The Cambridge History of Iran*, Cambridge: Cambridge University Press, vol. 5, p. 313.

32 Petrushevsky, I.P. (1968) 'The Socio-Economic Condition of Iran Under the Il-Khans', in Boyle, J.A., ed. (1968), p. 497.

33 Shami, Tauer, F. (1939), vol. 1, p. 513–14.

34 Hafiz-i-Abru (1939) 'Madjma' at-tavarikh', in Volin, S.L., *et al.*, eds (1939), vol. 1, p. 525.

35 Sassoon, D.S. (1932) *Ohel David*, vol. I, London, p. 500, no. 710; Fischel, W.J. (1945), p. 37.

36 Bacher, W. (1900) *Ein hebräisch-persisches Würterbuch aus dem vierzehnten Jahrhundert*, Strassburg. 'Bokhara', in the *Jewish Encyclopedia*, 1902, vol. 3, p. 293; Fischel, W.J. (1945), pp. 42–3.

37 Fischel, W.J. (1945), pp. 38–40.

38 'Isphahan', in the *Jewish Encyclopedia* (1903), vol. 6, p. 659. V.V. Barthold gave a description of the Jewish sites in the city. In addition to the Jewish district of the city he mentioned the 'Gate of the Jews', Darvaza-i Juhudan. See: Barthold, V.V. (1984), pp. 169–70.

39 Benjamin of Tudela (trans. and ed. A. Asher) (1840), p. 128.
40 For details see: Boyle, J.A. (1968), pp. 332–5.
41 Rashid al-Din (1957) *Dzami-at-Tavarikh*, ed. A.A. Alizade, trans. A.K. Arends, Baku, p. 557.
42 Fischel, W.J. (1953) 'Isfahan – the Story of a Jewish Community in Persia', *Joshua Starr Memorial Volume*, New York, pp. 111–28.
43 'Ispahan', in *Vallentine's Jewish Encyclopaedia*, ed. A.M. Hyamson and A.M. Silbermann (1938), London: Shapiro, Vallentine & Co., p. 303.
44 Benjamin of Tudela (1840), p. 128.
45 Roemer, H.R. (1986) 'Timur in Iran', in Jackson, P. and Lockhart, L., eds (1986) *The Cambridge History of Iran*, Cambridge: Cambridge University Press, vol. 6, p. 60.
46 Boyle, J.A. (1968) 'Dynastic and Political History of the Il-Khans', in Boyle, J.A., ed. (1968), vol. 5, p. 372.
47 Jordan Katalani (Severaque) (1329) 'The Story of Father Jordan about Grand India', in Kurkchi, A.I., ed. (1996) *The Kaspiysky Transit*, Moscow: Tanais, vol. 1, p. 80 [Russia].
48 Roemer, H.R. (1986), p. 58.
49 Shami (1941), p. 110.
50 'Derbent', in the *Jewish Encyclopedia* (1903), vol. 4, p. 525.
51 Mann, J. (1931) *Texts and Studies in Jewish History and Literature*, Cincinnati: Hebrew Union College Press, vol. 1, text, pp. 21–5, commentary, pp. 10–14. Graetz, H. (1894), vol. 3, pp. 123–4.
52 Graetz, H. (1894), vol. 3, p. 222.
53 Lambton, A.K.S. (1968) 'The Internal Structure of the Salijuq Empire', in Boyle, J.A., ed. (1968), vol. 5, p. 275.
54 Benjamin of Tuleda (1840), p. 129; Graetz, H. (1894), vol. 3, p. 433.
55 Juvaini, Ala ad-din Ata-Malik (1958) 'Tarikh-i Jahan-Gusha', in Boyle, J.A., trans. (1958), *The History of the World-Conqueror*, Manchester: Manchester University Press, vol. 1, p. 177.
56 Clavijo, R.G. de (1928) *Embassy to Tamerlane, 1403–1406*, trans. G. Le Strange, New York and London: Harper & Brothers, p. 167.
57 Graetz, H. (1894), vol. 3, p. 434.
58 Boyle, J.A. (1968), pp. 310–11.
59 Ibn Arabshah (1936), p. 57.
60 Ibid.
61 'Astrakhan', in the *Jewish Encyclopedia* (1902), vol. 2, p. 240.
62 Ibn Arabshah (1936), p. 82.
63 Priselkov, M.D. (1950) *Troitskaya Letopis'*, text reconstruction, Moscow – Leningrad: Izd. Akademii Nauk SSSR, p. 368. The text of the chronicle states: 'That same year [1346] there was a punishment from God to the people of the Eastern lands in the Horde, in Ornach, in Sarai, and in Bezdezh, and in other cities and lands; and there was a great death among the people, among the Besermen, the Tatars, the Armenians, the Obezes, and among the Jews . . . and other people living there.' This is a description of the epidemic of pestilence in Asia which then became the epidemic of the Black Death in Europe. Sarai and the Jews are mentioned in the same sentence but it is not clear from the text whether the Jews lived in Sarai or in 'other cities and lands'. Even if we assume that there were Jews in Sarai, another question arises: how many Jews remained in Sarai after the epidemic?

64 Lane, F.C. (1973) *Venice: A Maritime Republic*, Baltimore: Johns Hopkins University Press, pp. 19, 83.
65 Schiltberger, J. (1859) *Reisen des Johannes Schiltberger aus Munchen in Europa, Asia und Afrika von 1394 bis 1427*, München, p. 136.
66 Lockhart, L., *et al.*, eds (1973) *I Viaggi in Persia Degli Ambasciatori Veneti Barbaro e Contarini*, Istituto Poligrafico Dello Stato, pp. 263–4, 277.
67 Lane, F.C. (1973), pp. 199, 286.
68 Barbaro, G. (1973) 'The Travel to Tana', in Lockhart, L., *et al.*, eds (1973), pp. 26–9, 96.
69 'Georgia', in *Vallentine's Jewish Encyclopaedia* (1938), p. 241.
70 Marco Polo (1926), p. 28.
71 Sassoon, D.S.(1949) *A History of the Jews in Baghdad*, Letchworth: D.S. Sassoon.
72 Kirakos Ganjakec'i (1961) *Patmut'iwn Hayoc'* [History of Armenia], ed. K.A. Melik'-Ohanjanyan, Erevan, p. 381. English translation by R. Bedrosian, 1986.
73 Sassoon, D.S. (1949), p. 91.
74 Benjamin of Tudela (trans. and ed. M.N. Adler) (1907), p. 39.
75 Poznanski, S. (1914) *Babylonische Geonim im nachgaonaischen Zeitalter*, Berlin, p. 119. Sassoon, D.S. (1949), pp. 100–1.
76 Ibn Arabshah (1936), p. 62; Howorth, H.H. (1888) *History of the Mongols, Part III. The Mongols of Persia*, London, p. 663.
77 Khwandamir, *Habibu's-Siyar*, vol. 3, trans. and ed. W.M. Thackston (1994), p. 279.
78 Odorico (1996) 'Friar Odorico in the Orient', in Kurkchi, A.I., ed. (1996), vol. 1, p. 117.
79 Hitti, P.K. (1957) *History of Syria*, London: Macmillan & Co Ltd., p. 553. Grousset, R. (1970), pp. 361–3.
80 Bar Hebraeus (1976), p. 436.
81 Grousset, R. (1970), pp. 360–2.
82 The story is found in an anonymous colophon in the manuscript by Bahya b. Joseph ibn Pakuda (second half of the eleventh century). Neubauer, A. (1886) *Catalogue of Hebrew Manuscripts in the Bodleian Library*, Oxford, Ms. 1225, p. 433.
83 'Damascus', in the *Jewish Encyclopedia* (1902), vol. 4, p. 417.
84 Stillman, N.A. (1979) *The Jews of Arab Lands. A History and Source Book*, Philadelphia: The Jewish Publication Society of America, p. 273.
85 Ibid. pp. 267–8, 273–6.
86 Shami (Tauer, F.) (1937), vol. 1, pp. 230–7; Yazdi, II, p. 225.
87 Ibn Arabshah (1936), p. 161.
88 T'ovma Mecop'ec'i (1860) *Patmut'iwn Lank-T'amuray ew yajordac' iwroc', arareal T'ovma vardapeti Mecop'ec'woy*, ed. K. Ahahnazarean, Paris [Armenian]. Translation: *Expose des guerres de Tamerlan et de Schah-Rokh dans l'Asia occidentale, d'apres la chronique armenienne inedite de Thomas de Medzoph*, trans. Felix Neve, 1961, Brussels. English translation: R. Bedrosyan, 1977. See also: Kostanean, K., ed. (1892) *T'ovma Mecop'ec'u yishatakarane* [T'ovma Mecop'ec'i's Colophon], Tiflis [Armenian].
89 'Armenia', in *Vallentine's Jewish Encyclopaedia* (1938), p. 51.
90 Benjamin of Tudela (trans. and ed. M.N. Adler) (1907), p. 26.

91 Petachia of Ratisbon (1595), in Adler, E.N. (1930) *Jewish Travellers*, London: G. Routledge & Sons, p. 71.
92 Kirakos Ganjakec'i (1961) *Patmut'iwn Hayoc'* [History of Armenia], ed. K.A. Melik'-Ohanjanyan, Erevan. Translation: Historire d'Armenie par le vartabied Kirakos de Gantzac. Brosset, M.F. (1870) *Deux historiens armeniens*, St Petersburg.
93 As of April 2001 the publication about this cemetery has not yet appeared. The detailed report about this expedition can be obtained from the Department of Armenian Studies, the Hebrew University of Jerusalem, Professor M.E. Stone.
94 McEvedy, C., Jones, R. (1978) *Atlas of World Population History*, New York – London: Penguin Books.

7 THE JEWS IN TIMUR'S EMPIRE

1 The total number of Jews in the fourteenth century was less than a million. See: Fishberg, M. (1911) *The Jews: A Study of Race and Environment*, London: Walter Scott Publ., p. 3; McEvedy, C. and Jones, R. (1978) *Atlas of World Population History*, New York: Penguin, pp. 141–2.
2 Keller, W. (1971), p. 153; Frye, R.N. (1975), vol. 4, p. 327.
3 Arnold, T. and Guillaume, A., eds (1965) *The Legacy of Islam*, London: Oxford University Press, pp. 102–3.
4 Vernadsky, G. (1953), p. 343; Tyszkiewicz, J. (1989), p. 150.
5 The term *Bazirganlar*, 'Jewish merchants', is derived from the Persian *bazergan.* See 'The Legend of Basmi Beyrek, son of Kam Pure', in P. Mirabile (n.d.) *The Book of the Oghuz Peoples or Legends Told and Sung by Dede Korkut*, Istanbul: Voies Itinerantes, pp. 97, 253: 'Prince Pay Pure called his *bazirganlar* to his side; he gave them orders: "Now then merchants, God the Great gave me a son. Go to the land of the Rum [Anatolia], bring beautiful gifts to give my son for when he is grown," he said. The merchants took the road and travelled day and night. They arrived in Istanbul.'
6 Lane, F.C. (1973), p. 79. Tyszkiewicz, J. (1989), p. 150.
7 Barthold, V.V. (1996), vol. 1, pp. 308, 325–6.
8 Heyd, W. (1886) *Histoire du commerce du Levant au Moyen-Age*, Paris: Societe de l'Orient Latin; reprint: 1966, Leipzig: Otto Harrassowitz, vol. 2, pp. 172–5, 268–9.
9 Ibid. vol. 2, p. 710.
10 Jackson, P. and Lockhart, L., eds (1986), vol. 6, p. 413.
11 Clavijo, G. de, trans. Le Strange (1928), pp. 129, 131.
12 Ibid. pp. 158ff.
13 Ibid. pp. 152–3.
14 Khwandamir, trans. and ed. W.M. Thackston (1994), p. 230.
15 Tyszkiewicz, J. (1989), p. 150.
16 Garbell, I. (1965) *The Jewish Neo-Aramaic Dialect of Persian Azerbaijan*, The Hague: Mouton & Co., Ch. 3.
17 Nasr, S.H. (1975) 'Life Sciences, Alchemy and Medicine', in Frye, R.N., ed. (1975), vol. 4, p. 415.
18 Elgood, C. (1951) *A Medical History of Persia and the Eastern Caliphate*, Cambridge: Cambridge University Press, p. 308.

19 Qutb-ud-Din Mahmud b. Mas'ud ash-Shirazi (1952–60) *Commentaries to the General Part of the Canon*, Ms. 2969, ed. A.A. Semenov, vol. 1, p. 247 [the manuscript is written in Arabic]. The collection has the manuscript that was copied in the seventeenth century.
20 Elgood, C. (1951), p. 311.
21 Rashid ad-Din (1971) *Perepiska* [Correspondence], ed. and trans. A.I. Falina, Moscow: Nauka, pp. 122–4, 153–4, 289–94.
22 Elgood, C. (1951), p. 307.
23 Semenov, A.A., ed. (1952–60), vol. 1, pp. 241–93; vol. 5, pp. 271–92.
24 Roth, C. (1940) *The Jewish Contribution to Civilization*, New York – London: Harper & Brothers, p. 224; Bevan, E.R. and Singer, C., eds (1953) *The Legacy of Israel*, Oxford: Clarendon Press, pp. 204–41; Keller, W. (1971), p. 153.
25 Merriman, R.B. (1962) *The Rise of the Spanish Empire*, New York: Cooper Square, pp. 159–64; Fischel, W.J. (1956), pp. 204–6; Brion, M. (1963), pp. 34–40.
26 Alexandrescu-Dersca, M.M. (1977[1942]) *La campagne de Timur en Anatolie (1402)*, Bucharest; reprint: London: Variorum Reprints, 1977, pp. 123–5; Fischel, W.J. (1956); Iriskulov, A., *et al.*, eds (1996), pp. 71–4.
27 *Vallentine's Jewish Encyclopaedia* (1938), p. 296.
28 Barthold, V.V. (1966) 'Karl Velikiy i Harun ar-Rashid' [Charlemagne and Harun ar-Rashid], in Barthold, V.V. (1966), vol. 6, pp. 342–64; Barthold, V.V. (1966) 'K voprosu o franko-musulmanskikh otnosheniyakh' [On the question of the Franco-Moslem relations], in ibid. pp. 432–61; Buckler, F.W. (1931) *Harunu'l-Rashid and Charles the Great*, Cambridge, Mass., pp. 43–4.
29 Alexandrescu-Dersca, M.M. (1977[1942]), p. 124.
30 Abdallah Muhammed b. Muhammed b. al-Djazari ash-Shafi'i, *Basic Science of the Reading of the Koran*, Ms. 2669/IV of the Collection of the Oriental Manuscripts of the Academy of Sciences of the Uzbek SSR. See: Semenov, A.A., ed. (1960), vol. 5, pp. 370–1 [the manuscript is written in Arabic].
31 Mirza Bahadur-hodja b. Hussein Hodja-ii Pirmesti, Ms. 2667, Semenov, A.A. (1952), vol. 1, pp. 166–7. The manuscript has no title. Hodja Pirmesti and his ancestors lived in Bukhara and owned land in the Mahallya-ii Miran village near the city. The last known ancestor served in the Shir Dor *medrese* in Samarkand in the 1920s.

8 THE LAST TRIP OF THE PROPHET DANIEL AND THE LIFE AND CULTURE OF THE JEWS OF CENTRAL ASIA

1 Poe, E.A. (1827) 'Tamerlane', in *The Works of Edgar Allan Poe*, New York: P.F. Collier & Son, 1903, vol. 5, p. 334.
2 *The Book of Daniel* (1978), The Anchor Bible, trans. L.F. Hartman, New York: Doubleday & Co., pp. 7–8.
3 Matheson, S.A. (1972) *Persia: An Archeological Guide*, London: Faber and Faber, p. 150.
4 Many of the Jewish patriarchs, kings and prophets are mentioned in the Koran. There is one Sura in the Koran named 'The Prophets'. Adam, Noah, Abraham, Isaac, David, Solomon, Jesus and many other Biblical personages are mentioned, excluding Daniel. See: *The Koran*, trans. J.M. Rodwell,

(1957) London: J.M. Dent & Sons; New York: E.P. Dutton & Co., pp. 151–8, 285, 324–5, 346, 389. Daniel, however, was mentioned in Islamic literature, for example, in the Persian Nasir-I-Khusraw's *Diwan* of the early Seljuq period. See: Browne, E.G. (1928), vol. 2, p. 228.

5 Benjamin of Tudela (trans. and ed. A. Asher) (1840), vol. 1, pp. 118–20; Benjamin of Tudela (trans. and ed. M.N. Adler) (1907), pp. 52–3.

6 Graetz, H. (1894) *History of the Jews*, Philadelphia: The Jewish Publication Society of America, vol. III, p. 435.

7 Barthold, W. (1984) *An Historical Geography of Iran*, trans. S. Soucek, Princeton: Princeton University Press, p. 186.

8 Anonymous, 'Na mogile hodja Daniyara' [At the tomb of Hodja Daniyar], in the newspaper *Leninskiy Put'*, Samarkand, 26 May 1946, p. 4.

9 Adler, E.N. (1905) *Jews in Many Lands*, London: Jewish Historical Society of England, p. 224.

10 Barthold, V.V. (1906) 'Poezdka v Samarkand s archeologicheskoi tseliu' [The trip to Samarkand with an archeological goal], *ZVO* XVI, 4: 34–5. Barthold visited Samarkand in 1904.

11 Krist, G. (1939) *Alone Through the Forbidden Land*, trans. E.O. Lorimer, London: Readers' Union Ltd., pp. 90–1.

12 Borodin, S. (1961) *Zvezdy nad Samarkandom*, Moscow: Sovetskiy Pisatel', p. 64.

13 Abu-l-Fazl Muhammad b. Khaidar as-Samarkandi, *Tarikh-i kand*, Ms. 1773/I of the Collection of the Academy of Sciences of the Rupublic of Uzbekistan. Usupova, D.U. and Jalilova, R.P. (1998) *The Collection of the Oriental Manuscripts of the Academy of Sciences of the Republic of Uzbekistan*, Mss. 261–6, Tashkent: Fan, pp. 109–11. Imam Abu-l-Fazl Muhammad b. Abdaljalil b. 'Abdalmalik 'Ali b. Khaidar as-Samarkandi (twelth century) wrote a short Persian version of a larger Arabic book of Abu Hafs an-Nasafi as-Samarkandi (d. 1142/1143) entitled *Kitab al-kand fi tarikh-i Samarkand* [The sugar book of the history of Samarkand]. This large *Kandiya* did not survive. There are six copies of 'The Smaller Kandiya' in the Tashkent collection.

14 Ususpova, D.U. and Jalilova, R.P. (1998), p. 111.

15 Netzer, A. (1971) 'Daniyal-Name: An Exposition of Judeo-Persian', in Tikku, G.L., ed., *Islam and its Cultural Divirgence*, Urbana, Chicago, London: University of Illinois Press, pp. 145–64.

16 Concerning the Judeo-Persian and the Bukharian languages, see: Bacher, W. (1900) *Ein hebreisch-prsischen Würterbuch aus dem vierzehenten Jahrhundert*, Strassburg; Bacher, W. (1906) 'Judaeo-Persian Language', in the *Jewish Encyclopedia*, New York, vol. 7, pp. 313–17; Birnbaum, S.A. (1956) 'The Verb in the Bukharic Language of Samarkand', *Archivum Linguisticum* 2:60–73; Zarubin, I.I. (1928) *Ocherk razgovornogo yazyka samarkandskikh evreev: opyt kharakteristiki*, Leningrad: Materialy AN SSSR, pp. 95–181; Niyazov, D.M. (1979) 'O yazyke sredneaziatskikh evreev', *Voprosy vostokovedeniya* 600: 92–104.

17 Reif, S.C. (2000) *A Jewish Archive from Old Cairo*, Richmond: Curzon Press, p. 222.

18 Some historians do not discern these differences and call the Persian language with Hebraisms 'Judeo-Persian'. This is the wrong approach. Nobody would describe the sentence 'He uses many cliches in his speech' as an example of

the Franco-English language. About Hebraisms in the Tajik language of the Jewish communities of Central Asia see: Danielova, H. (1988) *Gebraismy v tadjikskom yazyke sredneaziatskikh evreev*. In: *Synchroniya i diachroniya v lingvisticheskikh issledovaniyakh*, Moscow: Nauka, vol. 1, pp. 96–101.

19 Prof. Edward Rtveladze from Tashkent, Uzbekistan, is the leading modern archaeologist who investigates the Jewish presence in Central Asia. There are just a few publications containing archaeological evidence of the Jewish presence in Central Asia: Rtveladze, E. (1999) 'The Jews in the Pre-Islamic Central Asia', in Rtveladze, E.V. (1999) *Velikiy Shelkovyi Put': Entsiklopedicheskiy spravochnik* [The Great Silk Route: Encyclopaedia], Tashkent, Uzbekiston Milliy Encyclopediyasy, pp. 86–90; Klevan, A. (1979) 'Hebrew Inscriptions in Ossuaries Found in Central Asia', *Qadmomiyyot* 12, 2–3: 91–2 [Hebrew]; Livshits, V.A. and Usmanova, Z.I. (1994) *Parthian inscription from Old Merv*, Irano-Judaica III, Jerusalem, pp. 103–4; Mukherdjee, B.N. (1970) *An Agrippan Source: A Study in Judeo-Parthian history*, Calcutta; Mukherdjee, B.N. (1993) 'An inscripted gem from Indo-Iranian Borderlands', *Bull Asia Inst* (new series) 7: 141–2; Weitzmann, K. and Keesler, H.L. (1991) *The Frescoes of the Dura Synagogue and Christian Art*, Washington: Trustees for Harvard University; Zand, M. (1989) 'Bukharian Jews', *Encyclopaedia Iranica*, New York and London, vol. 4, Fac. 5, pp. 531–3.

20 Henning, W.B. (1957) 'The Inscriptions of Tang-i Azao', *BSOAS* 20: 335–42.

21 Margoliuth, D. (1903) 'An Early Judeo-Persian Document from Khotan in the Stein Collection', *JRAS*: 735–61.

22 This part of the chapter is mainly based on the folklore data collected by S.R. Abramova in 1936–8. This impressive material is kept now in The Central State Archive of the Republic of Uzbekistan, Fund 2577, Section 1, doc. nos. 1–167. In addition to this collection, there are several main sources for the folklore of Central Asian Jews, namely: Abramov, M.M. (1993) *Bukharskie evrei v Samarkande*, Samarkand. Adler, E.N. (1898) 'The Persian Jews: Their Books and Their Ritual', *The Jewish Quarterly Review* 10: 584–625; Amitin-Shapiro, Z.L. (1934) *Pajdo sudani sidho ve zurfu sodathoji jahudigi* [The origin of Jewish festivals and traditions], Tashkent: Gosizdat UzSSR, [Judeo-Tadjik]; Bacher, W. (1901, 1902) 'Judisch-Persischen aus Bukhara', *Zeitschrift der Deutschen Morgenlandischen Gesellschaft* 55: 241–57 and 56: 729–59; Gaffarov, S.S., Rahmatullaev, T.R, eds (1998) *Murabbiy*, Samarkand: Samarkand State University [Russian]; Kontir, L. (1929) *Uzbekistanda mahalli yahudilar* [Native Jews of Uzbekistan], Samarkand [Uzbek]; Pinkhasi, I. (1978) *Ten Folk Stories from Bukhara*, Jerusalem [Hebrew]; Wolff, S. (1846) *Narrative of a Mission to Bukhara in the Years 1843–1845*, London: Saunders, Otley, and Co. (2nd ed. 1860–1).

23 The Central State Archive of the Republic of Uzbekistan, Fund 2577, Section 1, doc. no. 134; doc. no. 156 (second part).

24 Ibid. doc. no. 156 (second part).

9 WHY TIMUR CONQUERED DAMASCUS BUT DID NOT CONQUER JERUSALEM

1 Carpini, P. (1247), in Dawson, C. (1966), p. 59.

2 Peters, F.E. (1985) *Jerusalem*, Princeton: Princeton University Press, p. 368. Peter's mistake arose from the fact that in November 1239 Egyptian Sultan al-Nasir retook Jerusalem in a surprise raid. But he did not gain long-term control over the city and withdrew all his troops. On leaving the city he destroyed Jerusalem's fortifications. The Khorezmian task, therefore, was made easier. For details see: Maalouf, A. (1984) *The Crusades Through Arab Eyes*, London: Al Saqi Books, p. 231.

3 Barthold, V.V. (1900), in Barthold (1963–66), vol. 1, p. 569. Maalouf wrote that the Khorezmians attacked Jerusalem in June 1224 on their own initiative (Maalouf, A. (1984), p. 236) but several medieval European chronicles contradict this fact by stating that Jerusalem was attacked in 1244.

4 A special article on the subject was published recently: Meserve, R.I. (1993) 'The Latin Sources for Khwarezm', in Nazarov, B.A. and Sinor, D., eds, *Essays on Uzbek History, Culture, and Language*, Bloomington: Indiana University Press, pp. 79–94.

5 'Simon de Saint-Quentin', in Richard, J., ed. (1965) *Histoire des Tartares. Documents Relatifs a l'Histoire des Croisades publiés par l'Académie des inscriptions et Belles-Lettres*, VIII, Paris: Libraire Orientaliste Paul Geuthner, pp. 53–4.

6 See for example: Gransden, A., ed. (1964) *The Chronicle of Bury St. Edmunds 1212–1301*, London: Nelson, p. 13; Andersen, A.O. and Andersen, M.O., eds (1936) *The Chronicle of Melrose from the Cottonian Manuscript, Faustina B. IX in the British Museum*, London: Percy Lund Humphries & Co., pp. 92–5. Concerning Jalal-ad-Din see: Karamatov, K., ed. (1999) *Jaloliddin Manguberdi* [Jalal-ad-Din], Tashkent: Sharq.

7 Graetz, H. (1894), vol. III, p. 606; see also: Keller, W. (1971), p. 227.

8 Kobler, F., ed. (1978) *Letters of Jews through the Ages from Biblical Times to the Middle of the Eighteenth Century*, New York: East and West Library, vol. 1, p. 226; Peters, F.E. (1985), p. 474. A somewhat different translation is given by Keller, W. (1971), p. 227.

9 Jackson, P. (1980) 'The Crisis in the Holy Land in 1260', *English Historical Review* 95: 481–513. Runciman, S. (1975) *A History of the Crusades*, Cambridge: Cambridge University Press, vol. 3, p. 308; Maalouf, A. (1984), p. 244.

10 Graetz, H. (1894), vol. III, p. 606.

11 Amitai-Preiss, R. (1995) *Mongols and Mamluks. The Mamluk-Ilkhanid War, 1260–1281*, Cambridge: Cambridge University Press, pp. 152–5.

12 Runciman, S. (1975), vol. III, pp. 400–5. Maalouf, A. (1984), pp. 254–6.

13 Raynaud, A., ed. (1887) *Gestes des Chiprois*, Geneva, pp. 296–306. Atiya, A.S. (1938) *The Crusade in the Later Middle Ages*, London: Lund. Hill, G. (1948) *History of Cyprus*, Cambridge: Cambridge University Press, vol. II, pp. 12–15; Runciman, S., 1975, vol. III, p. 439.

14 Peters, F.E. (1985), p. 474–5.

15 Ibn Arabshah (1936), pp. 91–4.

16 Sultan Suleiman the Magnificent, of the Ottoman Empire, only ordered the wall to be built in the sixteenth century.

17 *Polnoe sobranie russkikh letopisey* [Complete Collection of the Russian Chronicles], Moscow: Nauka, 1965, vol. 8, pp. 65–6; vol. 24, p. 161. Cherepnin, L.V. (1961) 'Some reflections of the international life of the 14th and the beginning of the 15th centuries in the Moscow chronicles'. In: *Mezhdunarodnye svyazi Rossii do XVII veka* [Moscow international relations until the seventeenth century], Moscow: Akademia Nauk SSSR, p. 245. Cherepnin mistakenly added the Nikon Chronicle to the list of chronicles where Jerusalem was mentioned in the list of Timur's possessions. The correct translation of the Slavic fragment says: 'There are the names of lands and kingdoms captured by Temir-Aksak: . . . and Great Assyria; and the Kingdom of Babylon, where Nebuchadnezzar was a king, who had captured Jerusalem and three young men, Hananiah, Azariah, Mishael, and Daniel the Prophet; and the city Sebastia, where the martyrdom of the 40 martyrs had happened; and Armenia, where St Gregory was a bishop; and Great Damascus, where was John Damascene; and Great Sarai.' It is clear from the translation that Jerusalem was taken by Nebuchadnezzar and not by Timur. See: 'Patriarshaya ili Nikonovskaya letopis' [The Patriarch or Nikon Chronicle] in *The Complete Collection of the Russian Chronicles*, Moscow: Nauka, (1965), vols. 11–12, p. 159.
18 Bar Hebraeus (1976), vol. 2, pp. xxxi–xxxiii.
19 Ibn Khaldun (1952) 'The Meeting with Emir Timur, Sultan of the Mongols and Tatars', in Fischel, W.J., *Ibn Khaldun and Tamerlane*, Berkeley and Los Angeles: University of California Press, p. 30.
20 Fischel, W.J. (1952), p. 57. When Sultan Faraj fled Damascus, Timur gave orders to take the coastal towns up to Acre, but there is no evidence that his troops indeed conquered this port.
21 'Patriarshaya ili Nikonovskaya letopis', 1965, p. 151.
22 Yazdi, Sharaf ad-din (1887) *Zafar-Nama*, Calcutta: Bibliotheca Indica, vol. II, pp. 335–7.
23 Muhammad Asadulla Safa (1981) *Temur-Lang*, Beiruth: Dar an-nafais, p. 315 [in Arabic]. The retired colonel of the Syrian army, Muhammad Safa, wrote this book, concentrating on the military aspects of Timur's time. Chapter 23 is specially dedicated to the Timur-Mamluk relationship before and during the war in Syria.
24 Hojja Muhammad Parsa (Muhammad b. Muhammad b. Mahmud al-Hafiz al-Bukhari) [*The History of Mecca*], Mss. 2463/II and 3844/IV of the Collection of the Academy of Sciences of the Republic of Uzbekistan. See: Usupova, D.U., Djalilova, R.P. (1998), Mss.775 & 776, p. 336.
25 Lamentations Rabbah 1.
26 Politically and militarily it was possible. At that time there were no alliance between Sultan Faraj and Ottoman Sultan Bajazet (Bayazid). The Mamluks rejected Bajazet's offer of allegiance against Timur. Timur was able to continue his offensive in the Mamluk Sultanate without fear that Bajazet would attack him from the rear. See: Fischel , W.J. (1952), p. 107.

10 THE ATTITUDE OF TIMUR AND THE TIMURIDS TO THE JEWS

1 Marlowe, C., *Tamburlaine*, in Tucker Brooke, C.F., ed. (1975) *The Works of Christopher Marlowe*, Oxford: Clarendon Press, p. 129.

2 Gibbon, E. (1914), vol. 7, p. 72.
3 Ibn Arabshah (1936), p. 18.
4 Ibid. p. 49.
5 Woods, J.E. (1987) 'The Rise of Timurid Historiography', *JNES* 46, 2: 81–108.
6 'Ibn al-Fuwati', in Bat Ye'or (1985) *The Dhimmi*, trans. P. Fenton, London: Associated University Press, pp. 191–2.
7 Alexandrescu-Dersca, M.M. (1977), pp. 100–1.
8 See for example: Çelebi, E. (1988) *Evliya Çelebi in Diyarbekir*. The relevant section of the Sayehatname, trans. M. van Bruinessen and H. Boeschoten, Leiden: E.J. Brill, p. 139.
9 Khwandamir (1994), p. 279.
10 Fischel, W.J. (1956), pp. 230–2.
11 Schiltberger, J. (1879) *The Bondage and Travels of Johann Schiltberger in Europe, Asia and Africa, 1396–1427*, London: Hakluyt Society, pp. 22–3.
12 Giese, A., ed. (1925) *Die altosmanischen anonymen Chroniken*, Abhdlg. für die Kunde des Morgenlandes, Leipzig, vol. 17, pp. 52–3.
13 Abou'l Feda (1968) 'Al Mokhtasar fi Tarikh al Bashar' [Events of AH 658 /AD1260]. English translation: Said Abdel Fattah Ashour (1970) 'Jews in the Middle Ages: Comparative Study of East and West', in *The 4th Conference of the Academy of Islamic Research, Sept. 1968*, Cairo: Government Printing, p. 505.
14 Daulatshah (1901) *The Tadhkirat al-shu'ara*, ed. E.G. Browne, Oxford: Oxford University Press.
15 Roemer, H.R. (1986) 'The Safavid period', in Jackson, P. and Lockhart, L., eds (1986), vol. 6, p. 303.
16 Ibn Arabshah (1936), p. 299.
17 Barthold, V.V. (1963–66) 'O pogrebenii Timura' [On the burial of Timur], in Barthold, V.V. (1963–66), vol. 2, 2: 423–54. Barthold, using primary sources, analysed the burial and mourning procedures. He paid attention to the specific nomadic rituals such as, for example, scratching faces until they bled. Timur's dress, weapons and other belongings were placed at the tomb according to Mongol custom. Only four years after Timur's death did his son Shahrukh change the tomb's decorations according to Islamic regulations.
18 Zahiruddin Muhammad Babur Mirza (1993) *Baburnama*, part two, trans. W.M. Thackston, Jr., Harvard, Mass.: Harvard University Press, p. 391.
19 Sankrityayana, M.R. (1964) *History of Central Asia: Bronze Age to Chngiz Khan*, Calcutta – New Delhi: New Age Publishers, p. 260.
20 Ibid. p. 261.
21 Ibid. See also: Morgan, D.O. (1986) 'The Great Yasa of Chingiz khan and Mongol Law in the Ilkhanate', *Bull. of the School of Oriental and African Studies* 49/1: 163–76.
22 Anonymous (1893) *Vie de Mar Yahballaha*, trans. J.B. Chabot, *Revue de l'Orient latin*, pp. 609–10. For the relations between the Mongols and the Nestorians see also: Grousset, R. (1970), pp. 302–69.
23 Tolstov, S.P. *et al.*, eds (1955), p. 327.
24 Gibbon, E. (1914) *The History of the Decline and Fall of the Roman Empire*, London: Methuen, vol. 7, p. 4.
25 Graetz, H. (1898), vol. 3, pp. 580–1.
26 Matheson, S.A. (1972), p. 121.

27 Bar Hebraeus (1976), p. 418; Mirkhwand (1853–6) *Raudat-al-safa'*, ed. Rida Kuli Khan, Tehran, vol. 5, p. 59.
28 Barthold, V.V. (1900) 'Turkestan v epokhu mongolskogo nashestviya' [Turkestan during the period of the Mongol conquest], in Barthold, V.V. (1963–66), vol. 1, p. 563.
29 For more about Sa'd ad-Daula see: Bar Hebraeus (1976), vol. 1, pp. 488–9; cited then by Stillman, N.A. (1979), pp. 262–3; Boyle, J.A. (1968), pp. 369–70, 541; Ghazi b. al-Wasiti (1292), in Bat Ye'or (1985), pp. 209–11; Graetz, H. (1898), vol. 3, pp. 637–48; Grousset, R. (1970), pp. 372–3, 377; Sassoon, D.S. (1949), pp. 89–93.
30 Howorth, H.H. (1888) *History of the Mongols from the 9th to the 19th century, Part 3: The Mongols of Persia*, London, p. 333.
31 Concerning Rashid ad-Din see: Barthold, V.V. (1900), in Barthold (1963–66), vol. 1, pp. 92–5; Grousset, R. (1970), pp. 381, 384, 387; Howorth, H.H. (1888), p. 561; Petrushevsky, I.P., in Boule, J.A., ed. (1968), vol. 5, pp. 508–11; Lewis, B. (1984), pp. 89–90, 100–1.
32 Pan Guandan (1984) 'Jews in Ancient China – A Historical Survey', in Shapiro, S., ed. *Jews in old China*, New York: Hippocrene Books, p. 54.
33 Rashid ad-Din. (1952) *Sbornik letopisey* [Chronicles], trans. L.A. Khetagurov, Moscow-Leningrad: Izd. Akad. Nauk SSSR, vol. 1, p. 189. Rashid ad-Din called this tribe 'Barulas'. Concerning the Barlas tribe, see also: Manz, B.F. (1989) *The Rise and Rule of Tamerlane*, Cambridge: Cambridge University Press, pp. 156–7.
34 Yazdi (1957) *Zafarnama*, ed. M. Abassy, Tehran, vol. 1: pp. 160, 176, 239, 275, 320, 441; vol. 2: p. 504.
35 Khwandamir (1994), p. 278.
36 Ibid. p. 279.
37 'Ibn Khaldun', in Fischel, W.J. (1952), p. 46.
38 Browne, E.D. (1928) *A Literary History of Persia*, Cambridge: Cambridge University Press, vol. 2, p. 12.
39 *Tuzuk Taimuri* [The Code of Timur]. Morley, W. (1854) *A descriptive catalogue of the historical manuscripts in the Arabic and Persian languages preserved in the library of the Royal Asiatic Society*, London, 96, No 94. This manuscript was compiled at the Timurid court and contains the main body of Timur's legislation. It is doubtful that Timur himself wrote this book, but undoubtedly it was inspired by both Timur and his sons, the Timurid dynasty rulers. See also: Abdurrazak b. Iskhaq as-Samarkandi (1470) *Mattla al-saadain*, Collection of the Oriental Manuscripts of the Uzbek Academy of Sciences. Mss. 17 (previous catalogue No 1719). This version, kept in Tashkent, Uzbekistan, is significantly larger than the copy of the Royal Asiatic Society, mentioned in the library catalogue (Morley, W. [1854], 96, No 95).

11 TIMUR AND THE JEWS IN THE TWENTIETH CENTURY

1 Fishberg, M. (1911) *The Jews: A Study of Race and Environment*, London: Walter Scott Publishing, pp. 117–19.
2 Tyszkiewicz, J. (1989), pp. 89, 160.
3 Beneveni, F. (1724) 'Reports and Letters', in Halfin, N.A., ed. (1986)

Poslannik Petra I na Vostoke [Peter's the Great Envoy to the East], Moscow: Nauka, p. 85.

4 Walker, A. (1995) *Aurel Stein: Pioneer of the Silk Road*, London: John Murray.

5 Gerasimov, M.M. (1947) 'Portret Tamerlana' [The Portrait of Tamerlane], *Kratkie soobsheniya Instituta istorii material'noy kul'tury* 17: 14–21.

6 This interview was given in August 1997 in Tashkent during the 'No Missing Link' documentary USA–Israeli project with Dr Ruth Westhimer. This interview was not included in the film.

7 Lamb, H. (1955), p. 4.

8 'Ibn Khaldun', in Fischel, W.J. (1952), p. 47.

9 Krist, G. (1939) *Alone through the Forbidden Land*, London: Faber and Faber Ltd., pp. 68–9.

10 Lamb, H. (1955), p. 4.

11 See for example: Akhmedov, B. (1992) *Temur tuzuklari*, Tashkent [in Uzbek]; Akhmedov, B. (1995) *Amir Temur, A Historical Novel*, Tashkent: Abdulla Kodirii [in Uzbek]; Akhemdov, B. (1996) *Sahibkiran Timur – Timur the Great*, Tashkent: Abdulla Kodirii; Berezikov, E. (1994) *Velikiy Timur* [Great Timur], *A Chronological Novel*, Tashkent, Ukituvchi [Russian]; Faiziev, T. (1994) *Temuriy malikalar*, Tashkent: Meros, [Uzbek]; Faiziev, T. (1995) *Temuriylar shazharasi*, Tashkent: Ezuvchi [Uzbek]; Faiziev, T. (1996) *Velikiy Amir Temur*, Tashkent: Uzbekiston [Russian]; Muhammadjanov, A.A. (1997) *Amir Temuriylar davlati*, Tashkent: UzRE, [Uzbek].

12 'Commentary Assails Peres' Remarks in Tashkent', *FBIS/NES-96-134*, 13 July 1994, pp. 55–6.

13 Islam Karimov said this in his speech at the opening of the 'Timur in World History' exhibition at the UNESCO headquarters in Paris in 1996. See: Iriskulov, A., *et al.*, eds (1996), p. 9. See also: Karimov, I. (1996) *Stabil'nost' i reformy. Stat'i i vystupleniya*, Moscow: Paleya, pp. 359, 405.

14 For those interested in further English-language reading on current problems in Uzbekistan, see: Olcott, M.B. (1996) *Central Asia's New States*, Washington: U.S. Institute of Peace Press; Hunter, S.T. (1996) *Central Asia Since Independence*, Westport and London: Praeger; Malik, H., ed. (1994) *Central Asia: Its Strategic Importance and Future Prospects*, New York: St Martin's Press; Thubron, C. (1994) *The Lost Heart of Asia*, New York, Harper Perennial. There is also a book written by the Uzbek President, available in Uzbek, Russian, English and Hebrew: English edition: Karimov, I. (1997) *Uzbekistan on the Threshold of the Twenty-first Century*, Richmond: Curzon.

15 Karimov, I., speech given at the meeting with Israeli businessmen at the King David Hotel, 15 September 1998, English translation, p. 5.

16 'The Measures for Further Development of Co-operation with the State of Israel', Decree no. 421 of the Cabinet of Ministers of the Republic of Uzbekistan, 2 October 1998, Appendix 2, Tashkent.

17 The last example is: Roman, Z., Zvi, S. (2001) 'Uzbekistan erets mi agadot' [Uzbekistan – the land from fairy-tales], *Le Isha*, February: 36–9 [Hebrew].

18 Rosenthal, E.I.J. (1952) 'Avicenna's Influence on Jewish Thought', in Wickens, G.M., ed., *Avicenna: Scientist and Philosopher*, London: Luzac & Co., pp. 66–83.

19 This poem was written in Uzbek during the Second World War. Almost immediately it was translated into Russian. In 1996 it was translated into Hebrew. For the complete Russian version see: Gafur Gulyam (1983) *Izbrannye proizvedeniya* [Selected works], Tashkent: Izd. Literatury i Isskusstva im. G. Gulyama, vol. 1, pp. 48–53.

CONCLUSION

1 See especially: Barthold, V.V. (1958) *Ulugh-Beg*, trans. V. and T. Minorsky, Leiden: E.J. Brill.
2 Wolff, J. (1860), vol. 1, p. 357.
3 William of Rubruck, in Dawson, C., ed. (1966), p. 197.
4 Ibid. p. 126.
5 Potanin, G.N. (1912) *The Saga about Solomon*, Tomsk [Russian]. V.V. Barthold was very critical of this work. See his review in *ZVO* XXI, 4 (1913): 150–2.

GLOSSARY

Ashkenazi Jews (Ashkenazim) from 'Ashkenaz' (Heb., Germany), originally the German and northern French Jews, later all European non-Hassidic Jews.

Dari the classic Persian language.

Dhimmi (zimmi) A special social status for the Christians and the Jews of the Muslim lands. The *dhimmi* paid a special poll-tax, were protected by the government, and were able to practise their own religion.

Djizya a special poll-tax, or capitation tax for *dhimmi* in the Muslim countries.

Exilarch a title held by the head of the Babylonian and Persian Jewish community; also known as Prince of the Captivity, or *Resh Galuta*. The institution continued for the twelfth century.

Farsi modern Persian language spoken now in Iran.

Hadj (hajj) Muslim religious pilgrimage to the cities of Mecca and Medina.

Hadji (hajji) a Muslim who performed *hadj*.

Kharaj Muslim land-tax paid by land owners.

Karaites a sect within Judaism which rejects Talmudic authority and bases itself on individual interpretation of the Tanakh (The Old Testament). Karaism originated among the Babylonian (Persian) Jews in AD 767.

Mikveh (mikweh) the Jewish ritual bath prescribed for special occasions (recovery from leprosy, discharge of semen), and to restore the purity demanded by the presence of the sanctuary. Must be taken before praying, and before entering a synagogue. The water of the mikveh must be running, not drawn.

Mazar in Central Asia usually a tomb or a mausoleum of a local Muslim saint, or a religious authority.

Medrese (madrasa) traditional Islamic college or Koranic school.

Rabbinic Judaism the mainstream Judaism, which from Talmudic times is based on Talmudic interpretations of Jewish law.

Sephardic Jews (Sephardim) from 'Spharad' (Heb., Spain), originally Jews of Spanish or Portugal origin, later Mediterranean and North African Jews.

Tumen the Mongol army division of 10,000 men. Also a region or a province that can contribute 10,000 soldiers to an army. Later this term became just a name for a district or a region of a Central Asian state.

Ulus (ulus-irgen) a state ruled by the Mongolian khan of the Chingizid dynasty.

Zyaket (zakat) 'Allah's share', a Muslim poor tax, which was put at one-fortieth of a man's income and was collected by civil servants.

SELECT BIBLIOGRAPHY

Primary sources

Anonymous (1675) *Asterie ou Tamerlam*, Paris.
Anonymous (1965) *Povest' o Temir Aksake* [The Story about Timur Aksak]. In: *Complete Collection of Russian Chronicles*, Moscow: Nauka, vol. 11–12, pp. 158–61.
Anonymous (1970) *Molla Nasreddin*, trans. from the Persian by N. Osmanov, Moscow: Nauka.
Anonymous (n.d.) *Tarikh Salati* [The History of Sultans], Ms. 3349 of the Collection of Oriental Manuscripts of the Academy of Sciences of Uzbekistan, Tashkent.
Abu Tahir Hoja (1906) *Kandiya Malaya* [The Smaller Kandiya] trans. V.L. Vyatkin. In: *Spravochnaya kniga Samarkandskoy Oblasti*, Samarkand, Issue 8.
Andersen, A.O. and Andersen, M.O., eds (1936) *The Chronicle of Melrose from the Cottonian Manuscript*, Faustina B. IX in the British Museum, London: Percy Lund Humphries & Co.
Babur Mirza, Zahiruddin Muhammad (1993) *Baburnama*, part two, trans. W.M. Thackston, Jr., Harvard, Mass.: Harvard University Press.
Bar Hebraeus (1976) *The Chronography of Gregory Abû'l-Faraj*, trans. E.A. Wallis Budge, Amsterdam: Apa-Philo Press.
Barbaro, I. and Contartini, A. (1973) *I Viaggi in Persia Degli Ambasciatori Veneti Barbaro e Contarini*, ed. L. Lockhart *et al.* (1973), Roma: Instituto Poligrafico Dello Stato.
Beneveni, F. (1718–1725) *Letters and Reports*, ed. N.A. Halfin (1986), *Poslannik Petra I na vostoke* [The envoy of Peter I to the East], Moscow: Nauka.
Ben Jacob Petachia (1861) *Travels of Rabbi Petachia of Ratisbon, who in the latter end of the twelfth century visited Poland, Russia, Little Tertary, the Crimea, Armenia, Assyria, Syria, the Holy Land and Greece*, trans. A. Benisch, London: Longman and Co.
Benjamin of Tudela (1840) *The Itinerary of Rabbi Benjamin of Tudela*, trans. and ed. A. Asher, 2 vols, London. Reprint: New York, Hakesheth Publ., 1966.

—— *The Itinerary of Benjamin of Tudela* (1907) critical text, translation and commentary by M.N. Adler. Reprint: New York: Philipp Feldheim, 1965.

Çelebi, E. (1988) *Evliya Çelebi in Diyarbekir* (the relevant section of the Sayehatname), trans. M. van Bruinessen and H. Boeschoten, Leiden: E.J. Brill.

Chefdeville, É. M. de. (1789) *Tamerlan*, music by J.F, Reichardt, Paris.

Clavijo, R.G. de. (1928) *Embassy to Tamerlane, 1403–1406*, trans. G. Le Strange, New York & London: Harper and Brothers.

—— (1859) *Narrative of the Embassy of Ruy Gonzalez de Clavijo to the Court* of *Timur at Samarcand A.D. 1403–6*, trans. C.R. Markham. Reprint: New York: Burt Franklin, 1970.

Daulatshah b. 'Alā' al-Daula Samargandī (1901) *The Tadhkirat al-shu'ara*, ed. E.G. Browne, Leiden and London.

Ellis, H., ed. (1846) *Original Letters Illustrative of English History*, 3rd series, London, vol. 1.

Eubel, C. (1913) *Hierarchia Catholica Medii Aevy I. Monasterii*, vol. 1.

Fane, F. (1686) *The Sacrifice, a tragedy*, London.

Förtsch, J.P. (1690) *Bajazet und Tamerlane*, Hamburg.

Ghiyas ad-Din Ali (1399) *Ruz-nama gazawat Hindustan* [Diary of Timur's Campaign in India]. Ms.1520/II of the Collection of Oriental Manuscripts of the Academy of Sciences of Uzbekistan. Russian translation: Zimin, L., ed. (1958), trans. A.A. Semenov, Moscow: Izdatelstvo Vostochnoy Literatury.

Gransden, A., ed. (1964) *The Chronicle of Bury St. Edmunds 1212–1301*, London: Nelson.

Guevara, L.V. de. (1642) *La nueva ira de Dios, y Gran Tamerlan de Persia*, Valladolid o. J.

Hafiz-i-Abru (1939) *Majma' at-tavarikh*. In: Volin, S.L., *et al.*, eds, 1939, vol. 1.

Ibn al-Athir (1867–1871) *Al-kāmil fi'l ta'rīkh*, ed. C.J. Tornberg, Leiden, 14 vols.

Ibn Arabshah, A. (1936) *Tamerlane or Timur the Great Amir*, trans. J.H. Sanders, London: Luzac & Co.

Ibn Khaldun (1952) *Autobiography*. In: Fischel, W.J., 1952.

Ibn Khurdādhbih, 'Ubaidallāh ibn 'Abdallāh (c. 870) *Kitāb al-masālik wa' l-mamālik*, ed. M.J. de Goeje (1889) *Bibliotheca Geographorum Arabicorum*, Leiden, 8 vols.

Jaffar hojja, Seid Muhammed hojja b. (n.d.) *Dastan Amir Taimur*. Ms.5738 (1887) of the Collection of Oriental Manuscripts of the Academy of Sciences of Uzbekistan, Tashkent.

al-Jauzjani, Abu Omar (1941) 'Tabakat-i Nasiri'. In: Tizengauzen, V.G., ed. (1941) *The Collection of Materials Concerning the History of the Golden Horde*, Moscow – Leningrad: Izd. Akademii Nauk SSSR, vol. 2.

Joseph ben Joshua Ha-Kohen (1885) *The Chronicles of Rabbi Joseph ben Joshua ben Meir, the Spharadi*, trans. C.H.F. Bialloblotsky, London.

Juvaini, Ala ad-din Ata-Malik (1958) *Tarikh-i Jahan-Gusha*, trans. J.A. Boyle. In: *The History of the World-Conqueror*, Manchester: Manchester University Press, vol. 1.

Katalani, J., (Severaque) (1996) *The Story of Father Jordan about Grand India (1329)*, In: Kurkchi, A.I., ed., 1996, vol. 1 [Russian].

Khwandamir (1994) *Habibu's-Siyar*, vol. 3, trans. and ed. W.M. Thackston, Harvard, Mass.: Harvard University Press.

Kirakos Ganjakets'i (1260s) *Patmut'iwn Hayoc'* [History of Armenia], ed. K.A. Melik-Ohanjanyan (1961), Erevan. Trans: M.F. Brosset (1870) *Histoire d'Armenie par le vartabied Kirakos de Gantzac*, Deux historiens armeniens, St Petersburg.

Kobler, F., ed. (1978) *Letters of Jews through the Ages from Biblical Times to the Middle of the Eighteenth Century*, New York: East and West Library.

Komroff, M., ed. (1973) *Contemporaries of Marco Polo, Consisting of the Travel Records to the Eastern Parts of the World of William of Rubruck 1253–1255; The Journey of John Pian de Carpini 1245–1247; The Journal of Friar Odoric 1318–1330 and the Oriental Travels of Rabbi Benjamin of Tudela 1160–1173*, New York: Liveright Publishing Corp.

Lewis, M.G. (1811) *Timour the Tartar, A Romantic Drama, in two acts*, music by P. King, London.

Magnon, J. (1647) *Le grand Tamerlan ou la mort de Bajazet*, Paris.

Al-Maqdisi (al-Mukaddasi) (1877) *Ahsan at-Takasim fi Ma'rifat al-Akalim*, ed. M.J. de Goeje (1877) (BGA III), Leiden. Russian translation in: Volin, S.L., *et al.*, eds (1939) *Materialy po istorii turkmen i Turkmenii* [Materials on the history of the Turkmen and Turkmenia. Arab and Persian Sources], Moscow – Leningrad: Izdatelstvo Akademii Nauk SSSR, vol. 1.

Maqtubat Taimuriya [Letters of Timur and Timurids], Mss. 2278 of the Collection of Oriental Manuscripts of the Academy of Sciences of Uzbekistan, Tashkent.

Marlowe, C. (1590; 1606) *Tamburlaine the Great*, London: Richard Jhones; the second part: London: Ed. White.

Mignanelli, B. de (1416) *Vita Tamerlani*, Constance.

Mirkhwand (1853–6) *Raudat-al-safa'*, ed.Rida Kuli Khan, Tehran, vol. 5.

Mirza Rumuz (1712) *Taimur – nama*, Ms. 1526 of the Collection of Oriental Manuscripts of the Academy of Sciences of Uzbekistan, Tashkent.

Moranvillé, H. (1897) *Chronographia Regum Francorum, Vol III: 1380–1405*, Paris: Librairie Renouard.

Narshakhī, Abū Bakr Muhammad (944) *Tahqīq al-vilāyet* [Complete research of the land of Bukhara]. Mss. 2110, 4355/II, 4289, 1494/V, 5056/II, 1862/I, 2047/I, 3042/V of the Collection of Oriental Manuscripts of the Uzbek Academy of Sciences. English translation: [Narshakhī] Frye, R.N. (1954) *The History of Bukhara*, translated from a Persian abridgment of the Arabic original by Narshakhī, Cambridge, MA: The Medieval Academy of America.

Poe, E.A. (1827) *Tamerlane*, Boston.

Polo, Marco (1926) *The Travels of Marco Polo, The Venetian*, trans. and ed. M. Komroff, New York: Horace Liveright.

Pradon, N. (1675) *Tamerlan ou la mort de Bajazet*, Paris.

Qazwini, Hamdu'llah Mustawfi (1330) *The Ta'rikh-i-Guzida, or 'Select History'*, trans. E.G. Browne (1913), Leyden: E.J. Brill; London: Luzac & Co.

—— (1340) *Nuzhat-al-Qulûb*, trans. G. Le Strange (1919), Leyden: E.J. Brill; London: Luzac & Co.

Rashid ad-Din (1952) *Sbornik Letopisey* [Chronicles], trans. L.A. Khetagurov, Moscow – Leningrad: Izd. Akademii Nauk SSSR.

—— (1957) *Dzami-at-Tavarikh*, ed. A.A. Alizade (1957), tr. A.K. Arends, Baku.

—— (1971) *Perepiska* [Correspondence], Moscow: Nauka.

Raynaud, A., ed. (1887) *Gestes des Chiprois*, Geneva.

Roche-Guilhem, M-lle de la (1710) *Tamerlan (Histories galantes)*, Amsterdam.

Ruysbroek, W. van (1900) *The Journey of William Rubruck to the Eastern Parts of the World, 1253–55, as Narrated by Himself with Two Acoounts of the Earlier journey of John of Pian de Carpine*, ed. and trans. W.W. Rockwill, London: Hakluyt Society.

Saint-Quentin, S. de. Quoted in: Richard, J., ed. (1965) *Histoire des Tartares*, Documents relatifs à l'Histoire des Croisades publiés par Académie des inscriptions et Belles-Lettres, VIII, Paris: Libraire Orientaliste Paul Geuthner.

as-Samarkandi, Abu-l-Fazl Muhammad b. Khaidar (n.d.) *Tarikh-i kand*. Ms.1773/I of the Collection of the Academy of Sciences of the Republic of Uzbekistan, Tashkent.

as-Samarkandi, Abdurrazzak b. Iskhak (1470) *Mattla al-saadain*. Ms.17 of the Collection of Oriental Manuscripts of the Academy of Sciences of Uzbekistan.

Schiltberger, J. (1859) *Reisen des Johannes Schiltberger aus München in Europa, Asia und Afrika von 1394 bis 1427*, München.

—— (1879) *The Bondage and Travels of Johann Schiltberger in Europe, Asia and Africa, 1396–1427*, London: Hakluyt Society.

Severac, J. de. (1863) *Mirabilia Descripta, the Wonders of the East by Friar Jordanus*, trans. H. Yule, London: Hakluyt Society.

Shami, Nizam ad-Din (1937, 1956) *Zafar-Nama*, ed. F. Tauer , 2 vols. Prague.

Sir Mandeville (1967) *Mandeville's Travels*, ed. M.C. Seymour, Oxford: Clarendon Press.

ash-Shafi'i, Abdallah Muhammed b. Muhammed b. al-Djazari (n.d.) *Basic Science of the Reading of the Koran*, Ms. 2669/IV of the Collection of the Oriental Manuscripts of the Academy of Sciences of the Uzbek SSR. In: Semenov, A.A., ed. (1960), vol. 5, pp. 370–1 [Arabic].

at-Tabari (1879–1901) *Annales quos scripsit Abu-Djafar . . . at-Tabari*, Cum aliis editit M.J. de Goeje, Séries I–III, Lugd. Batavorum.

Thomas de Medzoph [T'ovma Mecop'ec'i] (1861) *Expose des guerres de Tamerlan et de Schah-Rokh dans l'Asie occidentale, d'apres la chronique armenienne inedite de Thomas de Medzoph*, ed. and published by F. Neve, Brussels.

[Timur??] *Tuzuk Taimuri* [The Code of Timur], Ms. 38 of the Collection of the Oriental Manuscripts of the Academy of Sciences of Uzbekistan, Tashkent.

[Timur ??] *Malfuzat-i Timuri or Tuzak-i Timuri*. In: Elliot, Sir H.M. (1871) *The History of India as Told by Its Own Historians*. Reprint: Calcutta, Susil Gupta Ltd., 1952.

T'ovma Mecop'ec'i (1440s) *Patmut'iwn Lank-T'amuray ew yajordac' iwroc', arareal T'ovma vardapeti Mecop'ec'woy* [The History of Tamerlane and his Successors by Vardapet T'ovma Mecop'ec'i], ed. K. Shahnazarean (1860), Paris.

Troitskaya Letopis' [Troitsk Chronicles], text reconstruction, M.D. Priselkov (1950), Moscow – Leningrad: Izd. Akademii Nauk SSSR.

Wolff, J. (1861) *Travels and Adventures of the Rev. Joseph Wolff*, 2 vols. London: Sauders, Otley, and Co.

Wouters, S. (1657) *Den grooten Tamerlan met de Doobt van Bayaset de I Turks Keizer*, Amsterdam.

Yazdi, Sharaf ad-din Ali (1425) *Zafar-Nama Taimuri*, ed. M.M. Ilahdad, (1887), Calcutta: Bibliotheca Indica.

—— (1425) *Zafar-noma*, the Persian text, Tashkent: Fan, 1972.

—— (1419) *Mukkadama Zafar-nama* [Introduction to the Book of Victories], Ms. 520/I of the Collection of Oriental Manuscripts of the Academy of Sciences of Uzbekistan, Tashkent.

Yule, H. (1866) *Cathay and the Way Thither*, 2 vols, London: Hakluyt Society.

Zacuto, A. (1580) *Sefer Yujasin* [The Book of Genealogies], Cracovia.

Ziani, M.A. (1689) *Gran Tamerlano*, Opera seria, Venezia.

Literature and secondary sources

Abramov, M.M. (1993) *Bukharskie evrei v Samarkande*, Samarkand: Samarkand University Press.

Adler, E.N. (1898) 'The Persian Jews: Their Books and Their Ritual', *The Jewish Quarterly Review* 10: 584–625.

Adler, E.N. (1899?) *The Persian Jews: Their Books and Ritual*, Oxford: Horace Hart, not dated.

—— (1905) *Jews in Many Lands*, London: Jewish Historical Society of England.

Akhmedov, A., ed. (1999) *The Cities and Routes of the Great Silk Road (on Central Asia Documents)*, Tashkent: Sharq.

Akhmedov, B. (1995) *Amir Temur*, Tashkent: Abdulla Kodirii [in Uzbek].

—— (1996) *Sakhibquiran Temur – Timur the Great: His Life, Social and Political Activities*, Tashkent: Abdulla Kodirii.

Alexandrescu-Dersca, M.M. (1977) *La campagne de Timur en Anatolie (1402)*, Bucharest, 1942. Reprint: London: Variorum Reprints.

Altman, V. (1947) 'Ancient Khoresmian Civilization in the Light of the Latest Archaeological Discoveries [1937–1945], *JAOS* 2: 67.

Amitai-Preiss, R. (1995) *Mongols and Mamluks. The Mamaluk—Il-khanid War, 1260–1281*, Cambridge: Cambridge University Press.

Amitin-Shapiro, Z.L. (1934) *Pajdo sudani sidho ve zurfu sodathoji jahudigi* [The origin of Jewish festivals and traditions], Tashkent: Gosizdat UzSSR, [Judeo-Tadjik].

Arnold, T. and Guillaume, A., eds (1965) *The Legacy of Islam*, London: Oxford University Press.

Ashour, S.A.F. (1970) *Jews in the Middle Ages: Comparative Study of East and West*, The 4th Conference of the Academy of Islamic Research, Cairo: Government Printing, pp. 497–505.

Ashrafyan, K.Z. (1988) 'Central Asia under Timur from 1370 to the Early fifteenth century'. In: Asimov, M.S. and Bosworth, C.E., eds, *History of Civilizations of Central Asia*, UNESCO Publ., vol. IV.

Atiya, A.S. (1938) *The Crusade in the Later Middle Ages*, London: Lund.

Aubin, J. (1963) 'Comment Tamerlan prenait les villes', *Studia Islamica* 19: 83–122.

Ayalon, D. (1988) *Outsiders in the Lands of Islam: Mamluks, Mongols and Eunuchs*, London: Variorum Reprints.

Bacher, W. (1900) *Ein hebräisch-persisches Wörterbuch aus dem vierzehnten Jahrhundert*, Strassburg.

Bacher, W. (1901, 1902) 'Judisch-Persischen aus Bukhara', *Zeitschrift der Deutschen Morgenlandischen Gesellschaft* 55(1901): 241–57; 56(1902): 729–59.

—— (1906) 'Judaeo-Persian Language', *The Jewish Encyclopedia*, New York, vol. 7, pp. 313–17.

Baron, S.W. (1957) *Social and Religious History of the Jews*, Philadelphia: The Jewish Publication Society of America.

Barthold, V.V. (1900) 'Turkestan During the Period of the Mongol Conquest'. In Barthold, V.V. (1963–66) *Sochineniya* [Writings], Moscow: Izd Vostochnoy Literatury, vols 1–6.

—— (1906) 'Poezdka v Samarkand s archeologicheskoy tseliu' [The Trip to Samarkand with an archeological goal] *ZVO* XVI, 4: 34–5.

—— (1958) *Four Studies on the History of Central Asia. Vol. II: Ulugh-Beg*, trans. V. and T. Minorsky, Leiden: E.J. Brill.

—— (1963–66) *Sochineniya* [Writings], Moscow: Izd. Vostochnoy Literatury, vol. 1.

—— (1964) 'O pogrebenii Timura' [On the burial of Timur]. In: Barthold, V.V. (1963–66), vol. 2, pp. 423–54.

—— (1966) 'Karl Velikiy i Harun ar-Rashid'. In: Barthold, V.V. (1963–66), vol. 6, pp. 342–64.

—— (1966) 'K voprosu o franko-musulmanskich otnosheniyakh' [On the question of the Franco-Moslem relations]. In: Barthold, V.V. (1963–66), vol. 6, pp. 432–61.

—— (1984) *An Historical Geography of Iran*, trans. S. Soucek, ed. C.E. Bosworth, Princeton: Princeton University Press.

—— (1996) 'The place of Caspian areas in the history of the Moslem World'. In: Kurkchi, A.I., ed., *Kaspiysky Transit*, Moscow: Tanais, vol. 1: 280–9 [Russian].

Bat Ye'or (1985) *The Dhimmi*, trans. P. Fenton, London: Associated University Press.

Berezikov, E. (1994) *Velikiy Timur* [Timur the Great], Tashkent: Ukituvchi.

Bevan, E.R. and Singer, C., eds (1953) *The Legacy of Israel*, Oxford: Clarendon Press.

Birnbaum, S.A. (1956) 'The Verb in the Bukharic Language of Samarkand', *Archivum Linguisticum* 2: 60–73.

Borodin, S. (1961) *Zvezdy nad Samarkandom* [Stars above Samarkand], Moscow: Sovetskiy Pisatel'.

Boyle, J.A., ed. (1968) *The Cambridge History of Iran*, Cambridge: Cambridge University Press, vol. 5.

Bresslau, H. (1887) 'Juden und Mongolen', *Zeitschrift für die Geschichte der Juden in Deutschland* 1: 99–102.

Brion, M. (1963) *Tamerlan*, Paris: Albin Michel.

Buckler, F.W. (1931) *Harun'l-Rashid and Charles the Great*, Cambridge, Mass.

Champdor, A. (1957) *Tamerlan*, 2nd edn Paris.

Creasy, E.S. (1878) *History of the Ottoman Turks: From the Beginning of their Empire to the Present Time*, London: Smith.

Danielova, H. (1988) 'Gebraismy v tadjikskom yazyke sredneaziatskikh evreev' [Hebraisms in the Tadjik Language of the Central Asian Jews] In: *Synchroniya i diachroniya v lingvisticheskikh issledovaniyakh*, Moscow: Nauka, vol. 1, pp. 96–101.

Dawson, C., ed. (1966) *Mission to Asia. Narratives and letters of the Franciscan missionaries in Mongolia and China in the 13th and 14th centuries*, New York: Harper & Row.

Dennett, D.C. Jr. (1950) *Conversion and the Poll Tax in Early Islam*, Cambridge, Mass.: Harvard University Press.

Dimont, M.I. (1962) *Jews, God, and History*, New York: Simon and Schuster.

Dunlop, D.M. (1967) *The History of the Jewish Khazars*, New York: Schoken Books.

Elgood, C. (1951) A *Medical History of Persia and the Eastern Caliphate*, Cambridge: Cambridge University Press.

Estrada, F.L. (1943) *Embajada a Tamorlan*, Madrid: Instituto Nicolás Antonio.

Faiziev, T. (1994) *Temuriy malikalar*, Tashkent: Meros [Uzbek].

—— (1995) *Temuriylar shazharasi*, Tashkent: Ezuvchi [Uzbek].

—— (1996) *Velikiy Amir Temur*, Tashkent: Uzbekiston [Russian].

Fischel, W.J. (1945) 'The Jews of Central Asia (Khorasan) in Medieval Hebrew and Islamic Literature', *Historia Judaica* 7: 29–50.

—— (1952) *Ibn Khaldun and Tamerlane*, Berkeley and Los Angeles: University of California Press.

—— (1953) 'Isfahan – the story of a Jewish community in Persia'. In: *Joshua Starr Memorial Volume*, New York, pp. 111–28.

—— (1956) 'A New Latin Source on Tamerlane's Conquest of Damascus (1400/1401)', *ORIENS*. IX, 2: 203–21.

Fishberg, M. (1911) *The Jews: A Study of Race and Environment*, London: Walter Scott Publ.

Frye, R.N., ed. (1975) *The Cambridge History of Iran*, Cambridge: University Press, vol. 4.

Gaffarov, S.S. and Rahmatullaev, T.R, eds (1998) *Murabbiy*, Samarkand: Samarkand State University [Russian].

Garbell, I. (1965) *The Jewish Neo-Aramaic Dialect of Persian Azerbaijan*, The Hague: Mouton & Co.

Gerasimov, M.M. (1947) 'Portret Tamerlana' [The Portrait of Tamerlane], *Kratkie soobsheniya Instituta istorii material'noy kul'tury* 17:14–21.

Gibbon, E. (1914) *The Decline and Fall of the Roman Empire*, ed. J.B. Bury, London: Methuen, vol. 7.

Giese, A. ed. (1925) *Die altosmanischen anonymen Chroniken*, Abhandlung für die Kunde des Morgenlandes, Leipzig, vol.17.

Goode, A.D. (1940) 'The Exilarchate in the Eastern Caliphate', *JQR* 31: 149–71.

Graetz, H. (1893) *History of the Jews*, Philadelphia: The Jewish Publication Society of America, vols. 2–3.

Grekov, B.D. and Yakubovsky, A.U. (1950) *Zolotaya Orda i ee padenie* [The Golden Horde and its Fall], Moscow – Leningrad: Izdatelstvo Akademii Nauk.

Grekov, I.B. (1975) *Vostochnaya Evropa i upadok Zolotoy Ordy* [The Eastern Europe and the Fall of the Golden Horde], Moscow: Nauka.

Grousset, R. (1970) *The Empire of the Steppes. A History of Central Asia*, trans. N. Walford, New Brunswick: Rutgers University Press.

Hambly, G., ed. (1969) *Central Asia*, London: Weidenfeld and Nicolson.

Hartog, L. de. (1989) *Genghis Khan Conqueror of the World*, I.B. Tauris & Co.

Henning, W.B. (1957) 'The inscriptions of Tang-i Azao', *BSOAS* 20: 335–42.

Heyd, W. (1886) *Histoire du commerce du Levant au Moyen-Âge*, Société de l'Orient Latin. Reprint: Leipzig: Otto Harrassowitz, 1966.

Hill, G. (1948) *History of Cyprus*, Cambridge: Cambridge University Press.

Hitti, P.K. (1957) *History of Syria*, London: Macmillan & Co Ltd.

Hookham, H. (1962) *Tamburlaine the Conqueror*, London: Hodder and Stoughton.

Howorth, H.H. (1888) *History of the Mongols from the 9th to the 19th Century, Part III: The Mongols of Persia*, London.

Hunter, S.T. (1996) *Central Asia Since Independence*, Westport and London: Praeger.

Idries Shah (1966) *The Exploits of the Incomparable Mulla Nasrudin*, London: Jonathan Cape.

Iriskulov, A., *et al.*, eds (1996) *Amir Temur in World History*, Tashkent: Sharq.

Iskhakov, P. (1996) *K istorii bukharsko-evreyskogo etnosa* [To the History of the Bukharian Jewish Ethnos], New York.

Jackson, P. (1980) 'The Crisis in the Holy Land in 1260', *English Historical Review* 95: 481–513.

Jackson, P. and Lockhart, L., eds (1986) *The Cambridge History of Iran*, Cambridge: Cambridge University Press, vol. 6.

Jeffery, A. (1951) 'Al-Biruni's contribution to comparative religion'. In: *Al-Biruni Commemoration Volume, A.H. 362–A.H. 1362*, Calcutta: Iran Society, pp.130–58.

Karamatov, K., ed. (1999) *Jaloliddin Manguberdi* [*Jalal-ad-Din*], Tashkent: Sharq.

Karimov, I. (1996) *Stabil'nost' i reformy (Stat'i i vystupleniya)*, Moscow: Paleya.

—— (1997) *Uzbekistan on the Threshold of the Twenty-First Century*, Richmond: Curzon.

Keller, W. (1971) *Diaspora: the Post-Biblical History of the Jews*, trans. R. and C. Winston, London: Pitman.

Kharitonov, M.S., ed. (1978) *Dvadtsat' tri Nasreddina* [23 Nasreddins], Moscow: Nauka.

Klevan, A. (1979) 'Hebrew Inscriptions in Ossuaries Found in Central Asia', *Qadmomiyyot* 12, 2–3: 91–2 [Hebrew].
Koestler, A. (1976) *The Thirteenth Tribe: The Khazar Empire and its Heritage*, London: Hutchinson.
Kontir, L. (1929) *Uzbekistanda mahalli yahudilar* [Native Jews of Uzbekistan], Samarkand [Uzbek].
Krist, G. (1939) *Alone Through the Forbidden Land*, trans. E.O. Lorimer, London: Readers' Union Ltd.
Kurkchi, A.I., ed. (1996) *Kaspiysky Transit*, Moscow: Tanais [Russian].
Lamb, H. (1928) *Tamerlane*, London: McBride & Co. Last reprint: New York, Bantam Books, 1955.
Lane, F.C. (1973) *Venice: A Maritime Republic*, Baltimore: Johns Hopkins University Press.
Law, D.A. (1992) *From Samaria to Samarkand: The Ten Lost Tribes of Israel*, Lanham, MD: University Press of America.
Lewis, B. (1981) *The Jews of Islam*, Princeton: Princeton University Press.
Lichtenstadter, I. (1943) 'The Distinctive Dress of Non-Muslims in Islamic Countries', *Historia Judaica* 5: 35–52.
Livshits, V.A. and Usmanova, Z.I. (1994) *Parthian Inscription from Old Merv*, In: Irano-Judaica III, Jerusalem, pp. 103–4.
Loenertz, Fr. R., O.P. (1937) *La Société des Frères Pérégrinants: Étude sur l'Orient Dominicain*, Rome.
Maalouf, A. (1984) *The Crusades Through Arab Eyes*, London: Al Saqi Books.
Malik, H., ed. (1994) *Central Asia: Its Strategic Importance and Future Prospects*, New York: St Martin's Press.
Manz, B.F. (1988) 'Tamerlane and the Symbolism of Sovereignty', *Iranian Studies*. XXI, 1–2: 105–22.
—— (1989, 1999 2nd ed) *The Rise and Rule of Tamerlane*, Cambridge: Cambridge University Press.
Marcus, J.R. (1961) *The Jew in the Medieval World, A Source Book: 315–1791*, New York: Meridian Books.
Margoliuth, D. (1903) 'An early Judeo-Persian Document from Khotan in the Stein Collection', *JRAS* n.v.: 735–61.
Matheson, S.A. (1972) *Persia: An Archaeological Guide*, London: Faber and Faber.
McEvedy C., Jones R. (1978) *Atlas of World Population History*, New York – London: Penguin Books.
Meserve, R.I. (1993) 'The Latin Sources for Khwarezm'. In: Nazarov, B.A. and Sinor, D., eds (1993) *Essays on Uzbek History, Culture, and Language*, Bloomington: Indiana University Press.
Mirabile, P. (n.d.) *The Book of the Oghuz Peoples or Legends Told and Sung by Dede Korkut*, Voies Itinerantes.
Muhammadjanov, A.A. (1997) *Amir Temuriylar davlati*, Tashkent: UzRE [Uzbek].
Mukherdjee, B.N. (1970) *An Agrippan Source: A Study in Judeo-Parthian History*, Calcutta.

—— (1993) 'An Inscripted Gem from Indo-Iranian Borderlands', *Bull Asia Inst* (new series) 7: 141–2.

Netzer, A. (1971) 'Daniyal-Name: An Exposition of Judeo-Persian'. In: Tikku, G.L., ed. (1971) *Islam and its Cultural Divergence*, Chicago – London: University of Illinois Press, pp. 145–64.

Newton, A.P., ed. (1926) *Travel and Travellers of the Middle Ages*, New York: Alfred A. Knopf.

Nicolle, D. (1990) *The Age of Tamerlane: Warfare in the Middle East c. 1350–1500*, Men-at-Arms, no. 222, Osprey Pub Co.

Niyazov, D.M. (1979) 'O yazyke sredneaziatskikh evreev', *Voprosy vostokovedeniya* 6: 92–104.

Olcott, M.B. (1996) *Central Asia's New States*, Washington: U.S. Institute of Peace Press.

Peters, F.E. (1985) *Jerusalem*, Princeton: Princeton University Press.

Pinkhasi, I. (1978) *Ten Folk Stories from Bukhara*, Jerusalem [Hebrew].

Poliakova, E.A. (1984) 'The Development of Literary Canon in Medieval Persian Chronicles: The Triumph of Etiquette', *Iranian Studies* 17, 2: 237–56.

—— (1988) 'Timur as Described by the 15th Century Court Historiographers', *Iranian Studies* 21, 1–2: 31–44.

Pool, J.J. (1892) *Studies in Mohammedanism, Historical and Doctrinal*, Westminster: Archibald Constable and Co.

Popple, W. (1732) *Tamerlane the Beneficent, a tragedy*, London.

Poznanski, S. (1914) *Babylonische Geonim im nachgaonaischen Zeitalter*, Berlin.

Prawdin, M. (1967) *The Mongol Empire: Its Rise and Legacy*, New York: The Free Press.

Rakhmanaliev, R., ed. (1992) *Tamerlane*, Moscow: Gurash, pp. 352–8.

Reif, S.C. (2000) *A Jewish Archive from Old Cairo*, Richmond, Curzon Press.

Roman, Z. and Zvi, S. (2001)'Uzbekistan erets mi agadot' [Uzbekistan – the land from fairy-tales] *Le Isha*, March: 36–9 [Hebrew].

Rosenthal, E.I.J. (1952) 'Avicenna's influence on Jewish thought'. In Wickens, G.M., ed. *Avicenna: Scientist & Philosopher*, London: Luzac & Co., pp. 66–83.

Roth, C. (1940) *The Jewish Contribution to Civilization*, New York – London: Harper and Brothers.

Roux, J.-P. (1991) *Tamerlan*, Paris: Fayard.

Rowe, N. (1702) *Tamerlane, a tragedy*, London.

Rtveladze, E. (1999) 'The Jews in the Pre-Islamic Central Asia'. In: Rtveladze, E., *Velikiy Shelkovyi Put': Entsiklopedicheskiy spravochnik* [The Great Silk Route: Encyclopaedia], Tashkent: Uzbekiston Milliy Encyclopediyasy, pp. 86–90 [Russian].

Runciman, S. (1975) *A History of the Crusades. Vol. 3: The Kingdom of Acre and the later Crusades*, Cambridge: Cambridge University Press.

Safa, Muhammad Asadulla (1981) *Temur-Lang*, Beiruth [in Arabic].

Safargaliev, M.G. (1960) *Raspad Zolotoy Ordy* [Disintegration of the Golden Horde], Saransk: Mordovskoe Knizhnoe Izdatelstvo.

Sankrityayana, M.R. (1964) *History of Central Asia*, Calcutta – New Delhi: New Age Publishers Private Ltd.

Sassoon, D.S. (1949) *A History of the Jews in Baghdad*, Letchworth: S.D. Sassoon Publ.

Saunders, C. (1681) *Tamerlane the Great, a tragedy*, London.

Semenov, A.A., ed. (1952–1960) *Collection of the Oriental Manuscripts of the Academy of Sciences of the Uzbek SSR*, Tashkent: Izd. Akademii Nauk UzSSR, vols. 1 & 5 [Russian].

Shapiro, S., ed. (1984) *Jews in Old China*, New York: Hippocrene Books.

Shterenshis, M. (2000) 'Approach to Tamerlane: Tradition and Innovation. Ending 600 Years of Historiography of Timur', *Central Asia and the Caucasus* 2: 193–200.

Sinor, D. (1997) 'Le Mongol vu par l'Occident'. In: Sinor, D., *Studies in Medieval Inner Asia*, Ashgate: Variorum, IX: 64.

Sodikova, N. (1998) 'Cultural and Historical Heritage of the Period of Timur and Timurids', *Bulletin of SCST* 2: 64–73.

Soubrian, A. (1935) *Avicenne, Prince des Medicins*, Paris.

Spuler, B. (1969) *The Mongol Period*, Leiden: E.J. Brill.

Stier, R. (1998) *Tamerlane: The Ultimate Warrior*, Career Research Institute.

Stilman, N.A. (1979) *The Jews of Arab Lands, A History and Source Book*, Philadelphia: The Jewish Publication Society of America.

Tolstov, S. (1944) 'In the Desrts of Khwarizm', *Asiatic Review* 40: 408–14.

—— (1948) *Po sledam drevnekhorezmiyskoy tsivilizatsii* [Tracing the Ancient Khorezmian Civilization], Moscow – Leningrad: Izdatelstvo Akademii Nauk SSSR.

Tolstov, S.P., *et al.*, eds (1955) *Istoriya Uzbekskoy SSR* [History of the Uzbek SSR], Tashkent: Izd. Akademii Nauk UzSSR, vol. 1.

Trachtenberg, J. (1961) *The Devil and the Jews*, New York: Meridian Books.

Tyszkiewicz, J. (1989) *Tatarzy na Litwie i w Polsce. Studia z dziejów XIII–XVIII w.*, Warszawa: Panstwowe Wydawnictwo Naukowe.

Usupova, D.U. and Jalilova, R.P. (1998) *The Collection of the Oriental Manuscripts of the Academy of Sciences of the Republic of Uzbekistan, Historical Manuscripts*, Tashkent: Fan.

Vernadsky, G. (1953) *The Mongols and Russia*, New Haven: Yale University Press.

Volin, S.L., *et al.*, eds (1939) *Materialy po istorii turkmen i Turkmenii* [Materials on the History of the Turkmen and Turkmeniya], Arab and Persian sources, Moscow – Leningrad: Izdatelstvo Akademii Nauk SSSR, vol. 1.

Voltaire (1905) *Tamerlane*. In: *Ancient and Modern History, The Works of Voltaire, a contemporary version*, trans. W.F. Flemming, Akron: The Werner Co., vol. XXVI.

Vyshenskaya, T., ed. (1995) *Evrei v Sredney Asii, proshloe i nastoyashee* [The Jews of Central Asia in Past and Present: Expeditions, Researches, Publications. Collected articles], St Petersburg: St Petersburg Jewish University.

Walker, A. (1995) *Aurel Stein: Pioneer of the Silk Road*, London: John Murray.

Weitzmann, K. and Keesler, H.L. (1991) *The Frescoes of the Dura Synagogue and Christian Art*, Washington: Trustees for Harvard University.

Wiesehüfer, J. (1996) *Ancient Persia from 550 B.C. to 650 A.D.*, trans. A. Azodi, London – New York: I.B. Tauris.

Wilson, A.T. (1926) 'Early Spanish and Portuguese Travellers in Persia', *The Asiatic Review* 22: 641.

Woods, J.E. (1987) 'The Rise of Timurid Historiography', *JNES* 46, 2: 81–108.

Zarubin, I.I. (1928) *Ocherk razgovornogo yazyka samarkandskikh evreev: opyt kharakteristiki*, Leningrad: Materialy AN SSSR, pp. 95–181.

Zand, M. (1989) 'Bukharian Jews', *Encyclopaedia Iranica*, New York – London, vol. 4, Fac. 5, pp. 531–3.

Zayat, H. (1949) 'The Distinctive Signs of the Christians and Jews in Islam', *Al-Machriq* 43, 2: 161–252 [Arabic].

INDEX